C000186010

Catching Memories

First published in November 2011

Edited - Rosie Barham and Terry Doe

ISBN NUMBER 978-0-9570398-1-0

Designed and published by mpress (Media) LTD.

Unit Four, Ashton Gate, Harold Hill, Romford, RM3 8UF

Acknowledgements

Where do I start? There are so many who have been involved in some way in the production of this book. The first person I really should thank is my wife, Joanne. She's had to put up with me as an angler since we first met 26 years ago, and for that I thank you, my darling.

My sincere thanks go to Rosie Barham and Terry Doe for all the hours they've spent editing and proof reading, and for the encouragement they've given me from the start.

And now to my friends. Where would we be without friends? A big thanks to Jay Willis, Paul Pynen, Michael Germain, Neil Lunn, and Stuart Court, for their guest chapters. Also, thanks to all the really good people I've met over the years on so many different lakes, and for the good times and inspiration they've given me.

I'd like to thank Kevin Nash, who has not only made me feel so much at home since I joined the Nash team, but he's also has written the foreword for this book. Huge thanks to all the Nash team, who have really looked after me over the past few years: Gary Bayes, Alan Blair, Nick Maddix (Reedy), Matt Downing, and Sarah in the office, who I have most likely driven mad, and everyone else at the Nash Camp. Oh, and thanks again to Kev for allowing me to fish his incredible lake.

Thank you to Paul Moulder for designing and laying out the whole book, to Mpress for being my publisher, and a special thanks to Steve Fantauzzi for his fantastic drawings. They are brilliant mate, and very much appreciated.

Thanks to my good mate, Jerry Bridger, for his photography and encouragement, and to Steve Falco, John Pack, Terry Hearn, Nick Helleur, Tony Moulder, Steve Fantauzzi, Stuart Holman, Paul Gillings and Simon Hartop for letting me use their photos.

Thanks to Neil Gentry, my partner in crime, and to Lauren his missus for putting up with us both while making the DVD, 'The Compulsive Angler'. Thanks also to Kevin Law our cameraman, and to Charles Thorpe for the billboard adverts.

Last, but not least, thanks to all the fishery owners, managers and clubs who have allowed me to fish their waters: Dave Mennie at Greenacres; Andy Pye, Wellington Country Park; Toby Cooke, Croxley Hall; Lee Jackson, Cotton Farm; Ben Lofting, Cleverley Mere; Abbey Cross Club, Green Lanes; Kevin Nash, Church Pool; and Lee Valley Parks, Nazeing Meads, Watford Piscators, Tolpits, CEMEX Angling, Sutton at Hone and Yateley Car Park.

Memories are priceless, and so is the friendship that goes with them. As you've all helped me, be assured that I'll do the same for you.

Contents

Foreword

I would describe Jerry Hammond as one of carp fishing's unique characters, as well as being a bloke, a proper man's man. We've been friends for a long time and I can tell you that he's always up for a fishing trip, and a laugh. At the same time, though, he really knows his stuff and has rightly become one of the leading carp anglers in the country.

In this book, Jerry outlines his successes and failures, starting with his carp fishing début at Hainault Park Lake in 1977 when he saw his first 20-pounder on the bank. It had been caught by an 'expert' who later showed the very young Jerry how to cut a cube of Spam from a tin, and secure it to the hook with a blade of grass. That was his introduction to the world of carp and Jerry hasn't looked back since, although it has to be noted that there has been the odd distraction!

At the age of 16, Jerry joined the army. I've spent many hours on the bank with him, reliving his army days, and as a result have the highest respect for this man. After seven years, Jerry quit the army to marry his childhood sweetheart and start a family. Once settled, carp fishing came back to the fore and the Hammond journey really took off around 1988.

Jerry allows us to share his memories of various venues. He outlines his captures - and the lack of them - at Sutton, Cleverly Mere, and other venues; a brace of 40s from Wellington Country Park, his capture of Shoulders at Horton Church Lake, fishing Yateley in the company of some of his childhood angling heroes and catching big 'uns from my own Church Pool. He also includes a chapter about his acting exploits on film with the likes of David Schwimmer and Tom Hanks. You won't find many carp books where Steven Spielberg turns up, but he does in this one!

I was lucky enough to be there on the Church on that amazing morning when Jerry banked the 51lb common, and I saw for myself that he, like me, will never lose the thrill that catching big carp brings. The buzz, that feeling that only the true carp angler knows. Despite the many years of carp fishing, and the thousands of carp you have caught, with rod in a battle curve you still shake like a jelly.

I would pick out Jerry as one of the best carpers around. If you watch him fishing, you will know what I mean. Jerry has an energy that drives him, keeps him going, and ensures that he never gives up, as well as not accepting anything other than the best. Jerry shares my motto, 'Make it happen!'

Real carp anglers do it because they genuinely love it. The thrill of catching forges lifelong memories and friendships, and that's what this book is all about. Jerry Hammond is as close to being obsessed by angling as makes no difference, but unlike some who have devoted years to chasing big fish, Jerry has also built a successful life for himself in the real world. He's got a fantastic family, a lovely home on his own, highly acclaimed, fishery, and he's got his life's priorities totally sorted. That he does all this and still manages to be a proper bloke with not a trace of big-headedness, is possibly Jerry's greatest accomplishment.

So, there you go; this book is written by a remarkable man with an even more remarkable talent for hunting big carp, and loving every minute of the chase, as well as the result. Now that I've read Catching Memories, all I can say is – come on Hammond, get the next book done!

Introduction

I really can't believe I've actually written a book. To be honest, at school I was a bit of a lad. I'd already enlisted in the army so my future was pretty much laid out and I was off not long after leaving school to join up. I was fishing mad then, and now I've written a book! My English teachers simply wouldn't believe it.

Everything has been written from memory and I haven't told any tall tales or exaggerated anything. I may have made a few mistakes with here and there, and if that is the case, I apologise, but any mistakes are just that.

We start way back in 1977, when I was 12 years old and enjoying my first ever taste of big carp fishing while fishing at Hainault Park Lake. I absolutely loved Hainault and I used to spend every day possible at the lake with my new fishing mates. Most of the time we were just fooling around and it was more like camping than fishing, but it was great.

In June 1981, all the messing about came to halt and I was off to become a soldier. I just missed going to the Falklands war when I'd finished my training because our battalion, The Queen's Regiment, was not up to full strength. We had a lucky escape. The ship on which we should have sailed was the Sir Galahad, and she went down.

I had a great army career ahead of me but then I met my missus, Joanne, and decided that I didn't want a married life in the army, so after nearly seven years I called it day. It was at this time that I really got into my fishing, and where else other than Hainault!

I became friends with a large group of carping mad characters and I still keep in touch with many of them, but the main mates at Hainault were Neil Lunn,

Craig Bateman, Michael Germain, Jay Willis, and Paul Pynen. We're still good friends today, and I see them all the time. Over 24 years we've had some right old laughs together. Sadly, Craig lost his life one day on his way to the lake, doing what he loved, and I dearly wish he was still with us. We all miss him so much. Four of my friends have written guest chapters that are relevant to certain parts of the story, but none of us are professional writers, we're just anglers telling a tale that we hope you'll enjoy.

Not long after I left the army, I was married and then two wonderful children came along and they are my life: my son, Jay, and my daughter, Brooke.

This book is not an autobiography. I have gone over some of the main highlights and memories that really stand out for me, but I've missed out so much and many other waters that I have fished. I've hardly mentioned my life as a fishery manager, running my own carp waters and stretches of the river that runs around the lock house where I've lived for nearly ten years. I did sidetrack in one chapter, though, to talk about my film work experiences. That's something of which I am very proud and I wanted to share it. I hope you enjoy the diversion.

I've fished some great waters over the years and some have been very tough ones, like Sutton at Hone, Tolpits, and the Car Park at Yateley. I met another good friend, Stuart Court, at Tolpits and he has kindly told his story of catching the mighty Plodder.

Anyone who knows me will be aware of just how how crazy I am about my carping and I've never eased off the gas. It's a huge part of my life and I hope this comes across. There are stories of success and failure, as I take you through some of my most memorable fishing seasons. As the title suggests, I'm catching memories. This book holds the greatest times of my angling life, and each chapter is a carp sack of my personal bests.

Thank you for reading my book, and if it inspires you to slip the net under a PB memory of your own, I promise I'll be as happy as you are.

Chapter One
Hainault. My Childhood Playground

When I was a youngster, I fished a park lake in Hainault forest, my childhood playground, and that's where the carp angling seed was sown. I saw my first 20-pounder on the bank one very wet and rainy night, caught by a guy who was set up next to me with all the latest high-tech equipment. He had all the gear, including bite alarms and a 'bivvy', which was a pub-garden umbrella that still had the Double Diamond logo on the side, and he'd somehow made a wrap that was attached all the way around it, giving him a proper shelter.

I kept my eye on this expert. His matching rods were up high, and his bobbins had been cut out and made from yoghurt cartons. I set up as close to this man as I possibly could - I bet he was happy - but he was very secretive and stayed in his bivvy most of the time, while I was float fishing, sitting there under a tiny umbrella and getting soaked as the rain came at me sideways. I was very young, maybe 12, and only allowed to do night fishing because I was with a neighbour who was older. He was fishing just down from me and we used to sit there all night, float fishing - God knows how.

Anyway, it must have been 2am when the expert's rod got ripped from its rod rest. The guy was out in a flash and he grabbed the rod just in time before it was dragged into the lake. I was out by his side, watching as he played the big carp, which was trying to take him around an island. The glass-fibre rod creaked under the strain, and then he got his huge net ready. The whole time, it was pouring down and I will never forget the size of the carp as it rolled into the net; it was a monster. The angler was very happy as he lifted this great beast up for weighing and the scales read 22lbs. 'What a fish!' I thought, and the memory of seeing that carp on that rainy night has always stayed with me. The expert put the carp in a hessian sack until morning when we could get a better look at it, and I couldn't wait to see it again. When he finally retrieved it from the sack in daylight it looked even bigger, although it was covered in little red bloody sores from the hessian.

Later in the day, I sat with him and he showed me how to cut out a cube of Spam from a tin, and the way he pushed his size 2 hook through the meat and secured it with a blade of grass. It was 1977, the year of the Silver Jubilee, and the year that Elvis Presley died, and I still wonder who the expert was and if he's still carping today. I owe him a big 'thank you' for sparing a bit of time for a young lad. His kindness contributed greatly to my life as an angler, and enabled me to see thousands of sunsets and sunrises, to be awake with nature, looking out across water and doing what I have always loved - fishing, Thanks, whoever you are, or were.

For four years, I spent every day possible at the park lake having the time of my life, camping and fishing with my mates. By then the fishing seed was sown, but we were still very young and although we always started off the night deadly serious, after a few hours of not catching we would soon be playing about, fighting, lighting fires, and creating all sorts of diversions for our impatient minds. We must have driven the real carpers raving mad, as by this time there were a few anglers carping most weekends.

It was just before I was about to join the army at the age of 16 that I really got into carp fishing. I even built my own rods. The rods were brown, Jerry Savage blanks, and I whipped on all the Fuji eyes, with tuition from my dad's mate, who was a carp angler. Then, Romford Angling Centre, at the time the only shop within range that had a carp fishing department, sent off my blanks to be fitted with leather-whipped, tennis racket handles and Fuji reel seats. They looked the 'dog's' when I got them back and all my mates were envious. I paired the rods off with

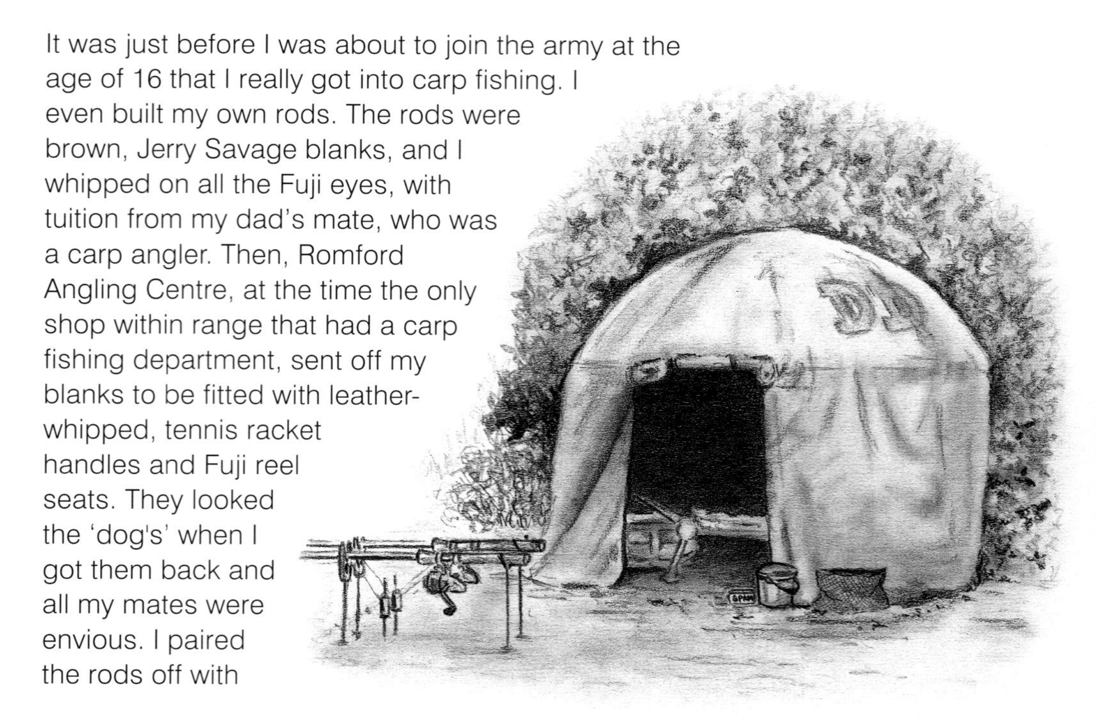

The missus has always supported my obsession.

two Mitchell 810s, got a set of Herons and I was a carp angler. Then I went off with the army for seven years!

I did go carping a few times when I was home on leave, mind. We would just go and poach somewhere back then because I was serving out in Northern Ireland at the time and was hardly bothered about where I fished. My mate, Roy, and me did catch a few big carp for the time, just into the 20s, and I remember reading about a method of attaching a bait to a long hair rather than on the hook - that was the beginning of the hair rig. What was that all about? It would never work, surely?

I left the army and got married to my lifetime companion, Joanne, and we had our first child, a son named Jay. He was my biggest catch ever. We lived just down the road from my childhood playground, my obsession instantly returned, and I found out that carp fishing really had grown since I'd been away. It was a few days before the 16th of June, the start of the new season, and as I took a walk around Hainault, I could see anglers already set up days before the start and waiting for the off. They had little dome tents and all of them had matching set-ups. Hainault did seem to breed a good standard of angler, though.

Many of the lads fishing were youngsters, and as I was about to start again on there, two of them were already leaving the lake, job done, and moving on to other waters in search of monsters. Terry Dempsey and Tony Moore were streets ahead and went on to destroy Darenth Tip Lake, but I had to buy all new gear as my once top of the range set-up would be laughed at now.

Some of the lads who fished Hainault back then were real characters and it was all so exciting for me. The lake's stock was very good for 1988, all the carp had names, and I dreamed about catching these wonderful fish. The big mirror was very well known and was caught regularly at over 36lbs, with the next biggest, the Small 30, that went 33lbs. Then there were five other mirrors that went between 25-28lbs and these made up the A-team that everyone campaigned for.

It was at this time that I met some of my best friends and we are all still very good mates over 23 years later. Jay Willis (Essex Jay) did very well over at Hainault and I'd say he caught most of the fish in there. He would get over Friday evening after work, and nearly every Saturday morning he would get a screamer.

A Dagenham Chase Front Lake fish of 25lbs.

I can still remember the rigs we used. Jay had done a few trips to another lake, South Weald, where he'd met an angler called Kenny Gates. South Weald was very silty, just like Hainault, and Kenny had shown Jay a rig they were using on there. It consisted of a 2oz lead, a swivel on the main line with a very short hook link of 3 inches. This was fished helicopter style, with a bottom bait, and later on pop-ups, then we would put a float stop up

A 22-pounder caught on a cold overnighter.

the line. The float stop was pushed up the main line a bit so that when you cast, the lead would sink in the silt and the hook length would fly up the line to the stop and then be lying on top of the silt. We used to fish our rods up high and pin our main lines down with back leads.

The rod tips would be slightly pulled over with the back lead, and when you had a drop-back the tip would spring back up, and on screamers the back lead used to come out of the water! In principle, it was a very similar rig to today's all-conquering chod. Anyway, that was the fashion over there at the time. More and more of us became good friends and there was always something happening. On one occasion, a load of Hells Angels rocked up and turned the lake into a Woodstock venue!

To be honest, I seemed to struggle over there, even though I was very particular about my choice of swims, my presentation, and the bait I used. When I think back, everything was okay really, I just never really seemed to have it off. Perhaps I was just trying too hard, but I'm sure this was all a good learning curve for later on.

We fished lots of other little waters at the time and I would always do well on them. Dagenham Chase (the Front Lake) was a very good 20s water where I caught plenty; at Bretons Farm I caught the lake record, a 24lb mirror, but back on Hainault, for some reason I struggled.

Towards the end of my time at Hainault, I was working in a family business where I was manager of a wine bar, and it was probably the worst job I've ever had. The hours were crap, I missed a lot the time when my young children were growing up, and dealing with the drunken public was not my favourite pastime. One good thing, though, was that all my angling buddies became regulars, and some Friday nights the bar would be full of my fishing mates. I would quite often finish work at midnight, go straight to the lake for an overnighter to fit in a night's fishing, then go home for a shower in the morning, and be back in the bar for 10.30am. I was absolutely obsessed with it. The fishing, that is, not working in the bar.

I ended up losing the Small 30 at the net once, at the beginning of winter. I was cut off by something in the margins, and not long after, someone caught my line on a plug they were using and landed the 30-pounder with my line still attached. Yep! He had photos of it, the lot. Another time, I was fishing in a swim called the Tench Hole. It was a good swim as there were no carp swims to my

A nice scaly Hainult carp.

The Chunk Fish at 21lbs from Hainault.

right and so I was able to control a fair chunk of water. I had seen a good fish show down to my right in the corner of the lake, so from where I was it was easy to walk a rod down there, drop it in, sprinkle a few baits over the top, and walk the rod back. Nothing happened during the night but the next morning the carp was back again, so I was confident of some action. Not long after I had seen the fish show, two youngsters turned up to float fish, and they set up right over where my hook bait was. I decided to leave it there and just hoped they wouldn't be making too much noise.

I lay on my new bed chair watching the day begin, and every now and then I glanced down to where the lads were fishing. Then, I saw that one of the young kids was standing up with a bent rod and was playing a fish. I thought he must be into one of the tench and so carried on scanning around the lake. The next time I looked, he was further around the end of the lake with a crowd round him so I thought that maybe he had a small carp on, because he'd been into the fish for ages. I saw someone else run from further round with a bigger net for him, and got the binoculars out as it went into the net with a big splosh. I got up and started to walk round when a young kid came running up to me.
"Hey, mister," he said. "Have you got some scales? My mate's got a carp!"

The view across from the Grassy Bank.

One of the A-team. The Friendly at 24lbs.

When I arrived, I couldn't believe it! He had the Small 30 lying there. He'd taken it on a size 16 hook, single maggot, and had landed one of the hardest-fighting fish in the lake! The young kid even had the cheek to moan about it. "I was only after roach," he said, "and this monster came along." It could only happen at Hainault.

There was an angler named Terry Butcher who was a lot older than us, and he had a serious case of OCD, probably the worst I've seen. His tackle was unbelievable; it was beyond immaculate and he was always tampering with it and making improvements. His ideas were well ahead of his time and he would have been an asset to any tackle manufacturer. Anyway, Terry was playing a very good carp one day in a swim right at the back of the island and sadly, he lost it, as his line somehow parted and the fish got free. This carp must have been tired after the fight and went to rest further around the island.

A short time later, another pleasure angler was fishing a swimfeeder and had hooked into a heavy fish that was just plodding up and down. A group of anglers were looking on when suddenly, the big mirror rolled exhausted on the surface, someone grabbed a bigger net and landed the big girl. Once on the bank, it seemed that this guy had managed to cast his feeder and put his size 18 hook through the swivel of Terry's rig that was still attached to the lost fish! Once again, photos were taken and the fish was claimed. How incredible!

Later that day, I caught one of the A-team, a fish called the Friendly at 24lbs, and I was over the moon. I ended up catching a fair few fish over at Hainault but just the one from the A-team. This makes me think of another friend at the time, Neil Lunn, later known as Sleepy Neil. Now, at the time, Neil was really young, about 15 years old, and he'd only had three bites at Hainault; the big 'un at 36lbs-odd, and then the Small 30 at 33lbs. There was always only two 30s in the lake, but one year a fish called the Flop turned 30, only for a short while, and that was to be Neil's third take, completing his three takes at the lake for three 30s. Unbelievable!

The big mirror was a cracking fish that many a time I dreamed of having in my net, but this fish had a thing about coming out at the most amazing times. I can remember more than a few occasions on scorching hot Sundays in the middle of the summer when you would least expect a take, yet someone would have her. The park would be rammed with cars all the way from the car park, across the field, right the way to the bank where we would be fishing. There would be football matches being played, games of cricket, music blaring ... and she would decide to pick up a rig.

Paul Pynen with the Hainault big girl.

There were literally thousands of people there and we had to keep the crowds back. Can you imagine a carp that big on the bank with all that lot about? My god, it nearly started a riot. "What are you going to do with that then?" they would say. "Are you going to eat it?" or "Put that fish back, the poor thing. It's cruel!" Some people would even ask, "What is it?" Yes, she was a proper Sunday mirror.

There are many funny stories about my time on there but I want to mention the lads because they are what made it so special. One of the anglers from those days was Paul Pynen. He had fished over at the lake before us lot, but he'd regularly walk round with his dog at the weekends, and the dog always ploughed through a set-up, knocking all the rods over. Paul was a respected angler who'd already caught the big girl from Hainault and was in with a few other good carpers, but had moved on to other waters, so it was always good to have a chat to him. Another character was Mick Germain, who was, and still is, a complete nutcase, and a book could be written just on the antics that we all got up to over the years. Craig Bateman and Lee Munders were good friends, too. I've named all these guys because they were part of the gang over the next decade.

Then, it was time to move home. The missus and me, and my little son, Jay, had another addition to the family, my daughter, Brooke, so we needed more room and we had a house to view near Nazeing. I knew very little about the area, but it was a nice drive through the countryside and I knew of a lake called Brackens Pool that was around that way somewhere, but the house was in a right old state and needed a great deal of work. I left my missus there to have a good look round and jumped in the car. I was sure the lake was close by, so I followed my instinctive ability to find a water and was amazed that it was no more than five minutes away from the house we were looking at. It was as if it was meant to be and this would surely be my new venue. I rushed back to the missus at the house and said, "It's in a mess, love, but we can get it all done," and so we moved in. It was great living so close to a water, but I didn't realise that I had actually moved right smack bang in the middle of the Lee Valley Parks. The area was full of lakes, a lifetime of fishing lay around me – and I was just the chap to make the most of it!

Chapter Two - Neil Lunn

A Hainault Hat-trick

When I was about ten years old and already into my fishing, Hainault Forest Lake was right on my doorstep. I often walked round it, and it was always busy with really keen carp anglers, even midweek. At the time, Hainault was probably one of the best carp lakes in Essex with the two big 'uns around 33 to 37lbs, and a small handful of mid-20s. By today's standards, this lake wouldn't stand out, but back then it certainly did.

Like other lakes, there seemed to be a style of how anglers fished over there and the tackle trend was rods with full Duplon handles, Cardinal 55s resting on original Delkims, and single bank sticks with the rods butts on the deck … cool at the time! It was carp tackle that I would have just loved to own at that age, but there was no chance.

I remember walking round there one freezing February day when a guy had just landed a mirror of around 25lbs, and from then on my interest moved toward carp fishing. Even by just walking around the place, you could tell that this was a lake where carp definitely didn't run up your rods and it seemed to be fished by the same guys doing long sessions.

I was about 12 when I got my first set of two matching rods, reels and buzzers, all bought with money saved from Christmas and a birthday. I'd had carp tackle before that, but it was all odds and sods. Now I was set up, really into it and I spent all my time over at another local lake, Fairlop Waters, where I caught loads, but nothing of any size. That's how it is when you start, though, or it was then.

Even at that young age, although I was always having a laugh with my mates, I was taking the angling very seriously, either fishing Fairlop Waters or walking round it and getting to know other anglers, as you do. Every so often, three guys from Hainault Forest Lake fished on Fairlop on a Sunday. After they'd fished the weekend on Hainault, not catching, they'd turn up to get some bites. I got to know them as Craig Bateman, Dave Barns, and Dave Baylis.

The close season of 1990 seemed to go on forever and my parents were planning a summer holiday for us all in the middle of June. Oh no! Even though my mother was going to get me out of school for two weeks, I was going to miss the start of the season. Damn! I remember asking her where we were going.
"Dorset," she said.
"Yeah, but where in Dorset?" I asked.
"It's a holiday park, called Warmwell," she replied. "Oh yeah, and there are two lakes that have carp in them, so you can take your rods if we have room in the car."
'If we had room in the car?' I'd make sure of that!

What a result! Not only did I have no school for two weeks, but also I could do the start of the season, and even fish for two weeks if I wanted. I'd never heard of Warmwell, and had no idea of the size of the carp in there. All I knew was that there were two lakes, one with smaller fish, and the other with bigger ones.

The more I thought about where we were going, the more sure I became that it sounded like the place another angler, Mark, on Fairlop Waters, had fished a few times. He'd done really well, and on his last trip, he'd had a 30lb common. He'd said that there weren't many carp anglers who fished there, only a couple of locals. Yes!

I had to get my bait sorted for the two weeks so I decided to make my own milk/bird food boilies. All ingredients were from Premier Baits which consisted of: 20% calcium caseinate, 20% casein 90mesh, 20% vitamino, 20% soya flour, and 20% cede bird food, plus 3ml Peach Melba to a six-egg mix and 20ml of walnut oil added in the bag over the rolled bait when dried. I'd used this before the trip to Warmwell and had caught lots in a short space of time, so I knew it worked well. I say 'worked well' - they loved it!

Soon we were in the car heading down to Warmwell and all I wanted to do was get there and check out the lakes. It was the day before the start of the new season and I really liked the look of the place. Even though it was quite small, it had two islands and the water was shallow and really weedy in some spots. There were many places where the carp could hide, without a doubt.

I was really excited as I walked down to the lake on the morning of the 16th of June and just wanted to get the rods out as soon as possible. There were a few anglers already set up around the lake, as they'd started to fish from midnight, and I decided on a swim that was on the left-hand side of a bridge that went on to the island. I got the bank sticks in, and the rods set up and then thought about where to cast them. The right-hand rod was sent straight out tight against a bush on the island, and the left-hand one cast up the left side of the island, just off an outcrop of reeds. I put a few free offerings round each and sat back.

It was only 20 or 30 minutes before the right-hand rod was away with a fast take. I soon had a carp in the net and it looked around 18lbs or so. I'd just got this fish on the bank to unhook, when my left-hand rod was away with another belter of a take. I picked the rod up and straight away it seemed to be a slower fight. There was a guy in my swim who had popped down to give me a hand with the first fish, so he slipped that back and helped to net the second one. As it rolled in the net he said, "I think you've a good one there. It could be a 30!"
I couldn't believe what I was hearing. It turned out to be a 26lb common, but I was more than over the moon as this was a new personal best and I was two fish up within just an hour or so of having the rods out. Result!

After a couple of days, the start of the season was well under way and there were only a few anglers on the lake so I started to fish different swims, catching most of the time. Nothing was as big as the common I'd had on the opening day, but hey, I didn't really care. I was more than happy.

At Warmwell, looking across to the swim from where I caught most of the fish.

The first week passed quite quickly and I was on around six fish at this point. As we got into the start of the second week, I near enough had the lake to myself most days, with just the odd pleasure angler doing a bit. Warmwell seemed to have a good head of fish, but not many anglers trying to catch them.

In just a few days, and as the lake got quieter, I started to find out where the fish were and really fancied one particular swim that faced the corner of the island on the opposite side of the lake to where I'd had the two on the opening day. I decided to cast both rods close together just over the back of heavy weed, one on the left-hand corner of the island, and the other on the right, hoping I could trap them whichever way round the island they went.

A few baits were catapulted around the two rods and then I tried to sit back and relax in a nightmare of a swim, because the bank was so steep. It was a warm day and I spotted two fish in the upper layers of the water above the weed and not that far from my two rods. One of these fish was a very big common, but a few minutes later as they went a little deeper into the water, I lost sight of them. Then I was away on my left-hand rod with a real savage take, and as I picked it up, line was stripping off it like there was no tomorrow. The fish weeded me up for some time but then I was able to get it on the move again. It really felt like a slow, heavy lump, but when it rolled into the net, I still didn't have any idea how big it was until I lifted it out and then - my god! I'd got what looked to be a massive common! Well, it was massive back then.

A guy who was walking round saw me with it on the bank and lent a hand. It weighed just over 30lbs, and I just could not believe it. Talk about smash your personal best, and with a common, too! After this, I decided to have a day or so away from the lake and return after I'd made more bait. With only four days of the holiday left, I fished and was so happy with what I'd had that anything else was just a bonus. I was only ever fishing the days. I didn't do one night session in the whole two weeks but this didn't make any difference. If anything, I was always fishing new areas and catching.

The next day trip, I wanted to fish a swim where I'd had a few fish, but nothing big. In this particular swim, I was able to fish one rod in the gap between the two islands, and one on a gravel patch tight against the island that was straight in front of me. There were plenty of options in the swim and I think this was one of the best on the lake. Back then, the swims didn't have any names, but they probably do now.

I remember this day because it was raining heavily for most of it, and I ended up with a run and got soaking wet. The rod that was cast on the gravel patch tight against the island was away, but this fish didn't seem to fight much and was soon in the net. My God! I struggled to lift the net from the water and carry the fish up the bank, and I could see this was another big 'un. It was weighed and I had another 30lb carp, just over 30 by a couple of ounces, but who cared? Over the moon was not the word. I had a fantastic two weeks at Warmwell and the fishing was awesome.

I couldn't wait to get home and tell my fishing pals about the result I'd had in just two weeks' fishing. I saw Craig and Dave over at my local lake, Fairlop Waters, and told them about the place. I didn't think that Warmwell was going to stay the fairly quiet lake that I'd fished on that trip.

"Where are you going to fish, now." Craig asked me. "With two 30s under your belt you should come and fish over at Hainault with us."
I told him that I wasn't sure about it, that I didn't know where to fish at that point and all I really wanted to do was to go carp fishing - rather than target any big carp.

Craig asked me a few times if I was going to do some fishing with him over at Hainault Lake, but every time, I said I wasn't sure if I wanted to fish there at that time for some reason - maybe because it was known to be a very hard lake to fish. For the rest of that year I carried on fishing Fairlop Waters, seeing Craig over there every so often, and he was always asking, "Come on, come over there!" Eventually, I said, "Yeah, okay. Why not? It'll be good to do the night over there with you."
It was around three weeks into the new season and all the big fish had already been on the bank once but to be honest, I didn't really think about that too much.

I remember it clear as a bell. Craig came to pick me up and we headed over to Hainault on a busy Saturday afternoon. We got to the lake and a lot of the swims were taken on the forest bank so we set up in the two middle swims on the grass bank.

That night around midnight I was sitting on my rods when I heard Craig's buzzer sound with a bit of a slow take that turned out to be a common of around 18lbs. I thought, 'It's the first night on Hainault, and I've seen one on the bank.' It wasn't one of the A team but it was a carp, and that was it. I was really keen and couldn't wait to get back the following weekend.

The next Friday came around and, once again, I was heading over to the lake with Craig in his van full of tackle. Most of the swims on the forest side were free and that was the side of the lake we wanted to fish, so we picked two swims and set up for the weekend.

I knew that the bait being used at Hainault was fishmeal based so I thought I'd stick to the milk/birdfood with Peach Melba because it was a bit different and not many people would be using something like that. Rigs were really basic, with running inline distance leads, 12lb Merlin hooklengths and size 8 hooks.

A few more anglers showed up on that Friday evening, but that didn't matter because we had our spots for the weekend. I was introduced to a guy called Jay Willis, who was fishing a few swims down to my right, and a few of the other chaps. They all seemed to be a good bunch of lads.

Not much happened that Friday night or during the day on the Saturday. It was all a bit quiet on the carp front but certainly not quiet in the respect of people walking round the lake, as it's a country park. After the gates shut in the evening, though, it seemed a lot more peaceful, that's for sure.

Sunday morning soon came round and I remember waking up, looking at the rods and thinking, 'Oh well, the carp are just not having it.' I got up to see if anyone else had had anything else in the night, and at this point Jay, who was fishing a few swims down to my right, came up and said, "I've got a fish on but it's snagged on the island in front of you. I need to go out on an inflatable Lilo to try to get it."

I'm not sure how the fish managed to get so far up the lake to his left and snag him. Maybe he was in the café toilet gelling his hair at the time of the take, who knows? Anyway, out he went, into the lake on a Lilo, straight over my two rods and the baited area and I was thinking, 'that's my chance of a bite gone out of the window now', but it was good that Jay was going to all this effort to get the fish. I was looking forward to seeing what he'd hooked, but when he got out to the snag he found that the fish was already off. From then on, he started to gel his hair in his bivvy on a Sunday morning, instead of going to the café toilet.

As I slowly started to pack away that morning, I had a short, fast take on one of the rods. As I got to it the line went slack, so I picked up the rod and started to wind. Whatever was on was running toward me fast, and I could I see a bow wave from what looked to be a large carp as it hit the surface.
I heard Craig shout, "Neil! You into one?"
"Yeah," I shouted back as I got a tight line on the fish.

Second session, and my first bite from Hainault. The Big One at 30lbs 10oz.

It started taking line, and kiting right, it headed down the margins to the point under all the overhanging trees. It felt like a very slow, heavy weight, and as the fish slowly came out from under the trees and into the open water, I did think I was going to lose it for a moment, but it soon it rolled into the net.
"Looks like you've got the big 'un, mate," Craig said.
"What?"
Yes, he was right. I had it in the net and I couldn't believe it. We got her on the bank and weighed her at 30lb 10oz. What a first fish to have! We did the photos and sent her back and I certainly packed up that day with a smile on my face.

I returned to the lake on a Monday afternoon and there wasn't another carp angler fishing. Result! Now I could do my three-day session in the swim I really fancied, the Mud Flap. I had a fair bit of bait with me, which would enable me to fish for the three days and to top up the same areas each day if I didn't have any bites, as I expected.

The weather was really warm during the day, with not much wind, but this didn't put me off. I was prepared to sit it out for the three nights, and that's what I intended to do.

The Flop fish at 30lbs 1oz.

Returning the Flop fish, this was my second fish from Hainault.

I was all set up by late afternoon and ready to get the rods on the chosen spots in the evening. I put the right-hand rod straight out, around one rod length off the island to the right of some snags, and the left-hand rod cast down toward the back of the island under a hanging tree – that was a bit of a tricky cast, but I managed it after a few attempts.

Not much happened over the first 48 hours, so I just recast the rods to the same spots and topped up with bait. I was only looking to recast twice at the most in 24 hours. The first two nights and early mornings, fish showed around the back of the island and not that far from my left-hand rod, so I thought that one would probably be the first to go. How wrong I was.

On the third morning, my right-hand rod came alive with a very fast take at around 6am. As I picked up the rod, the fish started to move on a tight line to my left toward the snags, but with some pressure, it moved out into mid-water and started to come toward the bank. My rod was dipped half under the water as the fish kept running in and out of a fallen tree to my left. It by no means wanted to come to the net, but after a 20-minute struggle, I managed to get it safely over the cord and it was mine.

I peered into the net and thought, 'My God, it's another big one.' I knew it wasn't the Small Thirty that was normally around 33lbs, but the only other one it could be was a fish called Flop, and that had last been out at 30lb 4oz. It could only be that one. I got the fish on the bank and weighed it at 30lb 1oz, and then I slipped it into the sack, got the rods back out and waited for a friend to turn up. He was due to walk round the lake on his way to work to see what was happening. When he arrived, he couldn't believe that I'd had my second bite on the lake and the third biggest fish. He wanted to chuck me in the drink and to be fair I could understand that. Most of the anglers over there had been trying for a good few years to catch even one of the big 'uns, and I'd had two of them in a couple of sessions. The photos were done and I sent the fish back. I was one happy fella; two bites, two 30s! Result or what!

I packed up later that day and headed home, but as soon as I was indoors all I could think about was my next session and which swim I fancied. I didn't fish over the weekends as I had time midweek, but I did spend time walking around the lake and seeing what was happening.

I got a load more bait rolled at home over a few days and decided to pre-bait a couple of spots. As I'd already had two bites and two of the big ones on the bait, I thought the fish must like it so it wouldn't be a bad idea to be putting a bit in a few days before I fished. I decided that I'd only put it in, though, if there was no one else set up and fishing.

I walked over there with a few kilos of bait thinking about the two swims I wanted to put it out in, and this time round I fancied the open water in the middle of the lake on the forest bank. Nobody was around when I got there, so I baited two swims next to each other, only around 20 yards out and in a line between them. Not many people were fishing only 20 yards out. Normally, they cast into the middle, so when I returned to fish a few days later, even if I couldn't get into one of the swims, I would go in the other and still be able to fish on the area I'd baited. That was the plan, anyway!

I returned to fish later that week and got set up nice and early in the swim I most wanted out of the two, as everybody was due over to the lake later that Friday afternoon. At this point, I had done a few sessions on my own and although it was nice fishing midweek with nobody around, I did fancy a bit of a social and to do some fishing with a couple of pals who were due over that weekend.

Later that day, the rods were out on the pre-baited area and just topped up with a few baits catapulted around each one. I settled into another session and waited for Craig and Jay and a few others to finish work and get over for the weekend.

The weather forecast for the next 24 hours on that Friday was looking really good, with fairly strong winds that were blowing straight onto my bank, and the weather stayed that way, but to everyone's surprise there were no bites at all. Really strange.

By late Saturday morning, with nothing happening, I decided to have a sort out, tie new rigs and get the rods ready for a recast. Both rods were reeled in and propped against the umbrella, and for some time I just looked at the lake, watched how the wind was still blowing into my bank and wondered why there hadn't been any action, because it looked really good.

Actually, it looked pretty good in the margins, so while I was sorting out new rigs and pottering around in the bivvy I decided to put both rods in the edge, one to my left in front of some hanging trees, and the other around one rod length out, with single hook baits on both. The lines were then slackened off and the rods rested into the buzzers.

What a good move this turned out to be! After around ten minutes, I was away with a fast take on the right-hand rod, and as I picked it up a powerful fish stripped line off the reel, headed out into the open water and into the middle of the lake. I didn't mind, though, because this was a safe area to play the fish and away from the marginal tree line.

A guy was walking round the lake and he stopped when he saw that I was into a fish, so I asked him if he would give my mate Craig a shout, who was fishing a couple of swims up to my right.

I turned around and saw a really serious look on Craig's face as he walked toward me and said, "You in, dude?"
"Yes, mate!" I replied. "It's stripped a load of line off the reel and it's out in the middle."
The fish was powerful and moving at a slow, steady pace. I really didn't know what I'd hooked into, but it felt as angry as hell.

After some time, I managed to get the fish closer in, where it hit the surface, and Craig who was on net duty said really quietly, "It looks like the small one, dude!" By that, he meant the Small Thirty, at that time the biggest fish in the lake and normally around the 35lb mark. This left me playing the fish while shaking in my boots and I just wanted it safely in the net.

It's a hat-trick! The Small Thirty at 31lbs 10oz.

Bigger second time around. The Small Thirty at 35lbs.

Job done!

At last, the fish was on the surface and was ready for Craig to lift the net. As she went in there was huge shout from us all – 'Come on!' I got the sling wet and the scales ready and then lifted the Small One from the water to be weighed. It looked awesome and was a really big-framed fish. On the scales, the needle went round to 31lb 10oz, a little down in weight by a couple of pounds but who cared? I sure didn't. I couldn't believe it! I'd just had my third fish out of Hainault Forest Lake and it was the biggest carp in there. That's a hat trick!

I fished the rest of the summer and all through the winter on Hainault, but didn't have another bite, just the three biggest fish in the lake. That was the only year when there was three 30-pounders in there because the Flop fish didn't get back up to that weight again. It definitely wasn't an easy place to catch from. I had done the summer and winter, the rod hours were racking up and I was still on three fish, but I'd had the three that counted.

I fished Hainault again the following season, but really struggled and only caught a few small fish to around the 20lb mark. I didn't manage to get any of the other known mid-20s on the wish list, and at the end of this season, I decided to leave Hainault alone and fish other places. Maybe I'd return at some time.

For the next couple of years I moved around. fishing different waters like Larksfield, Broxbourne Lagoons and a few other places, catching a few here and there. I'd been hearing of one fish in Hainault called the Boss that was getting toward the 30lb mark. It was getting caught at around 28lbs and I thought that maybe it was time to go back and have a go for the others, with the chance of this one getting even bigger.

I returned to Hainault lake around three years after I'd first fished there, with the hope of having a few of the other fish I hadn't caught, started fishing in August and ended up getting a bite on every other trip. September and October were great, as on most venues and once I'd worked out where the fish were, I was getting a bite on most trips throughout that period.

I ended up catching the cracking Peach at 26lbs, Wally at 27lbs, the Big Common at 26lbs, a recapture of the Small Thirty at 35lbs, and a handful of low-20s. The only fish that I didn't catch was the Boss, and that would have been around the 29lb mark. That was a shame, but I couldn't carry on fishing there for just the one fish, having caught near enough every other fish in the lake. It was job done and time to look for a new challenge, but Hainault will always be a part of my carping memories, and after all, that's what this book is all about.

Chapter Three
Nazeing Meads - The Lagoons

Brackens Pool had some very good fish in it. There were three that went 30lbs; Two Tone, Bill's Fish, and Spot, all in this little two-acre lake, so I got myself a ticket and fished there for a short while. It was a very tricky water, and there were some long-stay anglers who were practically living on the venue. I saw most of the big ones get caught and one night I landed a cracking 25lb leather for Mark Wilcox, who I'm still friends with today.

Sadly, for some reason, they drained the lake down and moved the fish over to the big pit beside Brackens that was known as the Centre Lagoon. The Lagoons were proper waters and were massive in comparison to anything I had ever fished. The North Lagoon was 25 acres, and was supposed to contain some monsters. Zenon Bojko and Phil Harper had been doing a bit of time on it and Roger Smith and Kerry Darringer were often seen walking about the pit. The Centre Lagoon channelled through a bridge and into the South Lagoon, so it's all one lake and the fish could go from one to the other. Combined, the lakes were about 60 acres.

All I knew about the place was that it was rock hard, and that it had done a common to 33lbs 8oz and that another good angler, Joe Brown, had a good hit one year at the start of the season on the Centre around the sluice area. The flood relief canal entered the North Lagoon through a sluice gate, then at the other end of the lake there was another sluice that allowed the water to pour into the Centre Lagoon. Right down at the bottom of the South Lagoon, the water poured into an overspill weir, and so back into the relief canal, so in theory, the lakes all had a river running through them when we had lots of rain, but as the Brackens fish went in the Centre and South, these were the ones I was interested in.

No one knew the actual stock of the Lagoons so it was always a mystery, and this was what lured us, the unknown. I started to spend every available moment walking the Centre and South and became addicted to the place, as was nearly all the old Hainault gang. The traditional close season was spent plumbing and searching every nook and cranny, but to start with, it was just Jay, me, Mick and Paul. Mick was a plasterer and more or less had to plaster my whole house, so naturally, with me going on about it all the time, he got interested and bought a ticket, and so did Paul.

In the spring, the water went gin clear and all the carp congregated in the area where the sluice gate poured into the Centre. It was like a meeting place that they loved, and as the weather became hotter, the carp would be seen in great shoals. We were able to stand above them and look down as they disappeared under the road to where the water was gushing in. This was where I learned just what lived in the lake, and there really were some cracking fish, and a fair few of them too. It was obvious that these fish were shoaling-up for spawning, but because the lake was so big, it would always be a late spawn. This gathering would last for weeks and weeks and then, when it was right, they would all move out of the Centre Lagoon and into the South where the lake was riddled with bars and weed, ideal for their spawning.

It was close season and I was planning my first ever session. Jay and me were down for the first few days, and I just knew I had to be somewhere around the sluice area so that I could ambush these fish as they came down the lake to the sluice. There were three swims that would be well worth a try for intercepting them, but I liked the one that I called the Gravelly. It had a very shallow bar that ran out in front of me, and at the end of this bar it widened and dropped off into about eight feet of water, where the fish had to pass on their route up and down the lake. Jay and me had put together a really nice bait, using Mainline's Liver Marine base mix, and we added Nash's Salmon Oil Palatant with Red Liver. It was very good bait, and we spent days and days rolling it in my little shed in the back garden. We would roll 100 eggs' worth of bait in a day, then go and bait up, and we kept a steady flow going in all around the area. To the right of 'my' swim, the bar just dropped off into deeper water and I didn't fancy that area but Jay did, so he did the start in the swim one up to my right.

To be honest, not many anglers were fishing these lagoons. They were quite daunting to many, so we knew our swims were safe, and on the final build-up to the start, Jay and me gave them two hits of a hundred eggs' worth in one go. I don't know how many kilos that is and it probably wasn't as much as it seemed, but it bloody felt like it having to roll it all, I can tell you. Mick and Paul also decided they would be fishing at the start, in the first two swims, with Mick in the Gate, and Paul to my left, in a little in-between swim. I had been seeing fish all over the area during the build-up so we had to be in with a chance.

We all arrived on the 15th of June. The preparation had been done, all the hard work was finished, and it was now time to chill and catch some carp. I can't remember if any other anglers were on the Centre, but I know a few were on the South. It was all so exciting then, those starts on the 16th of June every year. We were totally buzzing and all got our rods out on the stroke of midnight.

At first light, I heard one of Jay's alarms screaming next door. I wondered just how he does it, especially after I'd put so much planning in my choice of swim, and for all the right reasons. It was at the end of the bar that carp would be passing by all the time, the depth of water was just right, and so on. Whereas Jay, he just goes next door, on the wrong side of the bar in deep water, and bingo - he's first away! His fish was really fighting hard and was coming down my margin, dangerously close to a snag, but there was nothing he could do as his fish clipped the branches and was soon off the hook. He was gutted, as were we all; it would have been great to land the first of the campaign.

Jay didn't have to wait for too long for another bite, though. Half an hour later, he was away again on the recast rod. Luckily, this fish fought out into the open water and was stripping line at a rapid rate. Apart from the danger of the sharp gravel bar near where we were fishing, out in the open water were some buoys that the boats used to turn around, and we didn't want 'our' fish going round them.

Jay played out this hard fighter and I waited with the net, eager to see what he'd caught. In the clear water, we saw a dark mirror as it made its last few dashes for freedom, and as it tired and rolled on the top, I netted the first carp of the season for Jay, a lovely, dark, old-looking fish, which weighed in at 22lbs. We didn't have photos of any of the fish so every single one we caught was new to us, apart from the Brackens Pool fish that had been stocked. We decided to call this one Tug because it really did pull hard! We only named them for ourselves, though, in case we caught any of them again.

It was still early morning and I felt that the fish were only just turning up from wherever they had spent the night, as we hadn't heard any during the hours of darkness. I was fishing one rod over the end of the bar in about eight feet of water, and the other was halfway down the bar, off the left-hand side at around the same depth, two areas that I was so sure the carp would be searching around in. At 8am, my right-hand rod pulled up tight to the clip and roared off.

Jay lands the first fish, an old-looking 22lb mirror.

'Blimey!' I thought. 'They really fly off, these fish', and after a few highly spirited runs I had a small double rolling into the net. Again, it was a very old-looking fish, this time of 15lbs, and I was now off the mark. Jay took a quick couple of snaps for me and I got the rod back on the spot in case any more were about.

Mick, in the Gate, which was the first swim on our bank, landed a small common, and then Paul, next door to my left, had a small mirror of a similar size to mine. Everyone had caught and this was brilliant. As I said, this lake was known as very hard and I hadn't heard of many getting caught. As the day went on, it seemed that more fish turned up in the area, so I kept a bit of bait going in. They'd seen enough of it over the weeks and were, I hoped, looking for it. I had just fired out a few baits when the left-hand rod was one-toning. This was turning into a great session! The lads came to my swim to help out and this time I landed an 18lb common; we took a few quick snaps and slipped it back.

The action came to a sudden halt after that feeding spell, but six takes was a great start, especially on this water. All was quiet throughout the night and at first light, I lost one that cut me off on the bar. Then it really started to chuck it down and I got drenched rigging that rod back up. I recast it but didn't turn the alarm back on, and I was standing under the tailgate of my car, out of the rain,

Blimey, they fly off! My first one, another old-looking mirror at 15lb.

drying my hair off, when I heard a sound like something buzzing. For a second, I thought, 'what the hell is that?' before I glanced at my rods and saw the recast one was flying.

'How long had that been going?' I thought, as I picked up the rod. It was heading a long way out for one of the boats' marker flags, but I stopped it just in time and then it shot off in the opposite direction. The fish kited to left and right, all the way in, and each time I gained more line until it was ready to net. It was another nice common weighing 22lbs, and 20-pounders were big carp back then. They still are today, but in those days they were target fish. A 30-pounder was like a 40 today, and only Paul in our gang had caught a 30. A few years later, another angler we knew called Rob Kirby had caught nine 30s! That was an incredible CV.

Paul caught an 18lb common and I had to be off the lake as I was going to Ascot the next day. The trip had been planned at the wine bar where I worked, and the missus was looking forward to it so there was no getting out of it. Things always seemed to fall at the start of the season! Another year, my brother got married on June the 16th and I really did try my best to change the date but he was having none of it. Anyway, I was off to Ladies Day, and all I could do to take my mind off fishing was to drink lots of champagne.

My second common of the day.

Good angling, mate! The biggest so far at 25lbs.

Paul's swim was a kind of in-between swim to my left, and he told me that after I'd gone, the fish had started to show. Typical! As he now had a bit more room, he put one rod over my side (good angling, mate!) and later on caught the biggest fish so far, a really nice 25lb mirror with a single scale on one side; a nice result.

Later, Paul felt unwell and he must have felt rough because he ended up going home, with fish still in the area. Mick saw an opportunity for a move. He had been kind of out of the way in his swim, so he moved straight into Paul's bivvy, and when I returned the next day, he had some fantastic news. He had landed his first fish at 30lbs! He was going bonkers. Mick is crazy, anyway, so you can imagine what he was like after catching that fish! It was a cracking-looking mirror and so the swim was named Gertie's, after Gertie the 30. At the time, we only knew of one other original 30 and that was the common, and then there were the three Brackens fish. I won't say any more about Mick's fish because I've asked him to tell the story in his own words...

Gertie the 30 - by Mick Germain

It must have been around the late 80s when I first met Jerry Hammond over at Hainault Lake, in Essex. He had just come out of the army and was rekindling his love for fishing, which he'd put on hold for eight years while serving Queen and country. It was about that time that I was also lucky enough to meet up with a bunch of lads who are very good friends of mine to this day, Jerry included. Hainault was a crazy place to fish in those days, full of carpy characters and the occasional oddball. From time to time, there were devil worshippers, Druids, and escapees from Claybury mental hospital, which was just down the road, who used to wander around at night. You'd be mad to fish it on your own, that's for sure! I used to put a baseball bat under my bedchair, just in case. Luckily, I never had to use it!

Sometimes, there was an impromptu disco on a Saturday night. Someone would always bring a 1980s-style ghetto blaster down to the lake and pump out funky music until the early hours. If you wanted a bit of quiet fishing, you didn't fish Hainault! It was a fun place to fish, though, and it's where I met my best mates ever. We were, and always will be, a band of brothers. There was Jerry, Paul Pynen, Jay Willis, Craig Bateman, Sleepy Neil, Lee Maunders, Dave Bayliss, Terry Dempsey, Tony Moore, Paul Fagin, Gary the Poet, Davis Dave, Pike Steve, Foghorn Tyler, Mark 'Scruffy' Smith, and many, many more, all of them great lads. It was a fantastic place to fish back then, in the mid to late 80s. There are so many memories and we had so much fun.

When Jerry started to fish Hainault, we got to know each quite well. From time to time, I used to fish another Essex madhouse called the Chase, at Dagenham, and Jerry used to fish it a bit too. We had a lot in common; similar tastes in music, humour and, of course, a love for carp fishing. Hainault was the start of a friendship that is still strong today.

At the time, Jerry was living nearby in Chigwell with his lovely wife, Joanne, and his two kids, in a small flat which was getting smaller as the kids were getting bigger, so they decided to up sticks and found a three-bedroom house in Nazeing, near Broxbourne and not far from where their house and fishery, Carthagena, is now. To be fair, the house was in a bit of a state and needed major renovation including completely re-plastering which, as I'm a plasterer, Jerry asked me to do. Jerry used to mix the plaster for me and we had a right few laughs I can tell you. Jerry's a very funny man and could have been a brilliant comedian, as well as an actor, soldier and shit-hot carp angler!

Jerry loves masks and puppets and many an angler has been scared out of his wits by Jerry waking them up in the middle of the night wearing his freaky rubber old man face mask. He used to own a variety of puppets, his favourite being a Sooty hand puppet, and one day while working round his house, we decided to nip down to the nearby baker to get some rolls for lunch. While driving there, Jerry decided to wear Sooty on his right hand, and wave him at other drivers, but the best bit was when he was parking the car by the baker's. He nearly hit a car coming out and the other driver was not happy. He got out to give Jerry a piece of his mind, and as the bloke approached, Jerry wound the window down and waved Sooty at him.
"Sorry, mate," he said to the bloke. "It wasn't my fault. Sooty was driving, not me!" The other driver was speechless and I cried with laughter for about an hour afterwards. The guy's face was a picture. That was pure comedy and typical Jerry.

Shortly after that, while I was still working at his house, Jerry said we should take a look at the Broxbourne lagoons, which at the time were owned by Leisure Sports and now by CEMEX. There was a small, three-acre pit called Brackens, which held three or four good 30s and a couple of our mates had fished it. Lee Valley Parks were due to take it over the following season, drain down Brackens, take some of the bigger fish out and place them in the much larger Centre and South lagoons. This would ease the pressure on these old fish, because Brackens used to get pretty busy at times. Obviously, there were other fish in the lagoons, but it hardly ever got fished and Lee Valley was trying to get more anglers to fish them. Apparently, Roger Smith had stuck some fingerlings in there from when he used to fish Redmire pool with Jack Hilton, back in the early 70s, and that certainly added to the aura of the place. Tickets were going to be made available for the following season, and Jerry was keen to join as it was only about five minutes drive from his house. When he first showed me the place, I was really impressed with it and later on, a few of the Hainault boys came with us for a walk around the complex and we eventually decided to join. Jerry, Paul Pynen, Jay Willis and me joined first, and some of the others later on that season, as they were still fishing other waters.

At the time, the traditional close season was in place so we spent that time spotting fish and making bait. I kind of miss the old close season sometimes, and there was definitely a magical feel about June the 16th. I know waters are open most of the year but I feel that there should be some kind of closure, just to give the fish a break - even a month or so in the spring or summer. It was during those close season sorties around the Lagoons that we were starting to find fish, and soon realised that there were some lovely-looking carp in there. We were getting some bait in, everything was looking good for the start, and by the beginning of June we were really getting excited. Those days leading up to the 16th seemed to drag. We had earmarked four swims where we wanted to start, on the Road bank, on the centre part of the lagoons, and hoped that we would be able to fish them as long as no other anglers got there first.

Well, it was finally June the 15th - the eve of the new season. At around midday, the bailiffs agreed that the 20 or so anglers who were there were likely to be the only ones fishing, so they said it was okay to choose swims and set up. We had all been chatting among ourselves for a couple of hours before that, and everyone knew where they wanted to go. No one had a problem with the part of the lake we wanted to fish, and besides, the lagoons are about 60 acres so there was plenty of water for 20 anglers. It was all sorted out in a friendly way and there was no hassle at all.

So, we set up our gear in our chosen swims and waited for the off. We spent the day drinking tea, winding each other up and telling jokes; four good mates just enjoying being at a new lake which we were about to fish for the first time. Finally, midnight came, someone let off a huge firework, and we all cast out into the unknown for the first time that season.

Nothing much happened in the night but at about 7am, Jay had the first take, which he lost, but soon he was away again and after a while, he had a 22lb mirror, which we nicknamed Tug, a fish which we all had the pleasure of capturing over the seasons.

Over the next couple of days, everyone caught, except me, until I managed to catch a 15lb common from the Gate swim where I was fishing at about 30 yards on a gravel hump in six feet of water. I was pleased with that but felt the bulk of the fish were not in my area. I felt a bit cut off from the action as my swim was on a corner, but I'd fancied the area because I'd seen a few fish swimming about close in, a couple of days prior to the start. Once there was angling pressure, though, they all seemed to drift away, out in front of where Jerry, Jay, and Paul were, further down the bank. Still, never mind, I was enjoying myself and the lads were catching a few so it was all good.

Thursday came and Jerry had to go to the Ascot races because the wine bar he ran at the time had organised a race day, and there was no way he could get out of it. He was gutted, and rightly so, because he'd had fish and as an angler, there is nothing worse then pulling off a water when you're on fish. You could be offered the choice between a two-week break in the Bahamas or somewhere equally exotic, with sexy girls on the beach and glorious sunshine, or catching big carp on an English gravel pit, and I bet most of us would think, 'Very nice, but I'd rather catch carp'. Weird or what? That's fishing for you, but unless you're an angler, you don't get it do you?

Jerry left about four in the afternoon to finalise things for the race day and was due back on the Friday night, all going to plan. That left Paul, Jay, and me to fish on. Later that day, Paul had a lovely-looking mirror around 25lbs, which would grow into a big 30, a couple of seasons later. As I said, I felt that I was missing out a bit on the action where I was, but I didn't want to move into Jerry's swim, because he was coming back over to fish. Even though he'd packed up all his gear and the swim was vacant, and any angler could have moved in there, I refused to do it. Jerry had put a fair amount of bait into that swim and deserved to get back in there. Luckily, no other anglers jumped in, although more anglers were turning up to fish by now as the weekend was coming up. Still, it was a big pit and fish had been out in different areas so there was plenty of scope. A couple stopped to look, but we told them that our mate would like to get back in there. The calibre of angler was good. They were proper anglers who knew the score and wouldn't want a similar thing done to them, so they had no problem. There was no hassle. We made them a cup of tea and actually, they became good friends of ours over the season, proper old school.

The next day, which was the Friday, Paul didn't feel too good and decided to go home. He felt so bad that he couldn't even be bothered to take down his bivvy so, not one to miss an opportunity, I moved in to his swim and his bivvy to be nearer the fish – plus, he had a Lafuma bedchair which was more

I was pleased with this 15lb common, but felt the bulk of the fish were not in my area.

comfortable then my Argos sun-lounger! He didn't care, he just wanted to get home, poor old sod.

So, now I felt more confident, I decided to have a little plumb around and found a gravel bar to my left, 80 yards out, with about five feet of water on top of the bar dropping down to 12 feet either side. It was a bit of a difficult chuck due to the fact that I only had 2¾lb test curve rods, with Shimano 4500 Baitrunners, which I was using for the first time, and the wind was picking up a bit, blowing southerly along the lake. Paul had said that he'd had his fish long, although I wasn't totally sure whereabouts, what with the southerly. I knew they were still out there, though, when I saw a fish stick its head out long, and I knew I was in the zone, so to speak.

I broke out the throwing stick, put about 50 baits around the area, and at least 100 nowhere near the area, because of the distance and the wind. I think they call it 'spreading it about a bit' nowadays! The other rod was just a pub chuck, to be honest. The fish were out long and after about three casts with that rod, it landed with a nice donk about 90 yards out. My rods weren't really up for long-range fishing, but they were all I had, times were hard and I couldn't afford new ones.

I was using a nylon hook length about ten inches long, a size 4 Drennan Boilie hook with a 20mm bottom bait plus a two-bait stringer on the nearer rod, and a single bait on the longer rod; nice and simple and tangle-proof. I was using a 4oz running lead with a shock leader, and 12lb mono. I was taking liberties with my rods, I admit, but I had to find the distance and just prayed that I didn't blow them up in the process! Luckily, I didn't and after a few attempts, finally managed to get the baits where I wanted them, and then it was chill-out time and a cup of tea.

A couple of hours later, Jay wandered up, said he was going down the fish and chip shop, and asked if I wanted anything. Do bears shit in woods! So, off he went to get our dinner. This must have been around five o'clock and he seemed to be gone for a long time. Later on, I found out that he'd bumped into a mate of his on the other bank, who had just joined and arrived to fish, and they'd got chatting for a bit.

I was having one of those fishing 'half-sleeps', as I call them, when your eyes are shut and you feel sleepy but you can still hear the background noises of birdsong, water lapping on the bank, and the wind blowing. Pure Zen, I like to think. This chilled-out state seemed to last for ages but was probably only an hour or so, when in the background, a clicking noise got my attention. In half-sleep, it took a few seconds to figure out what it was, and then I realised it was the sound of a bait runner. My old Optonic had packed up and line was peeling off the nearer rod. Fish on!

I grabbed the rod and felt the fish kite along the back of the bar, until eventually it slowed down a bit, but it was still over the back of the bar. It felt like a good fish but I was struggling to get it over and the line was pinging off the bar. I knew that if I didn't get it over the bar soon, the line would give, so I held the rod above my head as far as I could, tightened the clutch and prayed. After a few heart-stopping moments, I managed to get it over the bar and into safer water. My old knees were a-knocking, the fight seemed to last forever, and I was wondering where Jay was. I positioned the net but I had a problem; there was a bank of weed just out in front of me which I hadn't taken into account, and the net wouldn't reach over it so I stripped off to my pants, kicked off my shoes and went in. I had to go in up to my waist before I had any chance of netting it, and as I got the net ready the fish saw it and dived off to my right, trying to escape. I held my nerve, though, and after a few nervous moments, I finally had it in the net.

I just stood there in the water, bit the line, and gazed at my prize. I knew it was big and I wondered if I'd caught my first 30. Then Jay appeared and he could tell by my grinning face that I'd had a good one.

I knew it was big and I wondered if I'd caught my first 30.

He got the scales, unhooking mat, and camera ready while I waited in the water with the fish in the net. I was still up to my pants in water and must have been there for nearly 40 minutes, but I didn't feel cold.

Once Jay had everything set up, we took the fish out of the water and weighed her. I let out a huge victory cry when Jay read out 30lbs 8oz; a lovely, dark old mirror and an original, not one of the Brackens fish. I was made up! My first 30, and from a 60-acre gravel pit! Photos were taken and the fish was put back. The fish and chips were cold by now but I couldn't have cared less - I was just so happy.

Jay went back to the shops to buy some beers and we celebrated the capture with plenty of cold lagers. Later on, Jerry came over after Ascot and he was really pleased for me, so we sat in my swim for a while, just going over the week's events. We all had a good result that first session over at the Lagoons, the first of many to come. Jerry had a lovely two-tone mirror at 28lbs the next morning, just to cap the session off. It was a great week and one of the most memorable sessions in my angling life. I will never forget it; fishing with good friends, lovely surroundings, and my first 30 - which we named Gertie, by the way, hence the title of this chapter!

I was made up! My first 30 from a 60-acre gravel pit!

Back to the plot

I was keen to get the rods back on their spots and to top up with some bait. I felt I had already missed enough, and this was my last day as I had to get back to work at the bar. The conditions were really good, still a bit overcast, but as soon as we got the next long, hot spell those fish would move down to the South Lagoon to spawn. The sluice area was only a meeting place and as it got warmer you would see the big shoals arriving at the sluice, and then leaving as a group, heading off right down the centre of the lake toward the South. It was a fantastic sight.

I was lucky to get just one more take from my swim, and what a nice fish! It was a two-tone mirror at 28lbs 8oz that we all thought was the one stocked from Brackens Pool, but I've a feeling that fish went into one of the other lakes in the valley, because in all the years I fished there afterwards, I never saw that fish again. We all opened up our accounts with some good fish that first session, and our hit was quite legendary. I bumped into one angler, Peter Noonan, who was later to become a good friend and who had been fishing on the South at the start. He told me that some of the lads had made a good start on the Centre. I told him it was me and my mates.
"Really?" he said. "You won't do that again!" Pete was a right old character.

A cracking 28lbs 8oz mirror that I never saw again.

I fell in love with the place and as I only lived locally, I was always walking the banks, watching and learning. Craig and Lee from Hainault got tickets, and then Neil. We started to get to know others who had recently joined and the whole atmosphere began to kick in. They were really exciting times. We did our first session on the bank that had swims down the whole length of it and at the end was a sailing club. We were able to drive all the way down it, so it was great for socials, and perfect for overnighters. We named it 'the Drive-in Movie bank'.

The lake started to get busier. There were seven of us, plus new mates, and at weekends the Drive-in Movie bank would be nearly all taken up. I always missed the weekends as I was working at the wine bar and weekends were busy, but that never stopped me from going over to the lake after work to see the lads, who were usually asleep by then. Sometimes, I would take the rods and chuck them out for the night, but mostly I just drove them mad because I'd just come from a busy bar and was still full of life. Some of the lads were using dome tents and I would drive up to them, and to wake them up, I'd put the front bumper on the tent and rock, pushing the tent back and forth, with the full beam on and a nice bit of reggae playing in the car. The lads got used to it in the end - they loved it! I think.

I used to drive a Sierra Estate and I had the idea of setting up my bedchair in the back for overnighters. What a joke that was! I got the rods out one night and then tried to lie on the bed, but I had to lie on my back with my nose about an inch from the roof. I had a couple of takes the first night, and with the rod screaming outside I was stuck in my car trying to get off the bed chair - and I do mean stuck. So I got myself an air-bed, and this was better, but the hydraulics on my tailgate had gone so I was unable to keep the tailgate up. Every time I tried to keep it open, it would always come back down. I was fast asleep one night, the rod outside was singing its tune, and I was locked in the back. What a nightmare! Eventually, I managed to get out of the side door but, in all the panic, it seemed to take a lot longer than it probably did. Another time, the rod went, I kicked the tailgate open and dived out, but this time I was parked right on top of my rods, so when the door came down, it cracked me on the head. The guy next door heard the run and came to see what was going on while I was bent over, holding my head as I played the carp - blood everywhere. I decided to get the brolly back out after all that.

I was known for playing a few tricks. I must admit that I just love to fool around, and that's how I remember certain fish, they would usually be caught on a night when something funny happened. All the lads were down on the Drive-in Movie bank one night, standing about in a huddle behind one of the swims and having a natter. It was pitch black so I was able to slip back to my swim without anyone noticing. I had a really good mask, which I put on and then pulled my jacket up around my neck. It was a full head mask with long blond hair and a great big nose. I scared my mum with it loads of times. I walked back to the group and quietly rejoined them, but I stood more in the shadow. I just stood there without speaking and for ages, no one noticed me. After a while, Craig looked at me and I could tell he was freaked. He took a step back and said, "All right mate?" I didn't answer, and just stood there while Craig stared at me. He was thinking, 'who the f**k is this?' I really did get him. After a while, all the lads had noticed and they cracked up. They knew it was me, of course, or did they? Yes, I was known for my pranks and I thrived on it. It must be something I learned in the army.

One night I knew Jay was fishing, so not being one to miss an opportunity, I took a detour on my way home after work one night. He was all bivvied up, fishing the bank opposite the Drive-in Movie bank, and his door was down as protection from the wind. I crouched down and started to make scratching noises around the bottom of the door, and every now and then I made it sound like the creature was spooked and made noises in the vegetation as if it was belting off. Then I went back to scratching his bivvy again. By this time, I could hear that Jay was awake and probably concerned, so I made 'the creature' go right over the roof of the bivvy. I did this for ages, slowly building the scene and I thought nothing of keeping it up for an hour or two. At about 1am - and who would have thought it was me – I made this creature go under the groundsheet a few times and scarper off again, and on the final attack my hand went right under, knocking pots and pans over. I was biting my tongue with laughter and Jay screamed out something and started to try to whack it with his foot or something, so I pulled my hand out, made the sound again in the bushes, ran off back to my car and drove home absolutely pissing myself with laughter. I saw him the next day and said nothing. He said "Did you come over here last night?"
"No, mate. I was knackered after work. Why's that?"

I started fishing all around the Centre Lagoon, leaving the South for the time being, but the two parts were totally different. The Centre was a rectangle-shaped open water with only one long island at one end. There were plenty of features in the Centre with lots of bars, and some years there was weed, but the South was totally different; it was riddled with bars. Three main ones went out across the lake, and there was a group of islands in one corner with bars coming off them. There was a lot more weed, and it seemed the more carpy looking part by far.

Throughout that first year, I flitted about the Centre and caught some nice 20s but I wanted to catch some of the bigger known ones. There was a fish called One Pec that had been out at 30lbs, a real old original, and one that I wanted to catch.

Everyone was pleased to see another close to the 30lb mark.

A deep Italian strain fish, grey in colour just shy of 30lbs.

We were learning more and more about the place all the time, and I really liked a swim that I called the Pallet. It was up toward the end of the Drive-in Movie bank and any fish that came into the Centre had to pass under the bridge. They were very spooky about this mind, and many times I'd watched them as they built up courage and then just went for it. Once on the other side, if they were coming down the centre of the lake, I fancied this area to be where they would be happy to stop and feed.

There was a nice feature out in front of the Pallet swim. It was a bar parallel to the bank at about 40-50 yards, and after a fair bit of plumbing, I found that the bar actually dog-legged out and created a nice little corner that would be a good spot to bait up. I was sure the carp would be following this feature and would come across the bait.

It's hard for me to get all the sessions in the correct order because I did do a lot of time on the complex over a period of almost eight years but I'll try to cover the highlights as I go, and as the title of the book is Catching Memories, I'll do my best to do just that.

I baited the Pallets for a while and then started to drop into the swim for nights after work. At this time, a few of the lads and me were on the Darenth Valley baits. We used something called the Gravel mix and loaded it up with fish oil and the same flavours as before; the Nash Salmon Oil Pallatant, and Red Liver. As some of the fishing was at long range, I used the rotary rig with 4oz leads, and mainly pop-ups. At the time, I was using that stuff called Stiffy, or something like that. I used to coat the pop-up section with it and this would make it stiff but flexible. It was very effective.

I went through a period on my overnighters when I would nearly always get a bite. The only trouble was that the lake was now getting busier and sometimes I'd drive down the track at midnight and not see a single angler... until I got to my swim. Damn! That used to wind me up.

I was catching a good number of 20s and doubles, and nearly all of them were old fish because up until then no other stock had gone in, apart from the Brackens carp. One morning about 9.30, just as I was packing up, I had a take. This fish was a plodder, rather than the other fast, erratic ones I'd been catching, and I landed a deep-bellied, Italian strain fish, grey in colour and very welcome. The Italian weighed just shy of 30lbs and at first I thought it was Bill's fish from Brackens Pool. Everyone was pleased to see another this lake was getting better all the time.

I fished the Pallet as much as possible, but started to look about for other spots around the lake, and I ended up on the opposite bank for a while in a swim called the Pylon. This was another good interception swim like the Pallet because if the fish moved in from the South down the Pylon side of the lake, there was a bar at long range and they would show around this area so you would know that they were on their way down. I fished another bit of a broken bar about 80-odd yards out, and then another bar, closer in and to my right, which ran along the side of the swim about 40 yards out. This bar was savage, and sometimes you got cut off on the take, but I did like this swim and had some good hits. It was also a swim where the big common had been caught and I hoped that she had habits and may well be back.

In September, Mick was on the Drive-in Movie bank for a few days and I went over to see him because he'd had a result. He'd banked One Pec at just under 30lbs and he was buzzing. Mick had a few more days to go, so I said I'd be down for a couple of nights to join him and I'd go in the next swim up from him. He was fishing in the middle area of the Drive-in Movie bank, and the swims were a good distance apart, so it was no problem to go next door.

I had a change in bait for a while and a few of us started using Solar's Dairy Cream mix, with Squid and Octopus, and Esterblend, a really nice combination, especially for the time of year, with very good attractors. I knocked up a 12-egg mix and made my way over to the lake. The conditions were good; wind and drizzle, typical autumn weather that we don't seem to get in September nowadays. It felt very carpy. On the way to the lake, I could smell my bait in the car. That Esterblend really does kick and it made me cough. I arrived at Mick's swim where he told me that he hadn't caught any more fish, so we had a quick chat and I said I would get sorted and come back for a brew.

I parked in the swim next door and I had a map. Well, it was an echo-type scan with all the depths, so I was able to line my swim up across the lake and see roughly what was out to my front. This was handy, as I had never fished the swim before. An area of the lakebed was under a uniform 11 feet of water, and this was where I wanted to place my two rods. I got set up and fished single bottom baits with a four-bait stringer, made a cast and feathered it down until it landed with a thump. I was happy, but for some reason I decided to pull the rig back a bit. It was like glass. 'That's staying just there,' I said to myself. I then did exactly the same with the other rod and I had the same result. Perfect.

I grabbed my cup and went to see Mick. By this time, it was raining heavily so I sat inside the doorway of his bivvy and shielded myself from the rain. Mick got

the kettle on and we started chatting away.
"Hold up," he said, suddenly. "Listen, what's that noise?"
I concentrated on listening.
"Blimey! It sounds like my rod!" I said and legged it.
The left rod was melting away with the alarm LED lighting up the swim.
"Wow, that was quick!" I said.
Mick was by my side and he couldn't believe it either. After a good scrap, I landed a beautiful linear mirror of 21lbs and because we were allowed, the fish was sacked up. I went about getting the rod back out, and it went down nicely, the same as before.

"Blimey!" I said. "That sounds like my rod," and legged it.

The kettle went on again and we carried on from where we'd left off, chatting away for a while, then one of my rods was off again. This was mad! Two bites in a session is very good, but within a couple of hours was unheard of. When I got to the swim the same rod was off again, flying like a train. Mick stood next to me, just laughing. This fish was another 20, at 22lbs, and another cracking-looking carp joined its mate in another sack.

It was getting late now so we decided to call it a day and get our heads down. I was asleep for what seemed no time at all before the right rod was away. This was madness, but the fish was heading off down my left margin and Mick was shouting to me.

"Are you in?"
"Yes," I said. "Mate, dip your rods. It's coming your way fast and I can't stop it."
My instructions came too late. It had gone through Mick's rods and taken them both out. What a mess! Poor old Mick's rods were trashed, and sadly I lost that fish, but I helped Mick to re-tackle up and get them back out, and then I sorted out my own mess.

Finally, I got back in the bag, and lay there thinking about the night so far and the fish I'd lost. Then I shut my eyes and the left bobbin dropped to the floor. Once again, I jumped out and lifted into the rod. There was nothing there, but I kept reeling and Mick called out.
"Are you in, mate?"
"Well, I thought I was," I said.
I kept on reeling and then, right in the margins, the rod arced suddenly, round to the left, and steamed off. The crafty bugger had swum straight into the bank.

Another cracking-looking carp, joined it's mate in another sack.

A special one; the Brackens Leather at 26lb.

I bent the rod round to maximum side strain. I wasn't losing this one, no way. Mick came and grabbed the net. He was laughing again and so was I, because this was mental. In the darkness, the carp rolled on the top and Mick slid the net under it. Brilliant! I'm always happy when the fish is in the net.

This fish was a special one, the Brackens Leather, the one I had landed for Mark Wilcox when it lived in Brackens Pool, a mega fish, very dark and an old carp for sure. The Leather weighed 26lbs and I had to borrow a sack from Mick. This was going to be an epic night. I went on to catch another double mirror and a double common by the morning. Six takes for me would give me a night to remember. I went to see Mick.
"Hey, mate," he said, "give us one of them hook baits, will you?"
"Of course, mate," I said.
He put one on and cast it to where his rod had been for the last day or so. Well, I'll tell you what, it was only out there ten minutes and he had an 18lb common. It was unbelievable! Mick said he wanted to get a 20lb common, as he had never had one before. "Give us another hook bait!"
He put on the fresh hook bait and within half an hour, he got his 20lb common. It couldn't have gone any better, we had a Billingsgate photo session.

A Billingsgate photo session.

After the photos, I tried to find those spots in the daylight, but there wasn't a chance, or if I was finding them, they didn't feel the same. The fish had done the off and we caught no more. However, I do know that I did something wrong when I made the bait up. I'd thought it was a bit strong when it made me cough. Instead of 12ml of Squid and Octopus to twelve eggs and 2ml of Esterblend, because I was in a rush, I'd done it the wrong way around. Bloody 12ml of Esterblend! Wow, that's strong, but hey, it produced eight takes in a night! It wasn't as if I was baiting up with it, and this mishap got me thinking and led me to trying something.

There must have been something in the over-flavouring of my bait, otherwise surely I wouldn't have caught anything, but to have six bites on 60-odd acres is pretty outstanding. As the Esterblend is the more powerful one of the two, I decided to drop the Squid and Octopus and just use the Ester. I made up some pop-ups from Solar's pop-up mix, dyed them orange, and rolled them around in a dry saucepan until they were like rock hard marbles. I let them cool down for a few hours and then put them in a plastic bag with some neat Esterblend over them and let them soak it up. My theory was that I would use single hook baits and draw the fish in with the Ester, and they would only have two choices - take or leave it. I was sure this had to be a winner, judging by those six takes in a night on over-flavoured bait. With my new hook baits, I was ready to go and decided that they would be my winter and early spring specials. Throughout the autumn and early winter, my hook baits worked well, and I had a few fish on them but a couple of sessions stood out in my mind.

It was a freezing cold December. Mick was already down for couple of days and we decided to double up for a social in my old favourite, the Pallet. I pulled into the Drive-in Movie bank at midnight, and it was so misty and cold that I could hardly see the track as the headlights reflected the haze. I drove into the swim and started to nudge Mick's dome tent with the full beam on and Desmond Dekker blaring out of my window, to get him up, He would expect no less. Mick got up and made a brew and I set up my gear. I knew the swim really well, we shared the area between us, and all night long, I was receiving little tiny liners that would just about move the bobbin.

The next day, it started to sleet. It was a proper wintry December day but, we were enjoying ourselves as we always did. At midday, the little liners returned, and then slowly, my right-hand rod pulled to the top and I was into a carp. The fish kited slowly along the back of the bar and then thankfully, it turned away and headed out into the lake. It was a heavy fish; I knew this by the way it was fighting, and gradually, I coaxed it back to within about 30 yards from the bank until suddenly, it all locked up solid. Damn! What was this, a snag or something? I got it moving, but still it felt as if it was connected to something, and then I saw it. A big flank of a good fish hit the surface tangled up with a big branch. This was not good and I felt very unlucky, especially when the fish got free and I dragged in the culprit branch. I was gutted. The chance of a good winter lump had been lost.

I got my rod back out and by this time, the sleet had stopped so we sat out by our rods (hardcore!), chatting away and Mick had his tips up high. I always keep glancing at rod tips, and I saw one of Mick's tips just pull down slightly.
"Mick," I said. "Your rod tip just pulled."
He looked at the rod and then his alarm gave a single bleep and the bobbin pulled up an inch. Mick picked up the rod, wound down a bit, gently pulled the rod back and was met with heavy resistance - he had a fish on. Another slow plodding fish kited left and right for a while until he had it clear from the bar and the old inky pattern on the surface was seen as he slowly brought it up for the net and in went a grey-coloured mirror; it was Mick's old friend, One Pec. Why does that always happen? One Pec was one that I wanted to catch and it falls to someone who has already caught it! I bet it was her out there all night, giving me those bleeps and liners. I will catch up with her one day.

"Mick," I said. "One of your rod tips just pulled over."

Although Mick had already caught her, he was happy to have a fish in these conditions and I was unhappy to have lost one, but I didn't go empty-handed. I had an 18lb common for my troubles, which came to my special hook baits. I'm not sure what Mick was using, but it didn't matter. We were on the fish that trip.

It was the last few days of that first season. I had turned up late after work and decided to fish the swim right next to the Brackens Pool car park. I had fished the swim before and knew roughly what was out there, but I wanted to fish long to the middle of the lake area. There was a shallower area like a plateau, with some little bars and gullies all around it. I had plumbed it from both sides of the lake and it was definitely a good holding area, winter and summer, as the fish would hardly be disturbed out there. What brought my attention to it at first was a group of kids who had turned up one day and decided to swim down the lake going in from beside the sluice gate. One lad swam out and then suddenly, he began to walk where he had hit the shallow water, and continued to walk along this area until it dropped off again. Well, I was fishing at the time and I was not happy about them swimming at first but when this area was revealed, my feelings changed.

I had to be fishing at over 130 yards to reach it, and all I wanted to do was get two rods with my hook baits in the general area. I launched both rods as hard as I was able to, right out there, and I felt I was in the zone. It was an 'icy frost on the unhooking mat' sort of night and I was glad to get in the bag. At 2am, the left rod pulled up tight and a long-range carp was on. I jumped out, lifted the rod up high and straight away I felt it kiting left - that was until it went solid around one of the boating flag buoys. I cursed myself. What an idiot I was! I should have considered the buoys. All had locked up way out in the lake and I held the rod without a clue as to what I could do. I stood there holding the rod for ages without feeling anything on the end. The fish must have been long gone and all I was able to do was pull for a break. Luckily, I snapped at the lead core knot so I didn't lose too much line but I hate losing fish, and I moaned away to myself as I re-tackled and got the rod back out.

The rest of the night was quiet, until 7am when the other rod pulled up tight. It was one of those bright, sunny but frosty mornings when it is hard to see where your line is going with the glare. I made good progress with this fish and before long, I had it within 40 feet of the bank. I was watching the line where it entered the flat calm water and as it zig-zagged about, it began to take a bit of line and then it simply cut me off. I was standing there with the limp line hanging from the rod tip. How's your bloody luck! Two lost now and I wasn't happy.

I leaned the rod on the bivvy and went round to the other bank to have a whinge to Craig, who was fishing there.
"All right, mate?" I said. "I bloody lost two. What a nightmare!"
He stuck the kettle on while I relayed the stories of my two lost fish and as we chatted, we heard the sound of an alarm screaming away.
"Whose is that?" we said, as we looked around the lake.
Then it dawned on me; there were no more anglers on and I still had one rod out. In my anger about losing another fish, I had just walked away from the swim to see Craig. I had Skeetex boots on and an all-in-one suit, and I had to sprint all the way back to my swim. The rod was melting still as I arrived and I thought, 'Don't let me lose this one!'

Fortunately, it went the opposite way to the marker buoy, and without too much trouble, I landed a 22lb common. At last, I had landed one! I was so pleased that the idea of fishing that area had worked, along with the single hook baits. I had to go to work but Jay was on his way over so I told him that it was a big swim, to head straight here and double up. It was to be the last night of the season and as I'd had three bites, I hoped that there was more to come.

I went off to the bar and Jay set up to my left. The weather had changed dramatically and a big wind had blown up. I was very keen to get back angling again. The night at work was soon over and once again, I pulled the car into the Lagoons entrance and down the track to the car park that was just near our swim. I walked into the swim and there were no bivvies there, no tackle, or anything. Where the hell was he? There were no mobiles about then, so I got in the car and drove round the Drive-in Movie bank, and there was his car, in the first swim by the gate.

"All right, mate?" I said. "What's happening?"
"We got blown away," he said. "Both the bivvies took off in the wind and I had to pack the lot away."
"Bloody hell. What a nightmare, mate! Where's my gear?"
"In the back of my car," he said.
I opened up his tailgate and there it was, like a big mass of junk. It was midnight and I had to sort the lot out. I went one swim up, where Paul had been fishing that first session, threw my fishing gear together and lobbed the rods out for the last night of the season.

After a quiet night, I was up to one of the rods absolutely ripping off at first light. I called Jay and from his swim he was able to see what was happening. The rod was flying and stripping line at such a rapid rate of knots that I had to cup the spool in my hand to slow it, or I would have been over the other side of the lake. The instant I stopped the fish, it cut me off. I reeled in and my hook link was cut in half. That was three fish lost now; two to cut-offs and one to the marker buoys. Deep joy.

As the day went on, the sun came out and I was lying by my rods on my bed chair, when I fell asleep with my radio on and on top of my ear. I was enjoying the little bit of sun on my face. I woke with a start, I sat up, looked left to Jay's swim, and saw Anthony, from Johnson Ross tackle shop in the town, standing next to Jay with the landing net in his hand. Apparently, Jay had been on a bit of a naughty trot off his rods past my swim, when his rod screamed off. He told me that when he'd run back to his swim, he'd shouted to me that he was away. At the same time, Anthony and one of his brothers had turned up for a look around, so when I woke that's why I saw Anthony with the net. I went next door to see what was going down, and just as I arrived a great big common flopped into the net.
"Well done, mate!" I said. "It looks a good fish!"
Jay had just caught the prize of the valley, the big common, the one that everyone wanted.

Jay in his normal blasé way went and landed the big cheese. A 30lb common was a special prize, and come to think of it, I never knew any others at the time who had caught one. It was a beautiful fish, in mint condition after the winter, and weighed 31lbs.
"I'm not leaving this place until I've caught her," I told Jay. "Well done, son!"

I arrived as a great big common flopped in the net.

After Jay's common, we more or less packed up for the long close season, but we were more than happy with our year. We had all done very well and I'd caught something like 27 fish that first year, with 20-plus fish over 20lbs, and twenty x 20s a season back then was some achievement, especially on there.

There was a lake near me called the Crown and it was open during the close season. It was an any-method trout fishery full of carp; we never ever saw a trout. Harry, the guy who ran it, was raking it in; not least because, apart from Farlows, there was nowhere else that was open back then, that I knew of. He used to turn up on this big old trike and you could see the pound signs in his eyes. He would collect the money and then whizz off, with his girlfriend on the back, to the shops to spend it. Some days, every swim was taken and at £10 a day, he did well. We used to spend the close season over there to pass the time, and Jay and me smashed it up. We had a good bait but not being allowed to bait up was a problem. No boilies were to be used because it was a trout fishery but we would have a six-egg mix of bait each, and while everyone was setting up their tackle we'd put out all our bait as quickly as we could, and hope that no one would see us. It worked well, and if we cast out a pop-up amongst our bait, we would be catching throughout the day.

We really did take it apart, and before long the regulars started to take notice. One day, an old boy came round to us to find out what was going on.
"Right," he said, "You and your mate are up to something. You must be. You two always catch. What is it that's doing the business for you?"

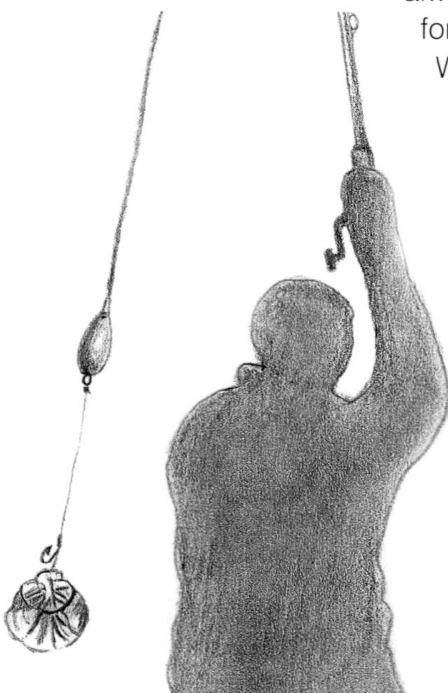

Well, as I've said, I love a wind up, so I said, "Listen. Don't tell anyone else but we're getting them on Brussels, mate. You know, Brussels sprouts."
"I bloody knew it," he said. "I knew you two were up to something."
We knew that, by the time we came over next, everyone would be on Brussels because he would have told everyone. Jay and me even went to the trouble of having a bag of sprouts in our swim on display, just to give the story some back-up.

It was good over at the Crown, but all we wanted was to get back on the Lagoons. We would walk it all the time and always see fish. The Lee Valley Parks authorities

A nice one from the Crown.

had stocked it that last autumn with 70-odd fish of the John Paton strain. I was there and took photos of the nicest fish. I'd spend hours sitting by the railings in the Sluice swim on the Centre, just watching the fish in their shoals go in and out. It was a sight to see.

That next season, I thought it would be a good idea to start off in the Pallet swim. I'd become a bailiff, and bailiffs had a choice of swims at the start. This was great because I was able to bait my swim during the close season and know that I would be okay to get in there at the start. As the fish were always in and out during the close season, and passing the Pallet area, it seemed a good choice, but really it all depended on the weather, and I wanted colder weather and rain to stop them spawning early. I really gave them some bait, and one evening another angler was about when I baited and the fish were all over it. They were rolling and jumping, and he said, "You're in here at the start! You should have it off."

When the start came round, the weather had turned hot and all the carp were South bound. I had no action for two days so I took a walk round the South and ended up in a swim called the Pylon. It was occupied, but I spoke to the angler in it and he told me that he'd had no action, and was looking to be pulling off. There were two islands out at about 70 yards, and a bar was evident that ran between them, and as we talked, I could see fish showing out long beyond the bar. I said my goodbyes and said that I would move in after him the following day.

I did another night on the Centre with no action, and the next day I loaded up the barrow, parked it in the Pylon swim and left it while I looked around the lake. Matey packed up and I was so eager to get a rod out that I whacked one long where they were showing. I started getting action immediately, and landed a few carp to 26lbs. I was so pleased. I'd worked hard in the close season and had done the first few days with no action. Now I was on some fish and getting my reward.

I was casting to the showing fish that were long behind the bar, and after catching a few, I think I moved the shoal off and it went quiet, although I had a couple of liners and saw a few fish show between the two islands. There was weed on top of the bar, so I brought both rods back and fished a pop-up off the lead right on top of the bar. I could see the fish as they moved about in the shallow water and felt sure that a bite was on the cards.

I was watching the water and they were stacked up along the bar area. My rods were hardly out when I received a bite and the water erupted on the bar as a carp made off in a big bow wave. The bar was savage as it dropped off behind and the fish was doing its best to get down the far side so there was a big danger of a cut-off. The swim had a high bit behind it and the trick was to get up on there and get the rod as high as possible to get the fish back over the bar. You would see them come back over it and once they were on your side, you were safe.

I landed a fish that I recognised as the mirror I'd braced with the linear back in September on the highly-flavoured hook baits, still at the same weight of 22lbs. I took a couple of snaps for the memory, slipped her back, recast the rod back on top of the bar and fired out a scattering of bait. Now for some stupid reason I thought it would be good to climb up the first stage of the pylon that was right behind the swim. This would give me a great view, but it's something I don't recommend! When I got to the first stage, it was bloody high I can tell you. It doesn't look it from below but when you're up there, it sure does! Admittedly, the view was amazing. I was able to see so much and I could have stayed up there all day just looking, but my attention was soon drawn to one of my rods that was screaming away as an angry carp fled the area.

Now, I'm up a bloody pylon and I had to get back down sharpish. The first obstacle was the barbed wire that they put around the first stage to stop people like me climbing them. I got through that bit and the rod was screaming away all the time, but in my panic while getting down the last bit, I scraped my shinbone hard and it hurt like hell. There was no time to check my wounds, though; I had a fish on!

Surprisingly, the fish hadn't gone as far as I'd feared and a battle commenced. It didn't want to come over to my side of the bar, though. I must have had him three times on the top of the bar and every time he would take line aggressively, and make it back to the other side. I had him once again on the top in a massive eruption of water and finally dragged him over. The rest of the fight was pretty textbook, the usual plodding up and down the margins until I had him beaten and in the net. The first thing I did after that was to pull my trouser leg up to check out my shin. It was not a pretty sight. All the skin was scraped off the shin and now I had landed my fish, the pain was returning.

Anyway, back to my fish. A lovely mirror lay in the net, a long fish that looked close to 30lbs. My fish was, indeed, 30lbs 8oz and I was over the moon. I decided to name this one the Long Fish as the list of 30s in the lake was growing, and it helped when we were talking about them. I continued getting action on top of the bar for the rest of that day and night and ended up with 11 fish, an amazing start to my season and an old original 30, to boot. That pylon behind kept trying to lure me back up there for another look, but I resisted the temptation. I had learned my lesson.

The list of 30s was growing so I decided to name this one The Long Fish.

The lake was getting very popular now, with at least seven or eight of the Hainault gang fishing it, and when we were all on the Drive-in Movie bank, it did get messy as you would expect. We met a lot of other anglers, who like us lot, were as keen as mustard and some weekends the Centre and South were banged out. It was so different to when we first started. Peter Noonan, who I mentioned earlier, was always down with his mate, Micky Daily. They were really funny, those two, like a double act. I nicknamed Pete, 'Saucepan Pete' because he did everything in one saucepan.

'Saucepan Pete' Noonan. What a character!

He made his dinner in it, boiled water for a brew, and then used it to have a wash or a shave in. I will never forget one day when I called in on him to see how he was getting on. He was in a swim on the other side of the bridge just inside the South lake, named the Earwig. It was about 11 o'clock, the sun was out and the Earwig swim was a roaster with no escape from the sun. As I entered the swim, Pete was under his brolly in his sleeping bag, wearing what looked like an all-in-one suit, fast asleep. He woke when I came into the swim, and I must say he looked a mess and he was a bit annoyed that I'd woken him. I was hot just standing there in his swim, so God knows how hot he was. His face was bright red and he said, "Jerry, I ain't been to sleep all night," then mumbled on about something that had kept him up all night, and turned back over to sleep. He really was mad.

Talking about the Earwig, a few weeks after the fish had spawned I got in there for a couple of nights. It was an interesting swim, with plenty to keep your mind occupied. Just down to the left was the bridge that split the two parts of the lake, and at about 40 yards into the South there was a bar that started and ran down the middle. At about 70 yards, a part of the bar kicked right, making a nice little elbow to fish to. I found some silt at the back of it in about nine feet of water, which had the potential to be a very good area. I could fish one rod left on the bar, which was a good ambush spot for any carp leaving or entering the South; the other rod was on that silt behind the bar.

I still fished the rotary rig, normally with pop-ups, and I was back on my oily fishmeals for the summer. My first take came from the left-hand rod on the bar, in early morning. Once the fish were away from the bar, it was deeper water so it was just a matter of not letting them get back near the bars. The first fish felt like a good one and I was well pleased when I landed one of the Brackens' biggies in the shape of Spot, a proper old carp, and one that people were talking about. Spot had spawned out to just shy of 29lbs and I was very grateful to catch her.

A Brackens original. Spot at 29lbs.

I had no more bites that day, but the next morning the silt rod, the one I was banking on, finally pulled away. I got the fish away from the bar system relatively easily and it didn't put up much of a fight. In close, I saw that it was a mirror and I had a feeling I knew which one one it was. Once in the net, my suspicions were confirmed; it was One Pec. This fish looked so old and leathery and it was also down in weight from spawning, but I cared not. I was chuffed to get her. That ended a very productive session, catching two target fish. I was loving the Lagoons!

One pec looked old and leathery, and spawned out.

As I said, I was on the Lagoons for a long time and I could probably fill two books with all the stories and captures but I'll just talk about the significant ones, the memorable ones - which is what this book is about, after all.

I was still working at the wine bar and you may be wondering how I managed to fit all the fishing in. Well, I worked the weekends, had Monday and Tuesdays off and didn't have to leave the lake until about 9.30 on the Wednesday, so it was a very good time. I was living just minutes away so I was lucky that my wife would

One of many nice carp from the Centre and South.

bring meals over to me, so I often had a full roast dinner on the bank. Behind the scenes, my missus was brilliant. She looked after me and I owe her so much. She's still looking after me today and without her none of it would have been possible. Thanks, love. xx

I had a mate, Gary, who worked next door to the wine bar. He was into his fishing, so he also got a Lagoons ticket, and one year, as I was a bailiff and was able to get a swim at the start, we decided to double up in the Point swim on the South. The Point swim was full of features with three main bars going out to the middle of the lake, plus nice gullies to fish to, and the area was perfect to bait up.

Gary and me went mad making bait. We turned my shed and garden into a bait factory and we'd roll all day long. We mixed our own base mix and ended up with a really nice bait, using essential oils as attractors; a blend of ginger, and geranium oil with salmon oil, all in a full-blown fishmeal - perfect. There would be bait drying out all over the garden and it was hard work. We'd roll a 100-egg mix in a day and then go and sling it all in the lake. The fish were going crazy for it.

As they turned up for their breakfast, I landed a cracking 23lb common.

Gary and one of the unusual gang of fish that had turned up.

Sometimes we had double takes. It was a mad session I will never forget.

When the start came, we couldn't wait to get fishing. On the first morning, the fish turned up for their breakfast and I was first away, catching a really nice common of 23lbs. Then, I lost one that took me around a stick on top of the bar. There were a few of these so that the sailing boats knew where the bars were. Later on, we got these changed to flexible plastic pipes, which made sense.

We seemed to have a shoal in front of us of really old-looking fish, mainly doubles, and I don't think I ever came across these fish again in all the years that I fished there afterwards. A couple of times, Gary and me had double takes. It was a mad and a very enjoyable session, one that I will never forget, but I still wonder where those fish came from – and went. Strange.

The carp were getting bigger every year, and I still hadn't landed that common, the one that Jay had caught. That fish was my target and I was now fishing all over the lake. All I had to go on was my watercraft, watching all the time, moving on new winds, and being ready to up sticks at any time, and by doing this I had some good hits. I'd moved into the Pylon swim on the Centre because while I'd been fishing the South, I'd seen some carp move through the bridge and I was anticipating the route they would take. So, I rushed to the Pylon, got the marker out in double-quick time and got some bait in.

Some of the stock fish were joining the A team. The Sergeant at 32lbs.

I had a mental session, taking nine fish, which included a 32lb mirror that we named the Sergeant. It was a cracking carp with big shoulders and some huge plated scales. Some of the stockies they had put in were by now piling on the weight, becoming target fish and members of the A team.

Over the years, I learned that the sluice gates played a big part in the make-up of the lake. When we were having heavy rains, the gates would automatically open and we would have a river, more or less, running through the centre of the lake. This stirred everything up and in the summer, it would shift great weed beds about. While all this was happening, there was no point in fishing too close to this flow. In the winter, I've fished right down the South and you couldn't even hold a five-ounce lead in the flow. I'm sure this was when some carp escaped from the lagoons, because when it was like that, there was hardly any drop at the area where it flowed into the river, and even today, years later, Lagoons fish get caught in the relief canal.

The best time to fish was just as the flow was dropping back. I'd set up in the Gravelly swim, near the sluice, and the water was on the drop. I'd done the night after work and was now on my days off. The rain had stopped but the skies were black and threatened a lot more rain, so if it poured down, I would either pack up or move.

In the morning, I was awoken by the sound of raindrops on my brolly and at 8am, I had a take that got me out in the rain and soaked to the skin, but I landed a nice 18lb mirror. I had one more T-shirt and tracksuit bottoms left, so I dried myself off and changed into the dry clothes before I got back in the bag. I'd got the rod back out and put some more bait in, just before it lashed it down again, and I was thinking that sooner or later the gates will be back open and then I won't be able to fish those areas. As the skies opened, I looked at my bobbins. The rain was bouncing all the mud off the floor and coating my reels in crap. 'Please,' I said to myself, 'don't let me get a take now'. I was snuggled into my sleeping bag, all cosy and dry with the rain hammering away, when the right rod just melted.

'That's bloody typical', I thought, as I dragged the bag with me to my rods. I was soaked and the rain felt cold. I was concentrating on keeping this fish away from the sharp bar and thankfully, the rain petered out and stopped. It felt like a good fish, this one, and as it surfaced, I saw it was a dark brown mirror. Once on the top, I had near enough won the battle and as it came toward, and finally into, the waiting net, I noticed that its mouth looked very blunt. I knew I had a good fish and I quickly retrieved my sling and mat, which were lying on some bushes to dry out, supposedly.

On closer inspection, I could see that this carp's mouth had no damage at all. It was just very 'pug-looking' and blunt. In fact, I remembered seeing this fish when I'd photographed it for someone once, down on the South. It was 22lb then, but was now considerably bigger. This was an old original fish and weighed 31lbs. She was certainly liking the anglers' bait, and so was born the fish named the Pug, that later on would go over 40lbs and now I believe lives in the relief canal. That fish topped the session for me. I was soaked through but happy with my catch, and then they opened the sluice gates once again, and I headed off home.

I noticed it had a very blunt mouth. An old one at 31lbs.

We had a very cold winter that year and the lagoons froze over so much that the fire brigade were practising rescues on the ice. They were pulling a fireman across the lake with a rope attached to a ladder that had wheels on it, so the ice must have been very thick. I was waiting for the ice to melt so I could get the rods out because in the past, it had fished well after the thaw. Eventually, it did all melt away and I set up camp on the Caravan bank of the South in my good old two-man Hutchy - good bivvies, they were. On the first night, I landed a nice mid-20 mirror, one I hadn't seen before. It had a big tail, and black colouring around the wrist - a nice fish. I had caught it on my old winter favourite, an Esterblend single pop-up, out in the silt at the back of the third bar from the Point swim.

The next evening saw us sitting in my Hutchy, sheltering on a cold January night from the wind and rain. Jay and Paul and a few others were having a social cuppa and the door was done up to prevent the rain from coming inside. We were all messing about having a laugh when Paul said, "Listen! Was that one of your rods?"

I unzipped the door a little, stuck my head out, and saw that my latching light was lit on the left rod, but nothing was happening. "No," I said. "Must be the wind." Suddenly, it was one-toning, and I burst through the door without undoing the rest of the zip. I picked up the rod and was once again doing battle with a cold water January carp. It's amazing how those single hook baits do their magic! I paid out the line that the carp was demanding and it did get a fair way out in the lake. The wind was making the line sing as it stretched out across the water, and as the fish came closer in, it made good use of the deeper water and ploughed about for a while in its attempt at freedom. With all my mates by my side, a big common rolled for the first time and Jay instantly said, "That's the big girl, mate!" I think I knew it was. I had a feeling and funnily enough it just seemed appropriate. After five years, I had finally landed my target fish and having all the lads there really did make it special.

With all my mates by my side, the big Common finally rolled into the net.

I must say I felt a bit sad, though, as she had sustained some fairly bad mouth damage, and when I'd seen her in the past she was always in immaculate condition. I do know that some stupid anglers were going for a fish at all costs, fishing right into the sluices until it was banned, and I'm sure this was the outcome. Anyway, I was made up, and with new fish coming through all the time there was always another I wanted to catch. The carp were piling on the weight now, especially the stocked fish. Later in the year, Paul got into a bit of a baiting campaign on the Centre Lagoon and caught a cracker; one known as the Pretty One and it was just that, at a massive weight of 37lbs-plus.

I made a very good friend, Keith Olney, over on the Lagoons. I used to see him all the time fishing around the lake, and he was mainly after the bream but he was a good angler and knew the lake well. He often caught carp on his bream outfit so we became very good mates and in the end he turned his full attention to the carp. (Watch out the carp!). Keith knew all the bream runs that the carp also used and he proceeded to empty the lake. He was catching carp every trip and, to be honest, made all us carp anglers look a bit stupid as he made it look so easy.

Mostly, he would just fish with loads of pellet, which he loved using, and he would larrup it in. He was fishing the left-hand side of the sluice swim one time,

The Boom swim.

and there is a deep margin that goes round to the right and then into the sluice area. He just filled in the bottom of the shelf with pellet and kept catching. Once, he had three or four 20s from the swim and then, for some reason that I can't remember, he moved right up to the other end of the Drive-in Movie bank, and within no time at all, he was catching again. Talk about know your water!

Keith was a special person and a real good mate. He'd do anything for you - and nothing was too much. Keith had severe diabetes and over the years I watched him getting progressively worse. Like me, he had a real passion for fishing, and one December, against the rules, me and Keith took a boat out on the Centre Lagoon with a fish finder. It was freezing so we were armed with of couple of hot Lagoon. As soon as we hit the bar under the bridge to the left of the Earwig swim, the echo sounder started to bleep as we picked up the odd fish. We were just curious, really, about where the fish would be at this time, and it was so cold that even the sides of the boat were frosted up.

It was a really good experiment. The fish seemed to be in the first bar area, but down the side of it in about eight feet of water, and then as we drifted on, they disappeared. We followed the bar right the way down the lake toward the boom area where the water spilled over into the relief canal. Before we got to this area we picked up fish again, they were in 16 feet of water, but the carp were all about six feet from the surface. Further over toward the Boom swim, there was a plateau on top, around six feet down, the same as the depth the carp were in, and this area was the nearest to where the carp were. I had a theory that the carp were happy at that depth and were, literally, just drifting in that area and staying at that depth all the time. If they came across the lakebed in the same depth of water, they would feed.

Keith agreed, so we decided to feed the area out in front of the Boom swim throughout December, and fish it hard after the New Year. At this time, I was a consultant for DT baits and Stud (real name Chris), the owner, had put together a really nice bait that we thought would be perfect for the colder water. It was called DNA 21, which Keith always said smelled just like Christmas pudding, and it did. We started to give it some bait along with loads of ball pellets for extra attraction, and the plan was to get over there on January the 2nd. I thought we might have put in too much bait for the time of year, but the only way to find out was to fish it.

Over the festive period, Keith became unwell. Sometimes, his diabetes really made him ill and he'd go on the missing list for a while. I'd only get a call from him when he was fully recovered, and he'd say, "I'm alive, I'm alive!" down the phone.

Well, he must have been bad because I couldn't get hold of him. It was a Sunday and I was all packed ready to go on the Monday morning but I knew Keith wouldn't be coming, so, as I lived locally, I got in the car and went on the Sunday night.

I was using a little Rocky dome tent at the time, and didn't get set up until about midnight. There was a small island 40 yards out to my right, and a little bar came off the left-hand side of it, with a gully about seven feet deep that ran behind it. This bar carried on across most of my swim where I had been baiting the gully, and Keith had been doing the plateau area. I flicked out two rods with bottom baits and stringers and fired out a few pouches of ball pellet, which was also DNA 21.

I got into the bag at 1am and was nearly asleep when one of the rods went screaming off. 'Blimey! That was quick.' I thought. The fish kited off left along the back of the bar and gave me the run-around for a while, but I soon had it in close. In this swim you had to drop down a few steps to get level with the water to land your fish and by this time, some of the fish in the lake were getting big, and this was one of them - a mid-30, maybe. There was a dead reed bed to the left, and this fish had got its head into the old reeds. All I could do was to keep scooping at it, trying desperately to get it into the net, but somehow it got off and swam away. I was bloody furious, especially as I had seen the fish, so I got the rod back out and went back to bed thinking about what had happened, until I eventually dropped off to sleep.

It was barely light when that same rod was flying again. I scrambled out of my dome tent and lifted into the fish that was kiting left along the bar. Everything was going well, until it just fell off. I was livid - so annoyed that I slung a load of bait out over Keith's area and mine,then packed up and left. To lose two fish in January like that was a catastrophe. They just may have been my only chance of action and I felt that I'd blown it. I decided to wait for Keith to get better before going back, but I kept some bait going in, and a week or so later I got the call from Keith to say that he was alive and would be over in a couple of days for a session.

No one had been fishing the South for what seemed ages. The weather was enough to put anyone off, but this was good for us as we knew our little campaign wouldn't get blown, and that we should have this area to ourselves for a while. So, Keith was better and looking fit and healthy again. He always lost a fair bit of weight when he was ill, but now he was like a new man, ready to go. We had doubled up in the Boom and it felt really carpy - you know, when you get that feeling of action.

Keith proceeded to empty the lake.

"These bloody coots, mate, are driving me mad!"

Keith's 30lb common was the fish of the campaign.

It was flat calm and cold, but tolerable sitting out by the rods. This turned out to be the calm before the storm, though, as a strong wind picked up later and pushed the temperatures down colder and colder. We had a thermometer and that showed us the wind chill was making it minus-7.

This seemed to make no difference under the water, though, because we both caught fish. The wind carried on and I was having trouble with the little island as the fish were kiting around the other side of it, and my line was catching on all the dead reeds. Without them, I would have been able to lift the rod and maybe the fish would just go around it, so under cover of darkness, I had to do a raid on the island and remove all the rushes; an easy assault that was soon over, and I was back on the bank, with coffee to warm me up.

The next fish I had was so much easier to deal with without the reeds. A mate came round later that day, one of the first visitors we'd had, and we chatted in our swim but not giving away the fact that we had been catching. He kept glancing at the island as if he thought something was strange. Then he said, "Where have all the reeds gone?"
"It's all them bloody geese, mate," I replied. "They were going nuts on that island all night. Kept us awake." He grinned but said no more.

When the wind eventually died off, we were in danger of the lake freezing over as it was like Siberia by now. I got up one morning and one of my swingers was hanging right down in a big drop-back.
"Those bloody coots!" I said to Keith. "They're driving me mad."
When I checked my alarm, though, I realised why I hadn't heard the drop-back; the wheel had frozen solid. The line was slack, so I picked up my rod to reel in and recast, and as I did that, I noticed that my line was nowhere near where I'd originally placed it, but was now down tight to my right margin. As I reeled in, I met with a resistance that moved off and started to take line. Keith looked on in disbelief and was singing, 'Fly Me to the Moon', by Frank Sinatra. He was always singing that.
"I've got one on 'ere, mate," I said.

It turned out to be a nice bonus 25lb mirror, and we'd now had six fish between us, all 20s. It just goes to show that these fish were well up for some grub as they really had been given a fair amount by now. A couple of anglers had started to mooch about on the Caravan bank and I think one of them saw one of our sacks hanging up - schoolboy error - so as we left the swim, we really baited it, hoping that it was over-baited if someone decided to move in after us.

A North Lagoon common.

I only dabbled with the North. This cracker came from St Albans Pool.

We got back a couple more times and Keith had some good fish, a couple of 29s and a 30lb common that really was the fish of that campaign. We'd decided to start putting some bait in the Point swim, in the gullies along the bars that run across the front of it. This area was to be our fallback position if our Boom swim was compromised. We gave the Point gullies plenty of bait and just left the area alone for later. We hoped that if the fish were working the Boom area, they may well be running along the gullies of the Point.

Keith had decided to give the Point a go and was down before me, and as we had also put a lot more bait out in the Boom, I was going to jump back in there. Keith had rung me to come and do some shots in the morning, when he'd had a 29lb mirror, and as I made my way to the Point swim, I passed the Boom. My heart sank when I saw a bivvy set up in the swim. 'What's going on here?' I thought. 'What a cheek!' You don't see anyone all winter, and then when they do come out, they're in your swim. 'Oh well, that's angling,' I thought as I walked down to see Keith. The angler who was in our swim was sitting in the doorway of Keith's bivvy. He was a mate and worst of all a very capable angler. I said my hellos and 'well done' to Keith on his fish, then I turned to matey.
"How you getting on then in the Boom?"
"Keep it to yourself," he said. "I've had a 36lb mirror."
I saw Keith's face behind him wince when he said it, but for the angler to tell me to 'keep it to myself', then surely he couldn't have known about our campaign, could he? Surely not.

Just as the lake was holding some very good fish, the Centre and South Lagoons suffered a fish kill. The fish weights were going through the roof with a good head of 30s and the lakes were buzzing. I never did find out exactly what was the cause but something went wrong and we were all devastated by it. A lot of the good fish disappeared and the whole atmosphere changed.

Now, I'd been fishing the lagoons for something like six years, and in all that time I never got bored with the venue. Jay and me did have some adventures on other waters, fishing Darenth and Larksfield, and had some very good fish, but we always ended back at the Lagoons. For years, it was like a magnet to us.

One year, I baited a bay called St Albans Pool in the North Lagoon. This bay was crystal clear and the North did hold some very nice fish. I was seeing these fish turn up every day as I fed them throughout the close season, and I definitely saw a low to mid-30 sandy-coloured leather that I'd never heard of visiting the bank, and I'm sure there were many more that had never seen a hook in their lifetimes.

Thanks for all the good times, mate.

The North always was a mystery water, and I did catch a few stunning fish from there, but I only flirted with it for a while. There's not enough time in life for everything, but maybe one day I'll have another go.

The fish kill was a big blow for me and the lake really wasn't the same any more, but the ones that survived were pushing on. One fish, a stockie called Smoked Ham, later went on to be close to mid-40, but my friend, Lee, had her at 19lbs and I later caught her at 28lbs. Some of the originals remained, but it was definitely time to find a new home and a new challenge.

I enjoyed my time on the Lagoons. It was almost like doing an eight-year apprenticeship because I learned so much as an angler, especially how to tackle larger waters and the watercraft of bigger lakes. I took all this knowledge with me and put it to good use for the rest of my angling life. There are many more stories to tell, but we were all settling down and spreading out. The gang was getting smaller and for the first time, we left the Lagoons behind.

Keith and me had more adventures together over the next few years, until one day the diabetes took his life. I was so shocked. His illness was making him ill more frequently and the poor sod was suffering. He was only 38 years old. Keith was a one-off person and I still miss him very much. Thanks for all the good times mate. I'll never forget. Fly Me To The Moon.

Chapter Four - Paul Pynen

The Pretty One

It was August Bank Holiday Monday, 1999, and I had woken up with a heavy hangover. The best cure was to take my dog for a walk around my local lakes, but first of all I needed to stop at the corner shop for a bottle of Lucozade, a packet of fags, and some Paracetamol. This, together with some fresh air and I would be feeling okay by lunchtime.

As I drove down the country lanes, I thought about the lack of fishing I'd been able to do that season. However, by taking regular walks with my dog, Jasper, I'd been able to keep in touch with the lakes and how they were fishing, so I parked the car in the factory entrance of the South Lagoon and walked down the path that leads to Reedy Bay. The floating weed was as thick as ever. It had been about all summer, making the fishing nearly impossible in warm, calm weather, because it spreads out into smaller rafts of weed and drifts constantly through your lines. This means a lot of casting, which is not very helpful when you're trying to catch wary fish in a big lake. When it's windy, though, the weed gets blown into tight areas such as snags, corners and around the islands, and that makes the fishing a bit easier.

It was one of those summer mornings without a cloud in the sky, baking hot and no wind (apart from my own of course, must have been something I'd eaten). As I crossed the footbridge over the river, the water looked like it was covered in hundreds of small green islands and it had turned a dirty-green colour, but as I wasn't fishing, I wasn't that concerned; it was just nice to be by the water on such a lovely morning. As I walked along the path, I could see that the first three swims were vacant, which was unsurprising, considering the state of the water. I carried on to the Point swim (every lake has one) and as I approached, I heard a buzzer sing out.

It seemed strange on such a hot, still morning and I made my way quickly into the swim, expecting to see a familiar face. To my surprise, I didn't know the two anglers so I just stood back, watched the action and tried to stop Jasper from eating their breakfast, which was cooking in a frying pan.

Landing the fish was hard work due to the amount of weed hanging on the angler's line, but luckily, the bloke with the net was able to help out and soon we were looking down at one awesome fish. As it was being weighed, Mick turned up. He'd been fishing the lakes for some years, but the lads who were fishing had just joined that season and were friends of his. On the scales, the fish weighed 36lbs, and as she was held up for the cameras, I said to Mick, "What a cracking looking fish! I'd love to catch it myself one day." Once the pictures were done and she was returned safely to her home, I carried on around the lake. I was feeling healthier by now so decided it was time to go home for some breakfast.

On the drive home, I kept thinking about the lump and hoped that I could catch one of the same size. At the back of my mind, though, I knew that the fish I'd just seen was the one I wanted. My only problem was lack of time. Due to work and social commitments, I knew that I wouldn't be able to get out during the whole of September, and this was bad news. We all know this is one of the best months of the year to have your rods out. I needed a plan of action.

As I pulled up in front of my garage door, part one of a plan hit me. Sitting in the garage was 30 kilos of Premier Aminos waiting to be rolled and once made up, this would give me well over 40 kilos of bait, so I decided that as September was a good time of year for the fish to feed, they could have the lot. I would start baiting the lakes straight away, even though I couldn't fish until the end of the month. The next few weeks were going to be hard work because on the nights that I wasn't making bait, I would have to be putting it in.

The next part of my plan was to decide where I was going to bait up. The venues get heavily fished so it can be awkward getting the bait in, and like most lakes, the weekend is when they are the busiest so there wouldn't be the space to get my bait out. Therefore, getting my bait established would be a less competitive task during the week. Then I had to think about where to put the bulk of it. The water is actually made up of two lakes joined by a narrow channel, which allows the fish to move freely between the two. The Centre Lagoon would be a good place to put bait, as a lot of big fish had been caught there before at this time of year, but you can drive your car up to many of the swims and anglers who fished overnight tended to occupy these areas, so it would be impossible to bait. The South Lagoon would be a better bet.

The Caravan Bank and Canal Bank are very popular autumn and winter areas, but the far bank where the Point swim is situated doesn't get much attention during autumn, because it's a long walk from the car park and very muddy. On that side of the lake, there are three main bars running nearly the whole length of the bank, and a few islands, joined by gravel bars that are a few feet under water. I started baiting that night and nobody was fishing so I was able to spread the bait between three swims, where I hoped some passing fish would find it.

Over the next few weeks, I managed to bait when I wanted, while the rest of the lakes were still being heavily fished, and I had booked a Thursday and Friday off work on the first weekend of October so this would give me three nights' fishing to find out if my baiting had paid off.

I arrived at 8am and took a drive around the Centre to see who was fishing, and if any fish were showing, although I was thinking about the South because that's where my bait had gone. The weather that morning was sunny and warm with a light south-westerly wind as I turned my car around by the sailing club, and as I pulled up in No. 2 swim, a fish leapt clear of the water, 80 yards out. I lit a fag, watched the water for a while and saw another four fish crash out. I was thinking about getting the rods out, but the fish I'd seen were well spread out and seemed to be moving and not feeding, so I decided to have a walk around the South Lagoon before setting up on the Centre. I walked around to a swim call the Stumps and there was a regular installed there. I had a quick chat and he informed me that he'd been there since the Sunday night and had caught two low-20s on Monday, but had seen nothing since. I thought this was strange because although the angler concerned was not a friend of mine, I knew he was a good angler and if he hadn't seen anything for three days, he would have moved by now.

I walked back to the car with my mind ticking over; there had to be a fair number of fish in the South, but I had also got them in the Centre. I had another smoke and a cup of tea and watched for a little longer. Over the next 30 minutes, three more fish showed and they were spread out just like the ones I'd seen earlier, so I got the rods out and made my mind up to give that swim a try for 24 hours. If I didn't have anything, or see any movement, I would still have plenty of time to move before the anglers arrived for the weekend.

I cast out three single hookbaits to areas that had produced in the past, but wasn't too hopeful as the early morning feeding spell had long gone. The kettle was just coming to the boil when Lenny drove down the path, and I hoped he had his rods with him, as he was good company to fish with. He got out of the van and asked if I'd seen anything. I told him and then he told me that he'd spoken to the angler in the Stumps who had caught four 20s since Monday. I laughed. "That's two more he's caught since I spoke to him a couple of hours ago!" I said. Len was only going to fish the day, but as the conditions were good and I was staying a while, he decided to do the night.

Early afternoon, I baited up and hoped to give my areas time to settle down. My right-hand rod was to be fished short, over a bed of hemp, groats, pellets, and chopped Aminos, so I put the marker float out in a gully about 20 yards from the bank. The bottom felt like fine gravel and once I had the spot marked, I clipped up my baited rod ready to cast out at dusk and then carried out the same procedure with the other rods, putting a kilo of boilies around the left-hand rod. This was achieved with a Gardener Boilie Rocket, which cast very accurately and is quite visible at range. The middle rod was to be a single pop-up fished at long range in the silt. So, the rods were cast out just before dusk, landing bang on my baited areas, and I felt really confident that I would catch in the night.

Now it was time to chill out and relax, so out came the beer, with me on Stella, while Len prefers Tennants Extra, (he drinks less of this so that he won't have to keep getting up at night to let it out). We sat up talking until one in the morning and heard a couple of large fish crash out, so our confidence was quite high when we turned in.

At six o'clock in the morning I was lying on my bed, smoking my third fag of the day, when my left-hand rod gave out two quick bleeps. I looked up just as my indicator pulled up tight, and before I could get my shoes on, the clutch was screaming. I pulled into the fish but it pulled straight back down, tore off toward Len's rods and I managed to turn it just in time. The fish went on three more long runs before I managed to get it into the margins, and then it was soon netted. I thought I had a mid-20 in the net but on the scales it was 26lbs 8oz so I woke Len to do some photos. He congratulated me and asked if I would be moving or staying put.

A little while later, I had a run on the particle rod, and this turned out to be a tench. No more runs occurred after that, but we did see some fish showing later that morning and like the day before, they were well spread out, so I decided to stay where I was for the weekend. The weather forecast for the next 24 hours was gale force, south-westerly winds and plenty of rain. Len said he would stay for one more night, because conditions were good and there was still a few fish in the area. I carried out the same routine as the day before, had all my areas baited by lunchtime and my rods clipped up ready to cast at dusk, so that even if the wind was strong, I knew that I could get on my areas. I also doubled the amount of bait as I thought more than one fish was on the cards.

By the time dusk approached, the wind had picked up and white-capped waves were pushing up the lake. I was glad I'd sorted my rods out earlier, and managed to get on my spots without too much trouble. The rain arrived just after dark, so I sat in Len's bivvy, drinking more Stella and chatting until midnight, and then crashed out. It was pointless sitting up listening for fish, as it was too dark and windy to see anything. I was woken a couple of times in the night by extra strong gusts of wind, (outside the bivvy, I mean), but the third time was my left-hand rod screaming away. I lifted into the fish, the rod was wrenched down hard, and I was forced to backwind straight away. The fish kited to my left and took a lot of line, but once I'd managed to slow it down, the next problem arose; the fish was kiting into the bank and in danger of snagging me down the margins. I tried to dip my rod tip but it was too late, my line had snagged a branch of a willow tree and wouldn't come free.

A few rod lengths along the margin, I could just make out the shape of a fish lying beaten and bobbing up and down in the waves, so I put the rod back on the rests and went to wake Len. I explained what had happened and he said he had an extension pole on his landing net and that it might reach. We tried the net but it was still a long way short, so the option was to go in after it. Len told me to be careful as the bank sloped away pretty quickly. I got out of my clothes and the strong wind made me shiver. It was freezing but I felt warmer when I was in the water and was soon up to my neck and nearly out of my depth. I managed to get the net under the fish and as Len slackened off the line, my prize sank down into the mesh. She was mine!

I cut my foot open as I scrambled back to the bank, so I handed Len the net, quickly dried myself and got some clothes on, while he sorted out the scales. I held them up while Len read out the weight as 30lbs 12oz, and I was well happy, especially as it was a cracking-looking fish. We did the photos and returned her to her home and then I fired up the Coleman for a brew to help me warm up. Before we had finished the tea, though, I had a take on my right-hand rod and although this fish put up a good scrap, I told Len that it didn't feel as big as the last one. I soon had it in the margins and rolling in the net, and as I sorted out the mat and scales, while Len held the net in the water, I asked him how much he thought it would weigh. His reply was, "You'll be pleasantly surprised."

It was warmer once I was in the water, and up to my neck.

As soon as I lifted the net, I understood what he'd meant. On the scales, she went 31lbs 8oz and I couldn't believe my luck. This one was a completely different shape to the last one, looking more Italian and very grey in colour, whereas the first one was quite dark and a classic carp shape. Len did the honours with the camera and my prize was released to fight another day as Len fired up the Coleman while I tied on a new hooklink with two 12mm boilies. Once cast out, I fired another 30 baits out just in case some more fish were visiting my area, as quite a bit of my particle had probably been eaten. Once we had finished our brew, Len decided to get some sleep, so I got in my bag too, but sleep eluded me. Two 30s in less than an hour! My mind was buzzing.

I was still wide-awake an hour later when my right-hand rod went off again. I could feel that the fish wasn't as big as the last two but it still managed to take me toward Len's rods. In fact, I took one of his rods out and I ended up in Len's swim to land the fish. We sorted out the tangle of lines and in the net was a 20lb 8oz common but I put this one straight back because the rain was pouring down and I was knackered. I got into my bag once more, and this time I did manage to sleep.

I was woken at about half eight by Kevin, a regular of the Lagoons, and he demanded a cup of tea and an update on what had been happening over the last 24 hours.

31lbs 8oz and completely different to the first one.

After we'd told him every detail, he congratulated me, said he would be fishing that night and, as Len was off at lunchtime, he might as well set up where Len was, as the rest of the Lagoons was rammed. We were discussing the night's events when Kevin said it was strange that Len hadn't had any takes, considering there were so many fish about. I thought it might have something to do with the bait that I'd had put in during the last few weeks, and also, all my takes had come to the rods that had a fair amount of bait around them, whereas my single bait had remained motionless. Len fished singles or stringers on all his rods, and it was possible that the fish wanted to fill their bellies for the onset of autumn.

Things didn't look too promising for the coming night. The forecast was for a cold, still night and a heavy frost, the first of the year, so we took the best course of action; a trip down to the local takeaway, stocked up with loads of lager and had a celebration. We sat up well into the night watching the flat calm water where nothing stirred except coots and ducks, a totally different night to the ones before. We crashed when the beer ran out, knowing that the fish had moved on and when we woke in the morning the frost was quite heavy. We sat out in the early morning sun and nothing moved, but we stayed there until lunchtime, just enjoying being out on the banks; there's more to our hobby than just catching fish. I started carp fishing in 1975, and know what it's like to blank, especially in the pre-hair rig days. As I drove home, I was thinking about the following weekend when, although I had booked Friday off work, I had to pack up early on Saturday morning to take my son to play football.

The week soon passed and at first light on the Friday morning, I was driving down the willow bank toward the swim I had been in the week before. As I pulled up at the boathouse, it looked like a refugee camp, with bivvies and cars in every swim. The bloke in the swim that I'd fished the week before, informed me that nothing had been out all week from that part of the lake, and as I looked around at the amount of pressure, that wasn't a surprise. With this information, I drove straight down to the South Lagoon and made for the Point swim. I was quite confident because I'd put a lot of bait out in that area over the previous few weeks, and had managed to stick some more in earlier that week while everyone was fishing the Centre.

I stood on the Point, and I knew that this was the spot. I lit a fag, watched the water and I could sense that fish were there, and that I would have one. The Caravan Bank was down to my left at the bottom end of the lagoon. Someone was fishing there and the lads on the Centre had told me that it was the same bloke who'd been in the Stumps the previous week. I'd just finished my smoke when a big fish came out of the water about 50 yards to my left. I could have cast a bait to where it had shown, but if I'd hooked anything, it would have been hard to land, due to an island to my left which a fish could easily kite round. So, I decided it wasn't worth the risk to the fish, and I would cast to an area on the same line, which would offer a more realistic chance of success. For some strange reason, I wasn't in any hurry to cast out. I let the fish finish off their breakfast in peace and left the water undisturbed. I didn't think they'd go far because this was the quietest part of the lake and had a regular supply of food.

By lunchtime, I'd gone through the same routine as the previous week and my swim was baited and ready. The right-hand rod was on particles, the middle rod just stringers and my left-hand rod was on the same line as where the fish had shown that morning. Around this rod I baited with a kilo of Aminos, and by using the spod I was able to get my baiting tight to the marker. Now all I had to do was cast my hookbait just as accurately. The cast was good for a change and my lead landed right next to the marker. I was concerned that I had hit the float but knew I would never get that accurate again, if I tried all day. I put the rod down on the buzzer and very slowly, tightened down my marker rod. It was a big relief when I wound in without moving my baited rod, leaving my hookbait bang on the freebies and my traps perfectly set. I just hoped that the bird life didn't find it before darkness.

The afternoon soon passed, so I had an early dinner, opened my first can of Stella, and was totally chilled out. My good friend, Jerry, arrived late afternoon, said 'well done' for my efforts the week before, and he agreed that I had a good chance of more fish. That boosted my already high confidence because Jerry had probably been one of the most consistent anglers on the complex over the previous few seasons, and he could fill a book on his captures alone.

As darkness fell and Jerry left for home, the water went flat calm but unlike the week before, the temperature was rising all the time and it became very warm and muggy. I sat up until about 2am and heard the odd fish roll, not crashing right out, but just heavy rolling. I wondered how much longer it would be before the real winter arrived.

I was woken by the noise of my buzzer screaming out its warning. I scrambled into my trainers and then pulled into the fish that had tried to nick the bait that was attached to my left-hand rod. It was taking a lot of line on its first run and I could feel that it had run down the back of the bar, causing a grating sensation down the line. The fish stopped suddenly and sulked behind the bar. I kept a tight line to it but nothing happened. Trying to pull from different angles also had no effect, so this stalemate went on for a few minutes until I decided to try and pull the fish over the bar.

I knew this fish was a bit special and probably 35-plus.

Cupping the spool in my hand, I slowly walked backwards a few steps and there was progress, the fish was on the move and kiting to my right and after a few more strong rounds, she was circling just a few rod lengths out, and feeling quite large.

I had one more shallow bar to guide her over and then, I hoped, she would be mine, so I sunk the tips of the remaining rods to give myself some space. I never use a torch to land fish in the dark because I think it spooks them, plus your eyes adjust to the dark and if you're patient and wait until the fish is near the spreader block, you should have no problems.

Finally, she was safely in the net and I left her resting in the water while I got my torch and unhooking mat. As I switched on the torch, I knew that this fish was a bit special and probably 35lbs-plus. My legs turned to jelly with excitement as I lifted the net and, on the mat, she behaved herself perfectly and allowed me to extract my Drennan SS size four. The scales spun round and stopped at 37lbs 8oz, for a new personal best by 2lbs. I put my prize in the landing net, lowered it into the margins, and carefully secured the net to a bank stick, making sure there was plenty of water over her head.

I looked out across the lake toward the Stumps, where Lewis was now fishing, and seeing that his light was on, I quickly wound in my remaining rods and went round to tell him the news and ask if he would do some photos for me. He said that he could do better than that as he had a video camera with him and would come round at first light. I went back to the Point so that I could keep an eye on my prize, and light was starting to break so it wouldn't be long before Lewis and his mate, Chris, arrived for the photo shoot. I still wasn't sure what the fish was as I hadn't had a proper look up to that point.

Just after first light, the lads came around to take a few photos, and I laid the fish on the unhooking mat, we realised what I had; the Pretty One! Unbelievable! Of all the stunning fish in the lagoons, this was the one I had dreamed of catching. Seeing her on the bank, back on that baking hot morning in August, had fired me up to get the rods out once more and to start my baiting up. I really believe that all my hard work in September, making bait and baiting up, had paid off big time.

The video shoot and photos were soon finished and I held her in the water for a few seconds until a powerful kick of her tail sent her gliding back home. Watching her swim off made me so happy and I knew the lagers would be flowing that night! I thanked Lewis and Chris for their help and as I headed for home, for once, the wheelbarrow flew down the muddy path.

Of all the stunning fish in the Lagoons, this is the one I had dreamed of catching the most. The Pretty One.

Chapter Five
The Struggle at Hone, Sutton

Around 20 years ago, there was a gang of us that fished together. We'd done it for years, and we all met up at Hainault Park Lake in Essex. Back then, Hainault was the be all and end all of carp lakes, and to my mates and me there wasn't another lake like it; we weren't interested in fishing anywhere else. Those times were fantastic and we had such a laugh but over the years things change, people get commitments and the old gang started to split up.

A small group of us stayed together and we marched onward in our pursuit to catch carp, fishing a few other waters before we settled on the Nazeing Meads complex in Lee Valley Park. We served an eight-year apprenticeship on there and I had some of my best-ever angling, but there came a time when we had to get serious. The gang had become even smaller because a couple of mates had moved to Norfolk, and that left Jay (Essex Jay), Neil (Sleepy Neil), Craig Bateman, and me, and we were up for a new challenge.

Back then, there weren't too many lakes that held 40-pounders, but one that did interest us was Sutton at Hone. All I knew about the lake was that it was small, days only, and an angler I had heard of, Danny Regan, had caught a big carp from there called Heart Tail Gertie at around 38lbs - a big fish. I also heard that there was another big mirror called Blind Eye, and one or two good commons were not far behind.

So, we went about getting tickets and the seed was sown; we were all Sutton mad and couldn't wait to start. We had never fished this 'days only' style before, starting at 4am and finishing at 10.30pm. That's a fair amount of time to be on the bank, just for the day, but little did I know just how hard and tiring it would be, especially if I wanted to string a few days together.

As I said, Sutton is a small lake of around three acres and we found out that it held something like 70 carp, a fair head of fish for its size. With such a large number of inhabitants, at least 20 of which were over 30lbs, we thought, 'here we go then – let's get it on!' Oh dear, how very wrong we were. I realise now in hindsight that it was one of the trickiest lakes I have ever encountered. Small lakes do seem to be very hard, well, the ones I've fished, at least. I think carp sense the angling pressure quickly, and that unrest is soon spread around a smaller lake so that nothing seems to play ball. In addition, we all had to leave for the night, just at the time when, I would suspect, the carp would have their feed. Then there were other anglers to compete with. We had a draw each morning at 4am and sometimes, midweek, we were disappointed not to get the swim we fancied. Then, at 5pm, all the evening anglers would turn up and start to cast about. Yes, Sutton was a head job!

A gang of good anglers already fished Sutton. Steve Edwards was the head bailiff, a member of a group called the Sound and Round crew, and these guys were all into their Richworth bait, which had ruled the roost over there for the past few years, or so it seemed. Steve was a very good angler and I was to pay a lot of attention to him. He knew the lake well, and he took a liking to us Essex lot.

For some reason that I can't remember, we stayed away at the start of that very first season on Sutton. I think we decided to let all the regulars get stuck in, hoping that perhaps it would calm down a bit. This turned out not such a good idea because by the time we did get on, most of the lake's residents had been caught. However, we found out a lot more about the stock of the lake. There were so many good fish to go for; Heart Tail, and Blind Eye were both doing 40lbs now and another fish, called little Gertie, was close behind at 38-39lbs. There were also two good commons. The Big Common was fast approaching 40lbs, and close behind that was one called Haswell's Common that had done 38lbs. That's not to mention other fish that were well on our list; such as the Big Fully Scaled at 37-plus, the elusive Brown Fish, over 35lbs, the Beast, the Unknown, Searcher, and the Little Fully - all good 30s - with other 30lb commons to back that lot up. No one can deny that's an impressive list of fish for any water, and we are talking 15 years ago now.

Sutton became an obsession, and all four of us got down there as much as we could. We got to know some of the characters that were also fishing the lake, and looking back, I realise that was a big part of the place; there was a right lot of banter, and it was competitive, to say the least. A load of bait went in and not many got caught, but the bait was getting eaten, because the weights of the fish were on the increase.

There were consistent anglers back then, who were always there, it seemed, every time that I was. One such character was an old boy called Dennis who fished for bream when he felt like it, and there were literally thousands of them that did became a right pest, but he also fished for the carp. He was good company on those freezing winter days, but what I especially liked about Dennis was that he was always inventing things, and his rigs were great. Where he got his ideas from I will never know; there were bits of tubing and plastic all over the place, with a hook and bait somewhere among it all. Quality!

Keith Sullivan (They called him Snoz but I don't think he liked that), was old school. He was the one in the Yateley video when Ritchie Macdonald had Heather on at the Car Park Lake in March. It was freezing and Ritchie's fish had gone round a big marginal tree, so Keith stripped off down to his boxers, went in on a Lilo, and more or less swam the rod back round so that Rich was able to play the fish again. Bloody hell! Keith deserved a medal for that.

There were loads of characters; Kodak, Poser Pete, Trigger, Craig Lyons, Leroy Swan, Terry The Boxer, John Elmer and Piccolo Pete, to name a few, and something was always happening. It was brilliant. One day, Piccolo Pete was fishing further down on my left in the High Point swim, when we heard a great big splash and wondered what had happened. I ran down and found him crouched at the edge of his swim, with his elbow on his knee resting his chin on his hand. It looked as if he was just scanning the lake. "What was that great big splash?" I asked him.
"What splash?" he replied, as if nothing had happened.
He was saturated, soaked through to the bone.
"Okay, then," I said, puzzled, and went back to my swim.

Later, he told me that he had fallen in and gone completely under, but had got out as quickly as he could and had just got back on the bank as I arrived. He was too embarrassed to let anyone know. Everyone did though, because I told them!

Because the lake was small, everyone knew everything that was going on. If a fish showed, everyone was aware of it. These fish were pressured and, as I said before, it was as if there was an atmosphere in the lake and all the fish were affected. From just after 4am, when the gates were opened and we all started walking the banks to our chosen swims, the carp knew what was coming. At times, nothing came out for ages, and we just knew we were not going to catch.

One day, I was talking to Steve Edwards as he was fishing a swim called the Pea, and we were chatting away when his right-hand rod signalled a liner.

He was only fishing close, so he got up and tweaked his line a bit, and suddenly this huge common leaped right out, clearing the water. It scared the life out of us and we got sprayed with water as it went back in. This was just off the end of his rod tip where, in fact, his hook bait was.
"Yeah," he said. "They come in close, here." You don't say! Later in the day, Steve caught that common, which turned out to be another huge carp at 37lbs. I did the photos for him and saw my first big Sutton lump.

Sleepy Neil was the first of our group to get a bite. At ten o'clock each evening, we would pack everything up and lay the rods on the floor for the last half-hour. Just before 10.30pm, Neil was into a fish and Jay and me went to assist. He was having a right old scrap and by the time he had landed it, it was near to 11pm. It was only a small fish, about 16lbs of nice mirror, but we were so worried about being on the lake so late that we didn't even take a photo of it. We imagined that the car park would be full of anglers and bailiffs ready to ban us when we got there, only to find that everyone had gone home long since. It would've been good to get a photo of that first Sutton fish; I wonder now which one it was, and how big it is today.

Jay was next to catch. Jay and Neil had done a five-day session, and after all their hard work, driving backwards and forwards to the lake from home with only a few hours sleep each night, Jay was rewarded with a strange-shaped common called Eric. He caught Eric from the High Point swim and it was the only bite between them, but we soon found out that this was the norm at Sutton. Anyway, Jay and Neil were off the mark, and although Jay's fish, Eric, looked a bit strange - it had a kind of dropped back on it - I wouldn't have turned it down to be off the mark.

For me, the way forward was to string a few days together, but even that wouldn't guarantee me the same swim the next day, and the other problem was that if I was to drive home each night, by the time I got there and all sorted for the next day, it would be 1am. I would have to be getting up again at 2.30am to make it for the 4am draw; it was hardly worth it, and it would cost me a lot in fuel. The only other option was to stay over, but where to spend those few hours overnight?

We were not allowed to stay in the car park because Sutton is in a residential area, and the neighbours would be disturbed with all the gates opening and shutting all night. It became a nightmare, but Roman Villa Road ran along behind Darenth where it linked up with Sutton and a little way along it was a lay-by. I ended up spending many a night of broken sleep in there.

Jay was off the mark with Crazy Eric.

I used to leave the car park and drive into Darenth town to get some grub. Either an A1 (a big, round container filled up with rice and God knows what else, but it did the job), from the Chinese, or I would get what they called an 'Evening Box' from the Indian takeaway. It was a box all sectioned up, with rice, curry, naan bread, and a side dish. The old Indian guy got to know me fairly well over the time I was there. Then, I'd head off back to my luxury lay-by accommodation and on the way, I'd call in at the garage for water, milk, and back then, fags, and any other bits I might need for the next day.

To be honest, that lay-by was a joke. I'd always thought it was a fairly big lay-by, but seeing it years later, I realised that it was just somewhere to pull over if a big vehicle came down the narrow lane. Anyway, I would pull in, keep the radio on, and eat my grub. I had a big quilt in the back and a pillow, and I'd try to sleep by reclining the driver's seat, wrapping the quilt around me, and doing my best to crash out.

Not a bloody chance! Cars were up and down that little lane all night, and their headlights blinded me each time. I felt really vulnerable on that roadside. One night it was so cold, my feet were freezing and I had to get them on the passenger seat to keep them off the floor. Not the most comfortable of positions.

The worst night of all, though, was when I'd crashed out in my lay-by, absolutely knackered. I had my head resting on the cold glass window, and a car with very bright headlights pulled up in front of me. To this day, I'm not sure whether I was dreaming, or if it was reality. The car was parked with its full beam on me, someone was getting out of the car and I was trying to wake up, but I just couldn't; it was as if I couldn't shake myself out of sleep. The person headed toward my car, came round to my driver's side, and started banging on the window. Who the hell was this? It seemed he was banging on the window for ages until I threw my head to one side and woke myself up. There was no one there. I started the engine and drove off sharpish, and I still don't know if it was a dream or not. It was probably the police wondering what I was up to, but nevertheless, I gave the old Villa lay-by a miss from then on.

After a while, we began to sneak back to the Sutton car park, and we never got in any trouble. I would start the car at 3.30am to demist the windows, and job's a good 'un. We used get a brew on pretty quickly, though, as it would always feel like we'd only just eaten the A1 or Evening Box; we needed that brew to wash away the lovely MSG taste – yuk!

Jay and Neil once told me that they'd found a nice little spot to hide up for the nights. I knew where it was, and on this particular night, I knew that they were staying over. They didn't think I was getting over to fish so they weren't expecting me. I left home really early, parked the car away from their lay-up position, and made my way down a wooded track until I saw their car ahead of me. They had both crashed out in the front seats and all the windows were steamed up. One of my kids had a little plastic alien, and when you switched it on, all these little LEDs would flash, and the alien made space invader noises. I placed the alien on the windscreen and switched it on. Well, I freaked them out big time! They didn't have a clue what was going on and I can still remember seeing Neil's face through the passenger window as I fell on the floor laughing. They were not impressed, but I thought it was fantastic!

I can't remember how many day sessions I'd done before my rod finally signalled a take, but I was more than relieved when it did, and I know it was a Thursday. For some strange reason, Neil and Jay's bites were also on a Thursday; that day seemed to bring us some luck. I was fishing the Pads swim, so called because of a large set of pads on the opposite bank, and I had a funny sort of fight with a fish that didn't involve a lot of effort. After a while, the large head of a common came up to the waiting net and as it slid in, the familiar shape of Eric soon lay in the mesh. So my first fish was also Eric and at about the same weight as when Jay had caught it at 25lbs.

I was happy that I was now also off the mark, even though it was Eric, who seemed intent on becoming a friend of ours; we named him Crazy Eric. I did hear a few remarks from around the lake about the fish we had caught between us, but it was early days yet and it just made us even keener. Talking of keenness, Neil got really eager for a while, and started doing from 4am until 8am every morning, before work. Now that's what I call keen. He must have been shattered! That's how the nickname 'Sleepy Neil' was born. Anyway, his efforts paid him well, and one morning he caught an awesome carp, named Searcher, at 31lbs 10oz, from a little close-in spot in the back pads, and no one could say anything about that one. I had to wait until September for my next bit of action.

Sleepy Neil gets his reward with Searcher.

The summer wore on and it was about this time that Terry Hearn was having a dabble. I had never met Tel, but I knew of his angling ability and all that he'd caught in the past. On one of his early trips to Sutton he'd caught the Brown Fish at 37lbs from a swim called the Wide, and that is probably one of the hardest fish in the lake to catch, and very seldom comes out. Later, after I'd got to know Tel, he told me that at the time, he hadn't known anything about the Brown Fish, and he was just doing his thing and along came this cracker of a carp at 37lbs. He was chuffed with his start on Sutton, and it wasn't until a season or so later, when it had not been out again, that he realised just how shy this fish was to the bank.

I was really lucky one day to witness the mighty Blind Eye on the bank at 44lbs 8oz to long-time regular Graham East, and as I stared at this huge carp while it was being photographed, I wondered if I would ever catch her myself. That particular day I was set up in the Pea and Tel was down in the Wide, next door to my left. He popped up, we had a chat, I got a brew on, and this was the start of a friendship with undoubtedly the country's best carp angler, and we became good mates.

For some silly reason, I kind of went all retro at first on Sutton with my tackle. I was using KM rods, 1¾, and Cardinal C5s for reels, and that evening I was to put them through their paces when I had a take off the willow tree hangers. It had been absolutely chucking it down for hours and I had just glanced at the rods when the right-hand bobbin was pulled up tight to the top. An extremely angry carp was trying its damnedest to gain sanctuary under the canopy of willow.

"It looks like you've got yourself a 30-pounder there!"

Craig with one of his Sutton stunners.

The very light rods were bending round to the butt, and the reel with a done-up clutch was no good; line was peeling off the spool at the carp's will. I held on to the soft rod and there was a kind of stalemate for a while until the carp begrudgingly started coming away from the danger of the willow branches. Tel came to assist and eventually I did manage to tame this beast, so Tel was able to slide the net under a good-sized common.

"Well, done mate," he said. "It looks like you've got a 30-pounder there!"
That was my first 30lb carp from Sutton; a fish called Jackson's after Lee, as it had a bald patch on one side. No offence, Lee, I didn't name it! I was well chuffed. Jackson's weighed just over 30lbs, and one memory that sticks in my mind was Tel remarking on my old-fashioned rods and reels, and he was right; they were not up to the job. Not many days later, Tel went on to catch the Fully Scaled at 38lbs from the Point swim. He really was opening his account in style.

Time was cracking on and with countless day sessions, and a grand total of only two fish since June, we had all really worked hard but with not a great deal to show for it. Jay managed to bank Jackson's at over 30lbs, and Craig, who was not doing as much time as us, landed Searcher. It seemed as if we were all catching each other's fish, but at least we'd caught. There were anglers that had done a fair bit of time who'd caught nothing all season.

Before I knew it, it was November and getting very cold. I really liked a swim called the High Point, and it is just that, a high point. From the left a bar breaks, leaving a gap, and then another big clump of gravel forms the high point that is shallow on the very top, a foot, or so. The gap to the left was, to me, an obvious route that the fish would be using, and this area was fairly deep in silt and held, I would imagine, a good amount of natural food.

I had placed a single bottom bait out in this silt channel because the bream in this area were a real pain. Sometimes, you might get between five and ten bream a session, and every time that bobbin pulled up tight your heart skipped a beat, as you thought that maybe it was a carp. It was a cold old night and with only an hour and a half to go things were looking doubtful, when at around 9pm, the left-hand rod signalled another bream-like take. 'That's all I need,' I thought, as I picked up the rod and started to reel in the offending bream. As I was reeling in, a couple of anglers came by.
"You into a carp, mate?" they asked.
"No," I replied. "It's just a bream."
I honestly hadn't felt anything as I literally just reeled in the fish, but as it neared the bank, there was a great big boil-up. Jason Barber was one of the anglers standing by my side.
"'Ere, mate," I said to him. "Shine your head torch down there will you?"
As he did so, I saw the flank of a big old mirror lying there on the surface.
"Bloody 'ell," I said. "Stick the net under that, mate!"

"Ere mate, slip the net under that!"

It was unreal. I looked down and couldn't believe my eyes. Carefully, we lifted the carp to the mat and it felt like well over 30lbs, for sure, and the lads recognised the fish as one called Cluster. On the scales, she went 35lbs 2oz and I was more than happy. For some reason, Cluster didn't give a fight when I hooked her but she was in fantastic condition and I wasn't complaining. Two days later, Jason went on to catch the Big Common at a massive 41lbs 8oz; the first time at over 40lbs. What a sight!

As it was now truly into winter, I more or less knew that there was going to be a long, hard time ahead, but I still stuck at it, and it was every bit as hard as I thought. I was still there for the draw at 3.50am, most of the time on my own, and I still tried to string a few days together, and this was before we'd started to stay over in the car park. Every evening when I left the lake at around 11pm to pick up my Evening Box from the Indian, I would always feel a bit sorry for myself because I had nowhere to go. It really it did seem a bit ridiculous having to pack up for those few hours and spend the night freezing in the car, only to go back later on.

I remember one night, when I was really tired, fishing in the High Point swim and I hadn't seen a soul all day. It was bitterly cold and I was as snug as a bug in my old bag under the brolly; it was so warm and cosy. At about 9.30pm, I started to think about packing up. 'Sod it', I said to myself. 'I'm staying'. I went over all the pros and cons; it would be great to have a whole night's sleep without having to pack all the crap away, but then, what if someone turned up to fish at 4am and saw me soundo? They would know I'd done the night and I'd be in the shit. Yeah, I argued, but I'll just tell them I couldn't wake up at 10.30pm, at packing up time. That was it. I was staying. I'd made up my mind, and besides, no one would turn up to fish. There was only one nutter on the lake – me!

I was really comfortable and fell asleep, but at around 10.45pm, I woke up and checked my watch. Suddenly, I jumped out the bag, packed everything up, and drove to the bloody lay-by on Roman Villa Road. I'd lost my bottle. Five hours later, I was all set up again, back in the High Point as I was before I'd left. What a nightmare, and just as I'd thought, no one had turned up! Typical.

Tel also started fishing, and we both put a lot of time in that winter. As hard as it was, I did learn a lot about the place and a fair bit of plumbing was done. Jay, Neil and Craig did the odd day at the weekends but all that seemed to be feeding was the occasional bream.

One night I was fishing in a swim called the Trees, and Tel was sitting on my unhooking mat. We were chatting away, passing the time while drinking lots of tea, when Tel noticed that the unhooking mat that he was sitting on was frozen solid.

It was dark, around 6pm, very quiet and there was a big full moon. I walked to the water's edge to check if the lake had frozen and it came as a kind of relief to find that it had, because that meant it was home time and there was no reason for us to be there. We were both packed up in no time and as we barrowed our gear to the cars we passed an angler just about to cast out in the Twins. He had turned up for the evening and was probably rushing to get his rods out without realising that the lake had frozen. Thinking about that winter on Sutton still gives me a shiver and reminds me not to do anything like that again.

So, my last fish was in November. I did the whole winter, all five months of it, and on the last day of the season, I was back in my swim, the High Point, again. Don't get me wrong, I fished all over the lake that winter, but that last day was very warm for the time of the year and I placed a single pop-up right on top of the high point, in only a couple of feet of water. At 8.30 am that rod burst into life, and at the same time there was a massive eruption as a carp made a big mistake.

This fish really did go for it and started to strip line as it kept high in the water and powered across the lake. I wasn't going to let it have it all its own way, though, so I slowed the spool down with my finger and got the fish to turn slowly, and once I'd done that, I was able to guide it back to my bank. In close, it tried several times to get in under the marginal trees on either side of the swim, but as it rolled on the surface, tired now, I knew she was mine.

After all my hard work, I was rewarded with Cluster again.

Searcher looked incredible.

A big mirror rolled into the net and I peered in to have a look at my hard-earned prize. Guess what lay in my net? Bloody Cluster! I was disappointed because I hadn't wanted catch her again, even though Cluster is a beautiful carp. It would have been great to catch one of the other desirable fish I was after, though. One good bit about it was the fact that she had well and truly fought this time, as opposed to waving the white flag as she had the first time we met.

So, basically, I fished through the whole winter, catching Cluster at the beginning of November, and five months later after all my hard work, I was rewarded with Cluster again. Still, as they say, 'that's angling'. Mind you, Tel also ended up catching one later in the day, with a good bit of angling, from round by the Pipe swim. The lucky sod caught Searcher at 32lbs, and the fish looked incredible.

That was the end of my first season on Sutton. We made some good friends, had a lot of laughs, I saw some huge carp on the bank and I learned a lot. My total catch that season was four fish, as was Neil's, and Jay had five. I was happy with my presentation, and really had thought a lot throughout the winter about finding the right spots to fish. With all the plumbing up I'd done, I had a lot of areas I wanted to fish, and I was already buzzing about the next season.

The close season dragged by, as it usually does, but eventually, it was time for the draw for swims and I had come out more or less last, again. I am truly crap at draws. I ended up with a swim called the Chicken, situated down one side of a little bay with a big set of pads at the end. It would have been okay but there was another swim just the other side of the pads. At the time, I was using DT baits and I really did like their Oily Chicken flavour, it was so different and the smell of it lingered on. If you got it on your hands, you would get a subtle whiff of it all day. This, with their Big Fish mix, was a great combination, and as I going to be fishing the Chicken swim, I tried to convince myself that it had some meaning.

That day turned out to be a scorcher and the fish were just cruising around all day. I had an angler just around the corner from me, and with four lines out in the little bay, we didn't stand a chance. All the fish caught that day came from shallow swims like the Bars and the High Point, with Blind Eye coming from the High Point at a spawned-out weight of 35lbs. The new season was under way and I was back to working really hard trying to get among them. Jay and Neil had started really well with something like four or five fish each, but none of the big ones. In fact, I think they both caught our mate, Crazy Eric, and Jackson's common again, and Jay caught this really mad fish called the Delinquent. Let me tell you about this fish, which has to be the strangest fish I have ever known.

I first saw it right at the back of the Pads under an overhanging willow, lying on its back with its belly facing up and with its pecs out to the sides. It just lay there for ages and I thought it was dead. I got as close as I was able to get a good look and I could see its gills moving, so it was alive, and then, suddenly, it started to swim round in circles, staying on its back and using its pecs. It carried on doing this for about 20 minutes or so, and then, with a massive eruption, it righted itself and just bolted off. To this day I have no idea what it was doing.

Another day, this fish was hanging around by the Point swim. As you walk on to the swim, there is a little bit of water either side, and on the right there is a bough of a tree that comes out over the water. The Delinquent was under it on this particular day, and then it jumped out, headbutted the tree and knocked itself out. It was lying there for a fair while before it came to and swam off.

It showed itself a lot, too. If a fish crashed out, most people would say. 'Yeah, that's the Delinquent' and much of the time they'd be right. On some occasions, the Delinquent was with a much bigger group of fish, and I learned that as the evening drew in, a group of fish always seemed to emerge from the Chicken Bay area. These fish would then move out into the main body of the lake, down the middle in front of the Twins, and the only way you could tell that this was happening was by the Delinquent throwing itself out of the water every now and then. When he stopped, you would see the feeding bubbles start; I saw this on many occasions and tried to use it to make my swim choices.

One morning I lost a fish from the Back Pads swim, and it left me totally gutted to have dropped my first take of the season. When possible, I was doing three days a week and introducing a fair amount of bait, always moving swims to try to better my chances. Most days it was not unusual for me to move three times. I had areas where I liked to fish early in the morning and I'd then be watching the water like a hawk. If I saw signs of activity, I was off again, and then as it got toward the evening, I'd be asking myself where I wanted to fish. There were always anglers who would turn up after work, just for the evening, and as I said, if the fish were moving down the middle, I'd have to move on them or be there before them. I was always trying to be on the fish and hoping that would eventually pay off.

It was a lot quieter now that the new season was under way. I was already on my third move of the day and it wasn't even 11.30 am. I'd put my gear into the Twins swim and noticed that there was a little bit of fizzing going on about two rod lengths out. While I was sorting out my tackle, Keith Sullivan had a take in the Pads swim and as I hadn't cast out yet, I whipped round there to help him out.

While Keith was playing his fish, I kept glancing back to my swim and noticed a fish roll right on the line of the bubblers I had seen earlier. Keith eventually landed a cracking 28lb common, and after we had done his photos I got back to my own swim, set two rods up with double bottom baits and four-bait stringers, and flicked them out on the line of the activity. I was shattered. The lack of sleep was starting to catch up on me and it was hot, so I lay down with a nice breeze blowing into my face and fell asleep. I awoke once and stared at the water as small common jumped out right over my rods, and I remember thinking, as I drifted off again, that it must have been one of the smallest fish in the lake, and I'd probably catch that.

The next thing I knew, I was up and holding the rod with the spool spinning away. Jay and Neil had heard the take and were soon by my side to assist. Still half asleep, I told them that it was only a small common, as the fish boiled on the surface out in the middle of the lake, and then I thought 'maybe not'. The fish came back, mostly on the top, until it was close in and all it did then was plod up and down the margins for a while. She felt heavy; it seemed that I'd waited ages for this moment, my first fish of the season. I was trembling, my heart was pounding, and it was great. Someone behind me remarked that it looked a big fish. I asked 'how big?' and the reply was just 'BIG!' By this time, I was a trembling wreck and I just wanted this fish in the safety of the net. The next time she rolled on the surface, she was mine.

A look into the net told me that without any doubt I had just landed one of the big 'uns. I was sure it wasn't Blind Eye, she'd only been out a little while back, so it had to be one of the Gerties - but which one? Keith Sullivan came round and confirmed her to be the magnificent Heart Tail Gertie. Most of the fish were

My first ever 40-pounder - Heart Tail.

Off home for a celebration.

down in weight from spawning, but after we put her on the scales, she weighed in at 40lb 4oz. This was a real dream come true. Finally, I'd caught an English 40-pounder!

That previous hard winter just seemed a distant memory now, and all the rough nights and effort I'd put in had finally given me a payday. Photos were taken and I was one very proud angler to have caught Heart Tail Gertie from Sutton at Hone. Keith (Snoz) suggested mad celebratory rituals such as jumping in without any clothes on, which to Snoz's disappointment, I declined. To catch a carp like that with my angling buddies, Jay and Neil, there to share my moment was great. The swim had calmed down, I was on my own again, and even though I'd seen another fish show that I did cast to, I just couldn't settle and I soon packed up to head off home with a great big smile on my face, to celebrate properly.

After a few days at home, my recent success soon saw me back at the lake. I'd decided to concentrate on the High Point swim and to keep a steady supply of bait going in. My set-up was quite basic really. I fished leadcore about four to five feet long with an inline lead, and the hook length was a supple 25lb Kryston Silkworm, that I rubbed some lead putty into. My hook of choice was a B175 but we found an equivalent back then called a Stinger, made by Big Fish Adventure.

I found the Stingers to be stronger and they were wickedly sharp. I used them in 8s and 6s and I would shrink a small piece of tube on the in-turned eye to kick the hook in even more. I am a fan of a long hair, to which I attached two 15mm bottom baits, because I noticed that everyone was fishing either pop-ups or single bottom baits and I wanted to be different. I believe when they take in a double bait on a long hair, it's that much harder for them to eject, so on every cast I attached a four-bait stringer - simple.

I got in the High Point as often as I possibly could and every night before I left the lake I would fire out a few pounds of bait, and then get back in the morning as the lake was a bit quieter now midweek.

At this time, I was fairly confident that mine was the only bait going in with any consistency, and apart from what I saw other anglers put in during the day, I was the only one baiting before I left. It was only fair to do this if I was able to string a few days together, because the last thing I wanted was anglers firing in bait all over the place and not planning on coming back for a few days. That would only make the fishing even harder.

I was sure my bait was getting eaten during the night, and I had this confirmed one evening when an angler fishing in the Trees swim caught an upper-20 common. I went round to help out and to see what he'd just landed. When he laid the fish on his mat, it was crapping out red fishmeal.
"That looks like my bait," I said.
"Yeah," said the guy, " but lots of anglers are using a red bait."
"I know," I agreed with him, "but not smelling of chicken!"

I just had to keep on doing what I was doing and consistency had to be the answer over at Sutton. Being 'days only,' not many anglers slept over and fished a few days on the trot. They may have been baiting a bit but nothing can compare with loading your swim up and getting back again the next day. I began to see a lot of activity in the swim, and was getting liners throughout the day, when at last the rod pulled away. This was to be a short battle and I landed a mint 28lb common.

A mint 28lb common.

Sutton's Big Common, spawned out. I cared not.

All afternoon I was seeing bits and pieces going on, and this was my first day of two or three, providing it still looked good. The next morning, luck was with me for a change when we had a draw for swims and I drew the High Point again. The rods were soon put on their spots, with double bottom baits and four-bait stringers, the kettle was on, and I could sit back and watch the day begin. As tired as I was, I was never able to sleep in the mornings. I think I was scared of missing something.

At midday, a big boil-up followed by a screamer had me once again doing battle with one of Sutton's crafty carp, and this one wanted a proper tear-up. It really pulled for all it was worth, but as this Sutton powerhouse eventually tired, I was able to see that it was another good common, and once in the net, we recognised her as the Big Common. What a result! She was down in weight at a spawned-out 34lbs 12oz, but she still looked a cracker and I didn't care about the weight. Whether it was 40lbs or 34lbs, it didn't matter, it was still the Big Common and another one of the A team to add to my list. Things were going really well for me and I felt as though I was getting something going, but I had trouble getting back in the High Point after that, strangely enough. I still had a plan, though. I was never going to be able to do it for long but it caught me two very nice carp.

My approach now was to fish as near as possible to that middle area and just like before, keep the bait going in. My next session saw me set up in the Trees swim, and I did like this area, as I was able to command a fair bit of water out to the front, and I had the tree-lined bank that the carp liked to my left, so fish would be passing as they made their way along there.

There was supposed to be a few bars out in front but they were just gravel strips without any real depth change. The closest strip of gravel, about 25 feet or so out, ran from left to right, across the front of the swim, and the furthest bit I could find to the right either finished abruptly or was a break in the gravel. Anyway, I liked the look of this area and hoped it would be a good ambush spot if the carp were following the gravel seam. I put about 50 baits out in a tight group, and fished one rod to it with the usual double bottom bait and a stringer. I was very happy with that and decided, no matter what, that the rod would stay out until it was time to pack up.

The days did seem to go quickly over at Sutton, even though it was an 18-hour day trip. At 22.05pm precisely, I was just starting to think about sorting my gear out to pack up and head off home when without any indication, that right-hand rod was flying. The whole lake must have heard the take in the quietness of the night, as well as the sound of my clutch spinning away.

A landing net full of scales.

The fish made a beeline right down the centre of the lake, with me just holding on for dear life, and after what seemed a scarily long run, I was able to slow it down, turn its head in my direction, and slowly regain some line. It was pitch black that night, and as the fish neared my bank, it made another hard run to the willow canopies to my left. I had to work hard to stop its progress and as it rolled a few times, I had to strain my eyes in the dark to make sure I got him in the net.

I was full of excitement as I wondered just what I'd landed. By now, a few lads had come round and we could see that my fish was a mirror, one of the A team known as the Unknown. It was a stunning carp, covered in big, plated scales, and I was over the moon with another 30 to my credit at 34lbs. I drove home that night feeling pleased with the reward for my hard efforts.

It got a lot harder over the next few months. There was another baiting team on the lake and they started to pump a load of bait in, a lot more than I was able to, and that did seem to take the edge of my little run. I did manage a 23lb common from the Twins swim, though, and caught that Crazy Eric again at 26lbs; he's a real crazy guy!

A hard winter's common.

On a crisp, cold evening in November, I got down to the lake for an after-work session and it was already well dark by the time I arrived. I had a small cork ball Strawberry pop-up on each rod, as I wanted my baits to be presented without any fuss.

Not long after arriving, I saw a fish show out in front of the Dead Tree swim, which is along the bank just past the Pads swim and opposite the Beach. My strawberry hook bait was cast to the area, the line slackened off, and over the next few hours I was receiving liners to that rod until it did eventually pull away. A heavy, slow fight ensued until finally, I slid the net under a large mirror. I couldn't believe it! I had caught Cluster for the third time. I weighed her, for the record, at 35lbs and then slipped her back. That evening trip was a Thursday, and Steve Edwards said, jokingly that we were no longer allowed to fish on Thursdays because it seemed we always caught then.

Once again, I fished another hard winter but only caught a 25lb common, and just as it was really starting to look good for the last ten days of the season, towards the end of March, I was called away to work. I really believe that I would have been in for another chance of one or two more fish before the end, but with three good 30s and a 40, I was more than happy.

Jay caught 14 fish that year, making him top rod, along with Terry H. Neil was on 11, and they were both unlucky to miss out on the bigger fish. I had to leave the lake and the fishing alone for a while due to work, but it was good work and very unusual. Anyway, this work prevented me from fishing at the start of the next season on Sutton and I was gutted - but that's life.

The next season was soon upon us and I went down to watch the draw, which happened a couple of days before the start. Jay came out third, the lucky sod, and I couldn't believe no one had chosen The High Point swim. Quite rightly, he picked it, and I told him he would be ringing me on the day to tell me he had landed Blind Eye. Guess what day the start was? Yep, it was a Thursday!

I'm passing you over now to my good mate, Essex Jay, so he can tell you the story.

A Day to Remember by Jay Willis

Before I share my story with you of a day I will never forget on Sutton at Hone, I would to like to let you in on a few of the tricks and wind-ups that my good friend, Jerry, has played on me. I've known Jerry now for around 20 years from when I first bumped into him over at Hainault Country Park. We don't get to fish together half as much as we used to, due to our busy lives these days, but we've had some great old angling trips over the years.

I was fishing on the Broxbourne lagoons, was 'between jobs' as they say, and putting in a lot of time for Mr Carp. I was lying in the bag one night, inside the bivvy, when I heard what sounded like someone slowly pulling up on a bike along the path. I thought it would probably be one of the lads popping over for a brew and a bit of a social, so I climbed out of the bag and emerged from the bivvy to be faced by someone sitting in a wheelchair, with a hood pulled up over his face, and some sort of mask on.

I began to feel a bit nervous and then, suddenly, the figure said, "any good mate?" but before I could say anything, he said it again, "any good mate?" and just kept saying it, over and over again. I was getting really worried but before I had time to collapse with fear, Jerry revealed himself as the hooded cripple. Unbeknown to me, Joanne, Jerry's wife, had undergone a small operation and been given the use of a wheelchair so Jel thought it would be funny to come and give me a bit of a fright. It worked!

Another time, again on the Lagoons, Jerry, Mick, Paul and me had all set up in a line on the Road Bank, and Mick had gone to answer the call of nature behind his swim. Jerry wound in one of Mick's rods, hooked a lifelike facemask onto his rig, cast it back into the margins (this mask was legendary and had fooled and scared many an unsuspecting angler in the past), and set the bobbin as if Mick had had a drop-back.
Mick came back into the swim and, straight away, he said, "Hold up! I've had a drop-back there. Did no one hear anything?"
"No mate", we all replied, innocently.
Anyway he pulled into it and felt some resistance.
"Yeah, there's something on here, lads!" said Mick, as he proceeded to wind in a mask!

Then there was the time when we were fishing up at Darenth, in Kent. I think we were on the big lake if my memory serves me right. We all used to wind in our rods in the mornings and go up to the café for a nice old English, but on one occasion, Jel did the usual and played one of his tricks on me. At the time, Darenth had their own unhooking mats in each swim and they were big old black foam mats. Now Jel thought it would be funny to barricade me in, while I was asleep underneath my brolly, with about four of these big mats. I was well known for liking a bit of a kip, so when I woke up and thought it was still dark, I turned over and went back to sleep. They all came back from the café, cracking up, and to top it all, once I had broken down the mats, I went to put on my boots only to find that Jel had put a load of dead mitten crabs in them. Timeless. Real good days we used to have, and to be honest, that's what big carp fishing is all about, the fun of it all! Thanks for the memories, mate.

I joined Sutton At Hone at the beginning of the 1998 season, if my memory serves me right, with Jerry, Neil, and Craig. I had quite a good first year taking five fish to over 30lbs and learning more and more each trip about the moods of the lake and the habits of the fish. As you know, Sutton was days only. We were allowed on at 4am, fished through until 10.30pm, and the carp had become wise to this over the years. Between these times, they really didn't need to feed, knowing that when 10.30 came they could trough away without the chance of being hooked. It was one of the trickiest venues I have ever fished.

My second year was much better, catch-rate-wise, with me taking 14 fish throughout the year. The only problem was that I wasn't getting through to what we called the A Team, or the Big Five, a group of fish all over the 38lb mark. I had taken a few 30lb fish out of the 14 but I was hungry for one in particular and that was Blind Eye, one of the lake's famous 40-plus mirrors. Little did I know what was in store for me!

At the beginning of the 2000 season, me and Neil headed down to Sutton for the draw for swims which takes place a couple of days before the start. Now, I'm usually really unlucky in draws, so my hopes of getting a good placing were pretty low, but all the lads were there so we put our tickets into the bag and waited for the off. The first name was called and he chose the Point. The second came out and he went in the Pads. The third name was called – 'Jay Willis' - I couldn't believe it! There was only one choice for me, even if I'd come out first; it had to be the High Point. It had done Blind Eye two years running on the first day, so I was over the moon with my draw. Neil came out later and went in the Wide so we were both sorted for the first day on Sutton. Happy days! I spent the next few days at work sitting in the office watching the clock, anticipating the start, and hoping that the weather would be as the weatherman said it would be - low pressure, south-westerlies with a touch of rain. Perfect.

I arrived on the gate with Neil at around 3.45am, full of anticipation for the first day of the season. All the lads were there and the wind-up for the start really began. Everyone knew where they were going, due to the draw, and we were all let in to head for our respective swims. I popped my gear down in the High Point and started to get the rods ready for the day ahead. I always made sure that setting the rods up was the very first thing I did, so that I could catch the tail end of the night-time feeding. I knew exactly where I wanted to put the baits, with one bang on top of the high point and the other down the left-hand side where the gravel turned to silt.

The swim only consisted of one main area really, a plateau which rose from the lakebed in about eight feet of water to within a couple of feet of the surface. This was situated about 30 yards out and slightly to the right. I had taken numerous fish off the top and down the bottom of the slope so I had full confidence on both rods. The rigs were just simple in-line 3oz leads, with a soft, braided hook length and a size 8, B175 hook. I was using single baits with six half baits on a small stringer. I never used to put any bait out at all because that was what everyone else seemed to do. They would turn up, put the rods out and then give it the good news with the catapult, firing about four or five pouchfuls around each rod, and I thought that the fish were feeding so cautiously around these small baited areas that the single bait or tiny stringer was the way forward.

The rods were soon out on my chosen spots so I sat back with a nice tea and a smoke and chatted to Jason who was next to me in the Bars. To be honest with you, the take came as a shock as it had only been out for 20 minutes, but the bait on top of the High Point had been picked up and the carp headed out into the middle of the lake on a powerful run. I had horrors going through my mind about it falling off, but I need not have worried. After about five minutes of it plodding about under the tip, I soon drew the fish into the waiting net. Magic! One in the net and I had only been fishing for 20 minutes. Now I could relax for the rest of the day. Jason helped me with the fish, a nice common of 29lbs 4oz, and after a few pics I slipped her back. I soon got the rod back out on top of the high point and sat back, really enjoying the day.

At 6am, the same rod absolutely melted as a hooked fish erupted on the high point and this one really did feel heavy as it slowly let me lead it into the margins. The lunges, deep down in the margins, were slow and heavy and I began to wonder what I was attached to. After about ten minutes, the leadcore started to show as the carp began to tire, and I saw the first flash of a big grey flank. This was a mirror!

She soon started to give in and a few of the lads that had gathered said, 'it looks like Blind Eye'. The old legs were giving it the shakes, I was numb down one side, and all I wanted was her in the net. Three years I had been fishing for the carp I was attached to, and there was no way I wanted her coming off! Steve went down with the net and in she went first time. I couldn't contain myself and screamed out, 'BLIND EYE!'

At last, I'd caught the one I'd dreamed about for so long. Neil came round from the Wide and most off the other lads started to appear in the swim and we got the mats out to give her all the protection we could. Up on the wheel of fortune she went and the needle settled on 42lbs exactly, a new PB for me and I was over the moon. All the lads congratulated me, which was great as that's how it was down there, us lot against the carp. Superb.

Everyone slowly drifted back to their swims and let me get sorted. Neil and I had a celebratory brew and he shot back to the Wide to get his rods back out. I got everything in the swim squared away and the rod back out onto the spot. The next

I couldn't contain myself and screamed out "Blind Eye!"

thing I did was to call Jel and as he picked up he said, "You've had the big girl!" He'd told me that I'd have her in the High Point, and he was right. I filled him in on the story and of the 29lb common and he was over the moon for me. As we finished our chat, Jel said, "I bet you have another one." Little did I know! I gave Kirsty, my missus, a call to tell her of my good fortune and she was genuinely pleased for me. She knew how much effort I'd put in down on Sutton and what that fish meant to me - and she also knew that I might be at home a bit more now!

Two fish in a day from Sutton was a good result and when the High Point rod roared off again at about 8am I couldn't believe it. Straight away, I could tell that this was one of Sutton's smaller residents as the rod gave the tell-tale knocks of a smaller fish, I soon had it under control. Steve went down with the net again and in it went first time. As I looked into the net I could see that it was one of the smaller of the lake's inhabitants, so I quickly did a few shots and back went a common of around 18lbs, but very welcome all the same.

Once again, I rebaited the rod, attached a small stringer and out it went, back on top of the high point. All three takes had came to the high-point rod and it was obvious that the fish were out there in numbers as when I had the last bite I could see other fish bolting out of the area! This was turning into a bit of a red-letter day for me with three fish by 8am. The first year that I fished the lake I had five takes in around 1000 hours of fishing, and to be honest, that was the norm for the weekend anglers so I was happy with my results so far.

The bait that I was using at the time really was doing the business down there. Neil and me had gone on a bait together the previous year and it was a nice proper fishmeal from Premier called Aminos 2000, with the green-lipped mussel powder. We added our own blend of flavours, just to be a bit different, which were Hutchy's Nouvelle Fizz and Autumn Harvest, and the combination really worked well. On our first year on the bait we took 26 fish from Sutton, all on our little three-half-bait stringers, a real good method. As I said earlier, it wasn't a super rig that was getting us results, just a good quality bait and applying it, or not applying it in our case, totally differently from everyone else on the lake.

Anyway, back to the first day. Around 10am, the high-point rod gave a two-inch drop and then ripped off. As I pulled into the fish, it really did give it some, steaming off the High Point to the right, and kiting into the margins a few swims down. I just felt like I was hanging on really; I just couldn't seem to get any sort of control over the fish, whatsoever. Steve, who was next door in the Thirty-six, had kindly wound in his rods which would make it easier for me, and stop the fish getting caught in his lines. Eventually though, after plenty of side, I started to gain the upper hand with a few turns of my trusty old Cardinal 57. The fish popped up just off the bush to the left-hand side of the swim and it looked like a very good mirror. I knew deep down that I was attached to one of the other big two, either Heart Tail Gertie or the Small Gertie, both possible 40lb carp. Now, I didn't panic much, just went numb down one side again and shook a lot, but I needn't have worried as Steve once again slipped the net under a very nice carp. I checked in the net straight away. It was the Little Gertie.

This fish had not been on the bank for 12 months and it looked in fine condition, not to mention extremely large. All the lads were back in the swim so we laid all the mats out again and settled her down to be unhooked and

Up she went and the dial settled on 38lbs.

weighed. A few of the lads were saying 40lbs, but I wasn't so sure. Up she went and the dial settled on 38lbs exactly. I gave another shout across the pond, and rightly so. She behaved like a dream on the bank as I held her for the cameras and I savoured every moment. Days like this were not going to happen all the time, that's for sure, and I soaked it up. I put her back and she soaked me with her tail. Brilliant. The lads were giving me some serious stick now about being a jammy git, and I suppose they were right. It was turning into a mad old day.

I got the High Point rod back out, redid the other rod down the side of it, and sat back to soak up the atmosphere. Things slowed down as the day wore on and a few other fish were caught around the pond. I think it was Jason who gave me a celebratory bottle of beer and, along with Steve, we sat at the back of the swim talking over the day's events.

It must have been around 7pm when the high point rod signalled another fast take. The water erupted as the fish took off and, again, it felt heavy! The fight was slow and dogged, and I would gain a bit and then the fish would take it back again, but soon the pressure began to take its toll and I caught my first glimpse of her under the tip.
Steve said it first, "That's the Big Fully."

I'd seen it and knew he was right. I tried to keep my cool, praying for her not to come off. I was numb down one side again; freak! Steve did the honours with the net again and she was mine. Out with the mats, and as I slipped the hook out, I noticed how wide she was. What an awesome carp! On the scales she went 38lbs exactly, and I was over the moon – yet again!

The lads were all patting me on the back and shaking my hand and it was an emotional moment indeed. As I held her up for the cameras, her big, plated flanks reflected the camera flashes. What a carp she is, and a proper old history fish. We lowered her into the margins in a zipped mat so I could do some returners, and the lads wanted to throw me in so I dived in head first - with my glasses on, which I proceeded to lose as they sunk to the bottom. I held her up for a few more shots and then she was gone, back out into the pond.

I didn't even bother putting the rods back out, I just sat on the old bed chair and took it all in. I had caught in a day what you would expect to have caught in a season. The catch of a lifetime for me, really. I had taken a 42lb mirror, a 38lb mirror, a 38lb fully- scaled, a 29lb common and a 18lb common. It really was a day I'll never forget.

I held her up for a few more shots.

Keeping the Hone Fires Burning

What an unbelievable start to the season that was for Jay, and there was definitely something weird about Thursdays; he truly hit the big fish that time. Well done, mate!

I wasn't able to get down until the following Saturday, due to work, and as you would imagine, the first weekend of the season was very busy at the draw. Unbelievably, I came out first on the Saturday and the Sunday, with Jay coming out second, and everyone was convinced that we were somehow fiddling it!

After Jay's fantastic hit in the High Point on the first day, unsurprisingly, the Friday saw no fish from the swim, but I thought it worth another go on the Saturday. My intuition paid off and I landed a long, 24lb mirror not long after casting out. Sadly, I had no more action that day but I was hoping that, as it was warm, they would be creeping back up on the High Point.

A long, torpedo-like 24lb mirror.

Given the choice of swims again on the Sunday, I just had to get back in there. I was sure the carp wouldn't stay away for too long and as I set up and got the rods out, I was seeing the telltale signs of fish in the area. Within no time at all, I was into a fish and landed my old mate, Crazy Eric, at 26lb 8oz. I'm sure that fish followed me around the lake! Eric was soon followed by a 23lb common, and then later I was into a hard battle with a very aggressive carp that was trying to take me all over the place. This fish was definitely not happy about the situation!

Crazy Eric. He's a real crazy guy!

The High Point contains a lot of gravel, and the swim to the left is the Bars which is shallow and lives up to its name. With this fish steaming about the place, I was sure I was going to get cut off and I must say it was a relief when it finally slid into the waiting net. My hard-fighting fish turned out to be a common, a cracking-looking carp of 33lbs 8oz, and it made my tally of fish up to four for the weekend. This would have been a fine start to the new season for me, but I knew that my time at Sutton that year was going to be limited.

As I said earlier, I was unable to fish the actual start that year, due to work commitments. I also had to pull off for the last few weeks in March and miss the tail end of the season, after doing the whole winter, and just as things were starting to happen. Craig Lyons caught Blind Eye at 40lbs-plus and I had to go away on a ten-day boot camp. Let me explain.

A few years back, I was manager of a health club where one of our instructors was a film extra/actor. I was chatting to him one day and I asked how he had got into that line of work. He told me that he'd joined a few agencies, and that it had kind of progressed from there. I said I would love to do something like that, so he gave me the contact details of a good agency to get in touch with, 20/20 Casting, and said that they did a lot of military work, which, with me being ex-Army, was right up my street. I was getting a bit bored with leading a 'normal' life and I needed to get into something a bit different, so I took the phone number and one Thursday afternoon I decided to give them a call. What could I lose?

A hard-fighting, powerhouse common of 33lbs 8oz.

I spoke to a woman who told me that their books were full, but they'd be opening them again in September to take on new applicants. She suggested that I should ring back nearer the time. Oh well, it was worth a try. She was just about to hang up when she said, "Do you have any military experience by any chance?"
"Yes," I replied. "I served eight years in the army."
"Okay," she said. "We may have something coming up. It's a military project."
She took my number. "Someone will be getting in touch with you," she said. "If you don't hear from them tomorrow, Friday, they will call you on Monday."
Well, I couldn't believe my luck! All weekend I was telling everyone about getting a chance to work on some war thing, but I didn't know what it was.

By late Monday afternoon, I'd written it off. I hadn't heard a thing, and I was a bit gutted; you know how it is when you build up your hopes. Then there was a call from the agency.
"Hi, Jerry. It's 20/20 here. Can you make it to the Officer Training Centre in Cannon Street, London, for an interview at 2pm this Friday?"
"Yes, no probs," I said calmly and casually, feeling anything but, and put the phone down.

Wow! I was elated. I had no idea what to expect, and I didn't stop going on about it all week. Friday couldn't come quickly enough. At the time, I was in really good shape because I'd been training really hard for a long time and I felt confident.

I arrived at the OTC (Officer Training Centre) 15 minutes before the appointment, determined not to be a second late. As I turned the corner, I could see that there was a great long queue of at least a hundred people, all waiting to go in for this interview/casting thing, whatever it was they were doing. My heart sank. I'd thought it would be just me and maybe a few others.

'Oh well', I thought. 'I might as well go for it, now I'm here,' and joined the end of the line. As I waited, I noticed that many of the people in the queue already knew each other, and they were all talking about jobs they had been on.
I was hearing things like, 'Hello, mate. How did you get on in London's Burning last week?' 'I did three days on the Bill.' 'Hi ya, mate. Well done on your bit in Eastenders!' Bloody hell. This lot were all professionals by the sound of it. I wouldn't stand a chance. Then the doors opened and about a hundred people came piling out. They must have been for the earlier casting; I must admit I really felt like slipping off.

We went in and the whole place was like a massive open-plan hall, with loads of tables and chairs, all laid out with paper and pens, and about 12 chairs to a table.

The beginning of the best summer, that I've ever had.

We were told to find a chair and sit down, and then someone from 20/20 stood in front of us and told us to fill out the forms that lay in front of us. The questions were just about personal details; age, height, etc, what experience and skills you had, and a load of other stuff. We were told that while we were filling out these forms, members of the agency would be walking around, and if they saw the 'type' of person that they were looking for, we would get a tap on the shoulder. If this happened to one of us, then we were to join another queue for an interview. I was filling out my form and straight away I was picked. It seemed as if all the guys at my table scowled at me as I went to join the other queue.

We were waiting to go into a room, one person at a time, and there was a soldier in full Second World War American uniform who was in full character standing outside. He would scream, 'Next soldier!' for the next one of us to go in. Just before it was my turn, I was told to march in, come to attention, and give my name, rank, and number. I heard 'Next soldier!' so I marched in gave my army rank and number, and before me sat a grey-haired American soldier wearing full uniform, whose name was Captain Dale Dye. Also in the room was another military guy who was English and working for 20/20; he would, I supposed, be helping with the selection of guys they needed.

It was a mad old interview and the Captain was as crazy as hell. He asked me to tell him about my military career, and anything the captain didn't understand was clarified by the other guy who, it turned out, was an ex-Major who had been attached to my battalion when I served in Northern Ireland. His name was Robin, and it couldn't have been better because he was explaining everything I said to the Captain, who, I later found out, was Steven Spielberg's military adviser.

I had got to the end of telling him about myself and finished off with the fact that I had also been an army physical training instructor.
"Tell me, Hammond," he said. "When you were a physical training instructor, were you a mean son of a gun?"
"I was the meanest, sir," I said, and this was just what he wanted to hear. He went mad.
"You're a good soldier, Hammond. I want you in my movie. Get this man sorted out!"
Away I went to get all my measurements taken for a German uniform. It was all bit surreal. One minute I was thinking that I never had a chance, and the next, I was getting fitted up to be a German soldier in Saving Private Ryan.

Anyway, the filming started a few weeks later in Hatfield, only 25 minutes from my house, and I was to be playing a soldier from the SS unit of Das Reich. They'd only wanted 60 Germans out of all those hundreds of applicants, and Robin, who was in charge of us, split the Germans into two platoons of 30. He put me in charge of one of the groups, and I was even given the rank of SS Sergeant Major, a Hauptscharfuhrer. Within the two platoons there were three sections of ten; that made it all a lot easier when they wanted troops for certain scenes.

I ended up working on 'Ryan' for eight weeks, and it was probably the best summer I have ever had. It was such an experience. We were mainly involved in the big battle at Ramelle at the end of the film, and I can't explain just how real it all seemed. I even got the chance to choreograph some small bits in that Ramelle battle because sometimes, the captain would be screaming orders down from the directors and we would hardly have any time to organise things. A few times, I was told to take my platoon and get them all in place and in position.

When the action started, it was unbelievable. We all had authentic, blank-firing weapons with plenty of ammo, and just before the scene started, the special effects guys turned on gas pipes in the houses. They walked down the street with what looked like a paintball gun, but it fired a ball of flint, and as this was aimed into a window of a house, the gas ignited, sending flames out of the windows, they would then set rubber tyres alight, and the street filled with black smoke.

Tom and Jerry.

There were special-effect explosives set up everywhere, the Tiger tanks were ready to roll and when the first assistant director screamed 'action!' through his loud hailer, all hell broke loose. I kid you not; it was so real it was frightening, especially when two Mustangs flew over, deafening us with their screaming, turbo-charged engines.

It just has to be the best thing I have ever done. The weather was scorching hot, we were treated really well, and the food was unbelievable. I did some weight-training a few times with some of the actors outside their Winnebagos, and although I didn't know who they were at the time, it turns out that I trained with Matt Damon, Vin Diesel, and a few of the others who were not that well known then.

I found out that a friend of mine, Bruce, was supplying a lot of the military hardware to the film, as he was a military antiques collector. We were in one of the food tents one day and Bruce had turned up to introduce a retired Major General to Steven Spielberg, something to do with a book he had written. Anyway, Bruce saw me and called out my name to come and join him at his table, so I did, but only for a short time. I felt a bit out of my league sitting on that table with the boss there, Steve S.

Because I had worked hard throughout the eight weeks, I was given the small bit at the end of the film, where the German guy, who they'd let go earlier, is

recaptured and I am standing to his left. Spielberg personally directed us and that's something to be proud of - not bad for my first job. I managed to get one of the very few photos of Tom Hanks, too, taken with me. Normally, they were just not allowed.

Sorry to have steered away from angling but this is something of which I am immensely proud, and I thought it might bring a bit of variety to the chapter. Anyway, that was how I got started in the film industry. Obviously, 20/20 Casting let me on their books after that, and I started to get regular work from them. I joined two more agencies and for a few years I did okay, working on so many different TV/film projects that I lost count; The Bill, London's Burning, Gimme, Gimme, Gimme with Kathy Burke, Blackadder, Ultimate Force, and more. Most of the time, I got good little parts and the agency stopped sending me for just background jobs. I worked on a lot of films over the years; Gladiator, Bond, Tomb Raider, Spy Games, to namedrop a few, and I enjoyed them all.

People always made me laugh when they said 'I've watched that film so many times and I've never seen you in it.' Who do they think I am, Tom Cruise or something? I'm hardly going to get the leading role, am I? At the end of the day, I worked for an extra agency, and we got chances now and then to say the odd word, but I was frequently seen whereas other extras just never got a look in.

The military experience was a major asset for me and it gave me so many extra chances for jobs. I was called up for an interview at Hatfield studios for a part in a series called Band of Brothers. If I got the job, it was for a ten-month contract working every day and some weekends.

Come on, the Huns!

The interview process was the same as with Ryan. We marched in, one at a time, and guess what, my old mate Captain Dale Dye was behind the desk. Ryan had been a few years before so I reminded him that I had already worked for him, but he'd remembered. They were looking for was a group of 20 military-trained guys to be mixed in with the 20 main actors to form Easy Company, which the series was about.

Easy Company was an airborne unit, from the 501st infantry parachute regiment in America; the story was to follow the company from D-day to the end of the war and Berchtesgaden - Hitler's nest. This was a great opportunity for me. Although there were thousands of extras used throughout the ten episodes, there were only 20 of us who worked every day with the main cast and we were known as the SAs - special abilities. Captain Dye said he was pleased to offer me a position in his Easy Company and I was extremely chuffed. So, this brings me back to the reason I would be missing the last ten days of the season over at Sutton. I was going away on a boot camp with the 20 actors to get everyone working as a team, and to put all the actors through as much military training as could possibly be fitted into ten days.

We were kitted out at Hatfield with all our Second World War uniforms and kit, our mobile phones were left behind, and from the moment we got on the coach we were back in the 1940s. Our training camp was an old army base in Aldershot called Longmore, and it really was the ideal place for what we were doing. Our accommodation was like the 1940s H blocks, and in my dorm was David Schwimmer - he's a great guy I really liked him - Donnie Wahlberg, Mark's brother, and others I hadn't heard of. It was so unreal to be there doing what I was doing, and when the lights went out David Schwimmer would start telling jokes. It was just like listening to him on TV's Friends.

We had a very tough week ahead of us. They didn't hold back with the training, so every morning was geared toward fitness, with a run followed by either an assault course or some sort of circuit training, and all of it was taken by the mad captain. He had us singing the American songs (cadence) that they all sing when doing any fitness. It was crazy and I had to pinch myself at times. Was I really doing this? We covered everything, including weapon training, marching, foot drills, manoeuvres, navigation, night attacks, parachute training, unarmed combat, the lot.

The days were long and every night we would have big lectures after chow (dinner). By the end of training, we were all shattered and were looking forward to getting back to the year 2000, as it was at the time. From the first day of filming, Captain Dye ran the whole ten months in character. We were all soldiers when at work and treated as such, being promoted and demoted - and all this was to keep everyone's mindset back in the 40s.

Me and one of my friends - David Schwimmer.

Tol could go weeks without offering a chance.

I was used to thinking about the 40s, but usually the ones I was chasing at Sutton, and for the first time, my fishing was taking a back seat, and those last couple of days I'd done with Jay were to be my last for a while. As luck would have it, Terry Hearn had told me of a little club water that was just down the road from Hatfield where we were filming, and this got me thinking about my fishing again. There was no way I could make any trips to Sutton, it was just too far, but Terry had a ticket and told me all about the place. This club water was called Tolpits, run by Watford Piscators, and it was perfect for me to do a few overnighters, which was something I hadn't done for a few years.

The carp were all lovely-looking, old, dark Italians with an upper-30 common, and two or three mirrors that were nudging 40lbs. Perfect! The lake was small, with miniature lily pads around most of the margins and its water was tap-clear. I should think it was about 2.5 acres, a lovely little venue that I was keen to get started on, and I found out later what a tricky little place it was. I managed to get myself a ticket, and as their season started on May 1st , I managed to get a two-night session in when it opened, a little taster to see if we liked each other. Nothing happened for me on the fish front, but I really enjoyed the atmosphere. It was great on this new water and I was gagging to get back.

I fished as many nights as was possible during May but no bites came my way. There wasn't a big head of carp, though, well, not as many as in Sutton, and the lake was receiving a fair amount of pressure so the carp would just totally switch off. Sometimes on Tol, nothing would come out for weeks, and I'm sure it even went a month once. When it's tough like that, you began to wonder if you'd ever get a bite. I remember saying to my friends, 'I'm not bothered. I'm just plodding along!'

I had that weekend at Sutton with Jay and after those four fish, I'd recharged my confidence and was keen to get back to the Watford lake to break my duck. I had a week's holiday coming up, starting on the 16th June, so I was looking forward to some proper time on the bank. I needed a rest from the war for one thing!

The day my holiday began was the start of the traditional season, and I'd found some carp in the river near me that I fancied having a go at. I'd been trickling bait in for a while and was seeing some good river carp, with one or two that may have been 30s. The car was loaded for my trip, but I thought I'd take a look at the river first, and if they were there I might have a go. I knew deep down that I wouldn't, though, because I wanted to be at Tol.

I took one look at the river - well, it's not the river really, it's the relief canal – and saw that it had gone pea green with algae, with hardly any flow. It had changed overnight. I looked for the carp for about 30 seconds and then, before I knew it, I was on the M25, Watford bound.

It didn't take me long to skip the river and head toward Tol.

When I arrived, I was amazed that the lake was empty and my first thoughts were 'what's happened, have they all been out or something?' A north-westerly wind was blowing down to the narrow end of the lake, so I grabbed my water bottle and started on a few laps. I headed down toward the windward end and as I slowly made my way, scanning the lake, I noticed a few dark shapes out in the middle, heading with the wind. It was only a gentle breeze really that stopped completely every now and then, the surface would go flat-calm. Every time it did, the carp seemed to stop travelling and were still for a while, then they would turn slowly and head back the way they'd come. When the breeze started again, the fish would turn and follow the wind.

As I walked on, I saw a few more fish doing the same thing further down. I came to the end swim, called the All Alone, left my water bottle there, carried on round the lake, and shinned up a few trees. I was happy about where I'd left the bottle so went to fetch my barrow. It was great walking round with no one on the lake, just me and the carp, and they seemed in a fairly happy mood, just doing their thing. The sun was shining, what more could I have asked for?

By the time I was set up it was midday and seriously hot, so I decided not to cast out until the early evening, but just sit back, relax and watch the water. A young lad had turned up on my lake - bloody cheek! - and he'd gone right up to the opposite end. Well, it felt as if it was my lake, with no other anglers about.

I liked the look of the marginal shelf that ran away from me on the right-hand bank, as I was in the narrow end of the lake and that margin was a main factor in my swim. I kept walking round and looking into the crystal clear margins, and saw that, among the weed and lily pads were little gravel spots. I found one that I liked the look of, was able to cast at and get my line down through the pads, then made a mental note of a particular pad to mark the spot, and went back to the swim to see if I would be able to get a rod to it.

It was going to be tricky and I had to swing it out underarm as the trees were in the way, but after two or three attempts, I landed one that I was happy with. I slackened off the line, and the other rod was fished close in, just round to my left margin. Both rods were fished the same as at Sutton, with double 15mm bottom baits, and I was able to walk round and put a handful of trout pellets over that right-hand rod.

By 5.30pm, everything was in place, and at 6.30 I received a big liner on the rod to the little gravel spot and I was worried that my rig might have been pulled off it. Half an hour later, a deep-bellied mirror showed a little further down from where I was fishing along the marginal shelf, so immediately, I reeled in that rod and went round to try to find another clear spot nearer to where the fish had shown. Once again, I found another little gravel spot, ran back, and tried to make a cast. This time it was a harder job, as I had to get it accurate over a longer distance, underarm. I didn't want to be making too much disturbance to the area and scare away this fish, and somehow by luck, I got the rig where I wanted it. Another handful of pellets and I was once again angling.

At 9pm, I was alerted to the sound of a Stevie Neville, something I hadn't heard for a little while, and it was coming from the right-hand rod. The rod tip pulled round and I was into a Tol carp! The fish soon found sanctuary among all the pads and weed, but I kept a steady pressure on and begrudgingly kind of bundled it out, off the ledge, and into the deeper margin under my rod tip. From there on it was just plodding about, up and down in front of me and it felt heavy as under its own bulk it seemed to be just lying on the bottom. When I did manage to lift it off, as soon as it rolled on the surface I knew she was mine and steered this great fish into my net. There was a big sigh of relief from me, so happy to have caught one at last.

I looked in the net, as we do, and was shocked at the size of this fish. It was bloody massive! It had to be one of the big ones, for sure. I knew it wasn't the one they called Lester's because I'd already seen that, so this had to be the other one they called Plodder. Sleepy Neil had also got a ticket and by sheer luck was on his way over for a social. He was literally walking down the bank just after I'd landed the fish. Fantastic!
"Oi, oi," I said. "Got one mate. I think it's Plodder."
We got all the bits ready and carefully hoisted out my fish. I knew then that it was a 40, and to confirm my thoughts the scales settled at 43lbs. I was over the moon to say the least. It was, in fact, Plodder, a new PB for me, and a lake record at the time for Tolpits. Bloody magic! I told all my mates I was just 'plodding' along. Neil and I celebrated my catch and I kept him there as long as I could, talking carp, even though he had work in the morning! Good old mate. Thanks, chap.

What a fine start. Over the next few days I moved swims, a bit further along from where I'd caught Plodder. I managed a double-figure common, and stalked an old-looking 25lb leather from right under the rod tip, but I was so made up with my catch that I just had to pack up, end my session early, and go home to celebrate properly.

Plodder and a new lake record - 43lbs.

Work took up all my time for the next couple of months, and I was still buzzing about Plodder, so that was enough for a while to keep me sane, and I must admit I was having such a good time at work. The whole experience was something I will never forget. We were mainly working at Hatfield, but we often went out to other locations for different landscapes and I felt as though I had gone back in the army. I made some great friends and we had some good laughs.

A typical day would be: breakfast at 8am, and then we were driven by bus to our wardrobe, which was a massive marquee. We would've seen a script the day before so more or less knew what the day would be about, and after we were dressed in our kit, it would time for hair and make up. Depending on what scenes we were doing, they would black our faces up and our clothes, and if we were 'injured' they would give us scars and bloody wounds. Some guys had to have major burns and all sorts done by the prosthetic department for close-ups.

Then it was a case of waiting until we were called up to the set. Sometimes that could be all day and we might not even get used until the next day, so we did have a lot of time just sitting about. That's how the job is, though.

An old-looking 25lbs leather.

They may be working on a scene that they need to get right before they could move on, but we needed to be ready as soon as they called us. We used to muck about a lot, because of all the spare time we had. All us SAs were ex-soldiers, and I don't know how many times they had to send a runner for us to get on set. We used to have massive bundles, rifles and kit everywhere, and we did get a lot of bollockings, but when we were on set they got their money's worth. We were very good, and they knew we were.

Although the actors were with us all the time on set, they spent their down time in their Winniebagos, and I must say they were really pampered, and the makeup and wardrobe people used to fuss about them all the time - it was laughable really.

We were in front of the cameras quite a lot so some of us started to get character names - mine was Sgt. Higgins - and the odd word here and there, because we couldn't just be there all the time and never speak or get mentioned. The whole series was filmed over ten episodes and there were two complete film crews - red and blue. We did get a lot of down time when they were filming scenes that only involved a couple of actors, but when they did need us we would sometimes work a seven-day week, and we did plenty of night work too.

On location, making 'Band of Brothers'.

One day, the captain offered me a really good scene, in which I would have been shot and seriously wounded. It would have been a very good close-up scene, and fantastic for my CV, but I would have had to die on camera. I was worried because that would have meant I couldn't be seen again and we were only halfway through the film. I wouldn't have been laid off, but they wouldn't have used me close to camera any more - and we all loved to get a bit of camera time.

I can't believe that I made it to Switzerland.

The main reason I didn't want to do it, though, was that toward the end there was a chance of half of us going to Switzerland, where they were to film Hitler's nest, Berchtesgaden. I really wanted to go to Switzerland - who wouldn't? - and what another great experience that would be, especially with my little gang. So I declined the offer, but sometimes when I watch the film now, I wish that I'd taken it. It was a good part.

It turned out that a group of us had to be killed off later, anyway. We were all shot by a sniper from a window. In the scene, Easy Company had taken an important village or town, and we were celebrating, all sitting around a captured artillery piece. I was sitting up on the barrel, and we were all singing a song when the sniper is seen taking aim and he picks us off. I had some special effects done on my shoulder and when I got to a certain part of the song, I had to press a button.

Out on location.

There was a wire running down the inside of my jacket, and when I pressed the button, it blew a hole in my shoulder, simulating me getting shot, and then I had throw myself backwards on to some mats. It was good to do and it took all afternoon for them to film it, so all the emphasis was on us, but it wasn't a patch on the scene that I'd turned down.

The captain came to us afterwards to congratulate us on our work, and he called me to one side and said, "Sgt Higgins, don't worry, you are still coming to Switzerland." What a touch! It turned out that the other nine who were going were all good lads, so we were in for a ball. Watch out Switzerland!

We were all given a week's holiday toward the end of August, so my missus, Jo, and me booked a week in Greece. It was a lovely week, the weather was scorching hot, and money was no object, mainly because I hadn't had time to spend any! They were exciting times. I got back from Greece on the Sunday, and early on the Monday morning I was picked up in a chauffeur-driven car and taken to the airport. I was starting to get a bit blown away by it all and began to think, 'you've cracked it, son. What a life!'

At the airport, everyone was in good spirits, already on the spirits, in fact, and we had a private chartered plane with all leather seats. It was amazing and I couldn't believe it was happening.

When we arrived in Switzerland, we had a five-hour drive by luxury coach to Interlaken, which was where we would be filming for the first few days. The location was an airbase between the mountains, and where we all played baseball at the end of the war. We got off the coach and were told to go to an enormous aircraft hanger for dinner and a briefing. The dinner they'd laid on was out of this world with everything you could wish for - you name it and it was there. While we ate, we were told the schedule for the next ten days, and that after our meal we should collect our overseas allowance. Overseas allowance! This was getting better and better. We were each given 700 Swiss francs for our spending money.

The actors and crew were staying in hotels in Interlaken, but we had our own driver and minibus and were staying in a hotel about 30 kilometres away, which suited us down to the ground. I had my own hotel room and that was absolutely fantastic; the view from my room was unreal. I used to smoke the odd fag back then, and I'd bought myself a bottle of the finest Remy cognac at the airport. I sat at my window, looking out with a glass of brandy and rolled myself a fag. I could see the mountains and waterfalls, paragliders circling above the town, and I just

The view from my hotel window. I thought I'd cracked it.

had to sit and evaluate everything. Yesterday I was in Greece. Now I was in Switzerland, sitting in a glorious hotel, with 700 hundred francs sitting on the table in front of me, sipping cognac, and smoking my fag. I was going to be here for ten days, all paid for - plus spending money - and I was going to be running around all week making a war film! What was going on?

We really did have the time of our lives out there. It was such a laugh, and we did get a lot of free time. Many of the Swiss drivers on the film set were skiing instructors, and were doing the driving work because the skiing was out of season, but they were also paragliding and free-fall skydiving instructors, so we all managed to get to have a go at that. We also got the chance to get up a few of the famous mountains; Schilthorn, the one that was in the Bond film, has a revolving restaurant at the top. The whole experience was just unforgettable. We were all quite close, having been working together for so long, and believe me they were a crazy bunch of lads. Every night was very messy and I would need another book to tell you about it all.

After Switzerland, being back home was a bit of a comedown. We'd been on such a high and now we were back at Hatfield, still with six to eight weeks of filming left to do. Although we'd already filmed the end of the war, they never film things in sequence, and the part that we were to be filming next was all indoors.

The war had ended, and so had the experience.

I took my son to work, where he got to fire all the weapons. He said it was one of the best days of his life.

We were in another huge airctaft hanger filled with mud and fir trees, and they had a massive refrigeration system hidden in the middle of it to bring the temperature down. We were filming the part where all of Easy Company were dug in, in trenches and shell scrapes, (the siege of Bastogne), so it was freezing cold, dark and gloomy in there, and to be honest, a bit boring at times, especially after Switzerland.

We started to play up a lot, and the third assistant director was getting the right hump with us. We were held up in rooms, up some stairs around the outside of the hanger building, and whenever we were summoned for work, some of us would disappear. It was getting near the end now, and it had been a long old road so a lot of us were ready to finish. I was getting itchy feet; autumn was nearly upon us and the carp would be on the munch.

One particular day we were having the usual bundle and trying to do our own stunts by throwing ourselves down flights of stairs, and I ran at my mate to take him out from behind. I jumped to grab him around the neck, head butted his rifle that he had shouldered, hit my cheek under the eye and made a nice little slit that poured with blood.
I had to go and see one of the set medics and made up some story about how I'd done it. She fixed it with butterfly stitches and said I wouldn't be able to work for the rest of the day because I would not be able to wear any make-up, so I might as well go home. Happy days! I was off in a flash. It was only 11am and I knew exactly where I wanted to go - home to grab my gear and then off to Sutton to catch Blind Eye. This was the carp I'd wanted ever since I saw Graham East holding her and I was soon en route toward the Dartford crossing, feeling nicely confident.

There were only a few cars in the car park when I arrived, so I loaded up the barrow, parked it by a Portaloo, and took a stroll round to see what had been going on.

Long Man Steve was fishing in the Gate swim and he updated me on all the recent activities. The wind was blowing a north-westerly and the sky was getting dark with heavy clouds, which to me was awesome weather, although noticeably colder. As we chatted, I saw a fish roll near the opposite bank, in front of a swim called the Unknown. The wind was pushing on to that bank, and no one was on there yet, so I said my good byes, wished good luck to Long Man and got myself round to the Unknown swim.

By the time I was set up it was 3pm. I tied up two fresh hook links - the usual 25lb Silkworm; size 8 Stingers, a long hair, double hook bait and a four-bait stringer. I cast both rods on the same line to where I'd had seen the fish show earlier, and slackened the line right off so it was hanging from the rod tips. In the front of the swim was a little ledge to sit on, so I made myself a brew, laid the unhooking mat on the ledge, and watched the water as the wind pushed into my face. It was great to be back. Thank God I cut my face open!

Out of the blue and ever so silently, a huge carp slipped out of the lake right up to the wrist, and then slid back into the water. If I hadn't been looking in that direction, I would never have seen it. The fish seemed to hover for a while in slow motion before she dropped back in. I can still remember some detail, especially the pink colours of her belly. It was Blind Eye and her colour suggested she'd been on the bait. Not long after that there was a period of sheeting up, but where she'd shown was a little way out for this swim. Fortunately for me, the guy who was in the Trees swim was fishing close in, so I reeled both rods in immediately, put on fresh hook baits and stringers, and cast either side of where she had shown. I was very confident.

At around 5pm, some of the regulars started to turn up for the evening and Terry the Boxer dropped in to my left in the Twins swim, with John Elmer the other side in the Wide. There was a lot of activity that evening, a bit of bubbling here and there, and John was receiving a few liners. In my swim, and John's, the norm is to fish very close in, so John came and sat with me for a brew and on a few occasions we both ran back to his rods as he was receiving some massive liners. He asked me if I had my rods in close, as there was definitely fish up and down, tight in. I told him I wasn't, because I was happy where they were. I must say though I did start to think that maybe I should have had at least one close. We sat and watched as the night drew in and fish started showing everywhere, but mainly over the other side of the lake in the Chicken Bay area, and John was even thinking of moving round for the last two hours or so. The fish continued to crash into darkness. Surely, something would happen? One went right over my rods so I remained hopeful.

Once it was properly dark, it seemed that all the activity just stopped abruptly, so at 9pm, I packed up all my kit for a quick getaway at 10.30pm, just leaving my net and rods. John had a fish boil up twice over one of his rods and we were sure he would get a bite. At about ten o'clock, I was standing there talking to John and Tel when my left-hand buzzer sounded once, followed by a full-on screamer. I was on it fast and as I picked the rod up I felt a heavy fish immediately start to kite left. I had to be careful and gain line quickly because of all the trees down the margins, and as it came in

Oi, oi - Blind Eye!

closer I felt it trying to get to the overhanging trees to my left, so I had to dip the rod under and apply side strain. I felt the line ping off one of the branches and I know I was very lucky there! I had the fish right in front of me now, watching nervously while it made two more attempts for the branches and then rolled on the top, where John Elmer stuck the net under it. I peered into the folds and saw a very big mirror.
"Looks like you've got Blind Eye there," John said.
"No way!" I said, "it can't be!"
Tony Tap came round and although I couldn't really see, they all told me it was her. I just had to scream out across the lake, 'Blind Eye!' We weighed her on John Elmer's tripod and she topped out at 40lbs 4oz. I just couldn't believe it. A season when I'd had no time really to do much, and I get two 40s! Oh,
and by the way, it was a Thursday. I can't explain how happy I was about that capture.

It was weird really, when I look at the coincidences. To start with, I cut my face just below my eye, which could have easily blinded me. I was then sent home. I said I was off to catch Blind Eye, and I saw her not long after arriving. It was a Thursday, and then I caught her. It's a funny old game.

To be honest, after Blind Eye I was happy to walk away from Sutton. There were still fish I dearly wanted to catch, including the Fully, the Beast, and a few others, but I'd got the big three plus some glorious carp, to boot. My time on Sutton was truly magic and I would like to say a big thanks to all the lads that made it what it was. A big up to all the Sutton massive.

The next day I was back to work again and I really didn't want to be there. I wanted to be angling. We were filming outside now and I wasn't happy. Anyway, Band of Brothers eventually ended, and it was very sad. At first, we were all glad to be finished, but after a few weeks, it was all anyone involved could talk about, and we all still do today. It was a chapter of my life that will stay with me forever.

My work on Band Of Brothers really set me up in the industry, and I ended up getting an Equity card, my own agent, and I worked on lots of adverts. My career highlight was to get a very good role in 'Bloody Sunday' with James Nesbit. It was a proper acting role and we spent weeks over in Dublin enjoying all the pampering that actors get. I stayed in the business for about five years, until I became a fishery manager. OK, I was never going to be Tom Cruise, I was aware of that, but I truly enjoyed the whole experience.

Obituary to Craig Bateman

I said there were four of us in the gang: Jay, Neil, Craig, and me. I haven't said too much about Craig because he was never able to put in the time like we did. He worked hard, and was starting a family with his young wife-to-be, Laura, and he was an extremely talented angler; very technical, and precise with his fishing.

Craig had been a longtime friend of ours, from way back in the days of Hainault Park Lake. I spent many a night having a beer and talking carp with Craig. Over at Sutton he caught the impressive Searcher at a top weight of 35lbs, and one sunny day, he lost one of the big girls in the Dugout swim. Later on, he made up for that with the rarely caught Heart Tail Gertie at over 40lbs, his PB.

I always felt inspired when I talked to Craig about fishing. He always got me really keen because he was an old-school type of angler. He just loved to fish those little old lakes in the middle of some forest, off the beaten track, for fairly unknown warriors. He used to target these types of lakes closer to home, when he never really had the time, and he caught some impressive, prehistoric creatures that any true angler would love to have in their logbook.

Craig has a young son, Toby, who is the spitting image of him, and a little daughter, Freya. I remember Craig's daughter's christening, and how proud Craig was of his baby girl. Not long after the christening, Craig was out on one of his after-work fishing trips, and on his way to the lake, rods across his chest in his rod bag, his rucksack on his back. I imagine that he'd have been pacing off down the track, thinking about which swim he was heading for and where he would place his rig for that short evening trip. Tragically, he lost his life and no one really knows what happened but he was found later lying in the undergrowth, by a dog walker, rods and rucksack still in place. I doubt he would have known a thing about it; it must have happened in an instant.

Craig was just 36 years young, way too early to leave his young family. They said it was something called SADS - Sudden Adult Death Syndrome - but whatever the cause, we all lost a dear friend, and his family lost a dad and a husband.

You'll never be forgotten. You'll always be my mate, Craig Bateman.
From us all.

Chapter Six - Stuart Court

Tolpits Revisited

It was early in 2000 that I first decided to join my local angling club, Watford Piscators, with the intention of targeting the carp in Tolpits. Despite the venue being only a few miles from my home, I had very limited knowledge of the lake and the fish that lived in it. The local tackle shop owner had mentioned in passing that there were some nice carp present, but other than that all the information I had was that my dad had fished it back in the 70s and caught some decent pike. With not a lot to go on this was going to be a case of learning as I went.

At this time, the lake and its inhabitants were relatively unknown to the carp fishing masses. It certainly wasn't the well-known circuit water it became, and this meant that the banks were quiet and relatively overgrown. This type of fishing was right up my street and I fell in love with the place from the moment I walked across the rickety old bridge.

I remember my first trip vividly. That nervous, excited feeling you get in the pit of your stomach when you walk your first lap of a new water, when every swim is an unknown entity waiting to be explored. Shadowy visions of old carp swimming through the thick lily pads which skirt the margins, and of course the ultimate angler's desire - to make first contact with one of the resident monsters. It was so exciting.

As I neared the top end of the lake, I noticed that a tree had fallen into the water and judging by all the leaves that were still on the branches, it looked as though it had fallen quite recently. There just had to be some inquisitive carp around it taking advantage of this new feature. As I approached the water's edge, slowly and quietly, a sight that I'd never witnessed before greeted me. Right under my feet, literally inches from the bank were a group of seven carp, each one bigger than anything I'd ever caught before. They were happily sitting there under the fallen tree branches, completely oblivious to the fact that I was in such close proximity to them. I just stood there and watched in awe for what seemed like hours before deciding that my best bet for catching one of these fish would be to set up a sensible distance away from the snag in the next swim and try to snare one of them as they came out.

Pumped full of optimism and excitement after being so close to these fish, I felt supremely confident that I could catch one. They seemed so comfortable in the area and I knew I hadn't spooked them, so surely it would just be a matter of stealthily dropping a baited rig out and waiting for it to scream off. Oh how wrong I was! Over 48 hours later, the fish were still under the tree and I hadn't had a touch. My first Tolpits lesson had been well and truly learned. Just because you can see these fish doesn't mean you can catch them!

A few weeks later, I witnessed my good friend, Dan Cashmore, catch what was the most impressive carp I'd ever seen on the bank, the mighty Plodder; its first time tipping the scales at over 40lbs, weighing in at 42lbs on the dot. What an absolute beast of a fish and she was in peak condition. The sight of Plodder's slate-grey flanks, as I photographed her for Dan in the early morning light, stayed etched in my memory, so much so that I even remember the time and date of the

My good friend, Dan Cashmore, holding Plodder. The first time it had ever been caught at over 40lbs.

capture. It was 6.30am on June 7th, 2000 and was a really special angling moment for me, even though I wasn't the lucky one holding her up for the pictures.

The rest of my season on Tolpits was a huge learning curve, but overal,l it ended up being equally as frustrating as that first session I did. I saw the fish on almost every occasion but never once managed to get a take. By midsummer, the word was beginning to get out about the gems that Tolpits held and the likes of Terry Hearn, Jim Shelley, and Dave Mallin began to pay the place some attention. I fished right through to late December in some awful weather conditions, which saw the lake and its banks constantly flooded. This made for some fairly uncomfortable, and frankly unenjoyable, fishing if I'm honest, so eventually I gave in and decided to fish for something a little less challenging for the remainder of the season - chub in the River Colne.

First of May 2001 was the opening day of the season and to my surprise, I was the only angler on Tolpits. Maybe people were put off by the fact that half of the lake was still basically unfishable due to the banks being under water, or maybe it was the unseasonably cold spring weather. Either way I had a score to settle with these carp and I wanted to start as soon as possible. I'd had a re-think during the close season as far as bait was concerned and made the decision to try something a touch more natural than boilies, in the hope I'd be able to fool a wily old Tolpits carp into taking my bait.

My better half, Lina, was able to source good amounts of frozen New Zealand green-lipped mussels from her work at a food importing business, so that was the obvious choice. I'd been trickling them into two different spots in the lake while it had been closed for six weeks, in a bid to get the fish used to picking them up. These things were fairly large and lightly coloured so there was no way they could ignore them on the lakebed, I'd never actually used mussels as bait for carp but I felt sure they'd eat them once they realised they were a good food source.

With the whole lake to myself, I had the opportunity to take my time over swim selection, and I was mainly concentrating on watching the water in the Railway Snag swim and the All Alone, as these were the two areas I'd been pre-baiting. After a few hours of not seeing any signs of carp, a patch of bubbles eventually hitting the surface in the Railway Snag made my mind up for me.

My next problem was the flooded banks. The swim I wanted to be in, much like two-thirds of the lake, was about two feet under water, so my only option was to wade round the lake with all my gear and set up camp on a pile of straw bales that had been handily placed there by another angler during the winter. Like a tiny island, this pile of straw was just enough to elevate me above the water level and was just big enough for my brolly. At least I was fishing the spot I wanted, though, and that's all that mattered.

I spent an uncomfortable night on the sopping wet straw island and then, as the sun rose at dawn, my buzzer let out a couple of bleeps. 'It must be a liner,' I thought, but the bobbin lifted and fell a couple of times and the rod tip bent round ever so slightly and began nodding. I had to investigate and I could barely believe it but, as I lifted the rod, it was clear that I had a fish on. My heart started pounding as the dreams of my first Tolpits carp were seemingly going to become reality at last, and when the fish finally slid into the waiting net, a wave of relief and joy swept over me. It wasn't Plodder, Lesters, the Big Common or the Italian; in fact, at 23lbs, it wasn't even a particularly big carp, but I was just so happy to have caught my first original Tolpits warrior, and on the mussels too!

The following week I was back for another 48-hour session but decided to fish the All Alone swim, my second pre-baited spot. The water level was still high and with the slight breeze pushing a raft of debris into the corner of the lake, it looked perfect for a few fish to be sitting underneath it. My hunch turned out to be right as I landed two fish from under that raft in a matter of hours, again both falling to the mussels; they certainly seemed to be eating them. While I was playing the second fish, another angler had heard the commotion and come round to offer some assistance and that angler turned out to be none other than Mr Jerry Hammond. We got chatting about all things fishy and subsequently became good friends.

So, three fish in my first two trips! I thought I was on to a real winner with my new found super bait but unfortunately, the crafty old Tolpits carp had different ideas and for the next few sessions I was back to blanking again. I did witness something that was to shape the future of the fishing on Tolpits, though. Many of you will have heard the term 'The Renegades' mentioned when Tolpits is being talked about. Well, that term refers to a group of carp, mainly commons, that arrived in the lake via a natural stocking of sorts.

As I've previously mentioned, the lake suffered quite badly from flooding due to some serious drainage issues. There was a ditch that ran along the bungalow bank, continued some 250 yards the full length of the car park bank, and ended in the wooded area at the back of the All Alone swim. This ditch was supposed to funnel the rainwater around the lake so it could drain away into the woods and subsequently into the river Gade and Grand Union canal.

Not the biggest fish in there but my first Tolpits carp meant so much to me.

However, with prolonged heavy rainfall, the wooded area could no longer drain the water quickly enough and the levels rose so high that it began to enter Tolpits through a concrete pipe at the top end of the pit. This pipe is why the swim located next to the All Alone was known as the Sluice.

While fishing in these swims one day, I started to hear splashing noises like a fish slapping the surface of the water with its tail. Obviously, like all good anglers, I jumped off my bedchair each time to try to locate the area of carpy activity, but time and again I could see no ripples. I was a bit puzzled for a while, until eventually, I heard the splashing sound again and realised it was actually coming from the flooded woods behind my bivvy and not from the lake at all.

On further inspection, I could clearly see carp swimming around in what was basically a swamp. There must have been between 10 and 20 fish milling around in there, one a very easy to spot, bright orange koi of around 20lbs. They seemed fairly happy, sucking bits of debris off the surface and rolling around as if they didn't have a care in the world. Only then did it dawn on me that these fish could conceivably get into the lake by going through the pipe so I investigated immediately. To my surprise, I saw a group of eight carp swim, one by one, through the pipe and into Tolpits.

A thick-set Tolpits carp caught on mussels. Things were beginning to come together.

The second fish of a very productive morning.

Without anyone realising, these cheeky little devils had used the flood water to escape from the small club lake behind the Tolpits bungalow. They must have made their way under the chain-link fence which separated it from the Tolpits complex, into the flooded ditch, all the way around the outside of Tolpits, into the woods and through the pipe. It really is amazing how inquisitive carp can be given half a chance. We later named these fish 'The Renegades' due to their daredevil mission that lead them into their new home.

All the fish that entered the lake were around the 10lb mark but they thrived in Tolpits' rich environment and packed on the weight quite quickly. They did get a bit of a bad press from some of the anglers as they were fairly small compared to the originals that everyone fished Tolpits for, but in my opinion, they were nice-looking fish that became increasingly difficult to catch the bigger they got. Many of these fish are alive and well in Tolpits to this day and are now pushing weights of well over 30lbs.

My next encounter with a carp happened a few weeks later, during June when fishing the car park corner. I'd seen all four of the A Team in the snag on my arrival so it was a no-brainer, I had to have a go. In this swim, you had to wade your bait along the marginal shelf and place your rig just short of a rope, which was tied across the corner of the lake to stop people fishing right into the snag.
This made timing extremely important as you didn't want to go wading into an area where the carp were laying up, so after carefully watching the fish and waiting for them to move out, I dropped my rig just short of the rope and locked my clutch up tight.

Nothing happened that night. The fish tended to move out into open water after dark but I was sure they'd be back in the morning so it wasn't a huge surprise when my rod wrenched round at 7am. I was into a strong fish and despite me giving no line off the clutch it immediately snagged me solid. This thing was just so powerful that I had no chance of controlling it from the moment it felt the hook. It boiled up heavily just under the overhanging branches then, a few seconds later, it was off and I was left with that horrible empty feeling that all anglers know.

I was absolutely gutted with this loss and after watching the other big fish return to the snags later that afternoon, I was convinced that I'd lost the big common that morning as she was nowhere to be seen. That loss really took something out of my fishing at Tolpits, so after catching one more mid-20 original the following week, I decided I needed a complete change of scenery and left Tolpits for the banks of the River Ouse and its record-sized barbel. You could say I got sidetracked somewhat as I didn't set foot on Tolpits again for six years!

Tolpits is a very intimate little lake. You're never far away from the fish but getting them to take a bait can be extremely difficult.

During my time away from the place, I'd heard from friends that dry summers had caused the water levels to drop so low that the fish had nowhere to hide. The snags were completely on dry land. The Big Common and Arfur, among others, had sadly passed away. Plodder and Lesters had been caught something like 14 times a season each, which was massively out of character, and the banks had become extremely busy now that everyone and his dog knew about the place. It honestly sounded like hell to me so I stayed away and concentrated on other species.

Inevitably, though, I started to think about that slate grey mirror carp again. Plodder was back on my radar and from what I was hearing, the place was a bit quieter than it had been for the previous couple of seasons and the water levels were back to normal. It was time to go and pay her some attention. These fish were getting old and I knew I had to take this opportunity before it was too late. Proper original upper-40lb carp that have been swimming around in a club lake for nearly 50 years, located not ten minutes from your front door aren't exactly two a penny. I'd have been mad not to give it another shot, so a club permit was purchased and plans were made to revisit Tolpits.

I started my second campaign at the beginning of June 2007. The season was a month old already and a few fish had been caught but despite missing the normally productive month of May, it felt good to be on those familiar banks. Funnily enough, my first trip back coincided with some seriously heavy rainfall and the lake was flooded again. It was almost as if I'd never been away. Standing in front of the famous bungalow and looking out along the length of the intimate pit, I caught a glimpse of a couple of carp swimming just under the surface, not six feet from the bank. They were casually heading down toward the railway corner so I thought I'd follow them and see where they were going. The next swim down was the Grassy, which has a nice bit of foliage along the water's edge so I hid behind the bushes and waited for the gang of cruising carp to enter my view again.

It wasn't a long wait as they appeared almost immediately from my left, bang on cue. To my surprise, they didn't carry on past me to the snags, but stopped directly in front and started feeding on the clean gravel. At normal water levels, this would only be a couple of inches deep, but as it was, they were quite comfortable in 18 inches. They were so close to me that I could see the unmistakable shapes of Lesters and the Big Italian among the group. These were two fish that I'd dearly love to catch, and although Plodder wasn't with them, I couldn't pass up this opportunity on my first trip back, so I set about getting my gear very quietly into the back of the swim.

A single rod fished right back so the tip was just poking over the edge between some reeds, leadcore hanging slack from the tip with half a tiger nut as bait was the chosen method, very stealthy, very sneaky, just like the old days. The main problem, as always at Tolpits, was getting the bait in the water without spooking the fish. I'd learned the hard way that patience was most definitely needed in these situations, so I decided not to drop a rig in until the carp moved out into open water as darkness fell. That way, the fish would find an inconspicuous single piece of bait on the spot when they, fingers crossed, returned in the morning.

Return in the morning they did, as my trap worked and the single rod I was using rattled off at a serious rate of knots. After a decent but uneventful scrap, I netted a pretty little common carp, a Renegade weighing in at 25lbs and a few ounces. It wasn't the fish I'd been after, but I was quite happy with that as a welcome back gift.

One of the 'Renegades'. They could be future Tolpits 40s.

The rest of the summer was fantastic fun. Stalking among the lilies with floating crust is what I found myself doing during the daylight hours. This type of 'up-close and personal' fishing really got my heart going in the same way as stalking a big barbel in clear water does. For the countless hours spent chasing the big carp around the lake, I only ended up catching two more Renegades during the summer. I did come incredibly close to hooking Lesters when she slurped down my floating crust from right under my rod tip one afternoon, but somehow managed to whip the hook out of her mouth before it could get a hold. So near, yet so far - again.

As far as Plodder was concerned, I saw her most days but I never felt like I'd been particularly close to catching her. She was the least interested in a lump of crust of any carp I've ever seen. Quite often, I'd see her cruising just under the surface along the far side of the lily pads, but she completely ignored the bread on every single occasion. She'd never been caught off the top before as far as anyone knew, and I did get the distinct impression I was wasting my time when she came waddling past. I imagine she was laughing at my pitiful attempts at fooling her.

As autumn arrived and the frosts started to lie on the ground, it was time for me to pack the carp rods away. Tolpits hadn't produced a single fish for anyone for over seven weeks and I'd had enough for the time being. I pulled off relatively happy with what I'd learned, and my three fish, and went in pursuit of big perch for the winter. Unfortunately, I did hear the sad news that Lesters had died not long after I pulled off. She was a lovely old fish, full of character and she'd done me fair and square that day in the pads.

With my enthusiasm fully recharged over the winter, I was really looking forward to the new season. It was another chance to put into practice everything I'd learned the previous year and I was confident that I was going to do better.

During the weeks prior to opening day, I had been popping over to the lake regularly to keep some bait going in on a couple of spots that I fancied, just like I had years ago. Each time, I introduced a few handfuls of boilies, hemp and some pellets to get the bream in to clean the spots off. I couldn't really tell if it was getting eaten as the water was quite coloured and as ever, the banks were flooded. I knew that if my bait was being introduced into the same spots each time, the carp would get on it at some stage so a 'little and often' baiting strategy was what I needed in this situation. I wasn't trying to feed the fish or get them on to a particular boilie as such. It was more about getting them to feel confident feeding on the spot where I could catch them when the season started.

Opening day arrived and surprisingly, more people turned up than there were actual fishable swims. This wasn't helped by the fact that the entire bungalow bank and the railway bank had been closed by the club because of flooding, so a few lads who didn't draw out of the hat very well had to go home disappointed. I came out fifth, but my pre-baited areas were already taken. I wasn't too unhappy with my swim but I started off the season with a five-night blank session.

My second session of the season began on Sunday afternoon the following week. It was really hot but things looked good with only two other anglers on the water. The water level had dropped considerably since I was there the previous week, and the banks resembled something from a World War 1 trench, with thick mud everywhere. However, to my delight, the bungalow bank had now been officially re-opened, and what was even better, I was the first angler to get myself round there. I slopped my way round through the gloopy black mud and stopped to look in the snaggy corner. This was one of the areas where I'd been trickling bait, so I was keen to see if there were any fish around.

I saw Plodder as soon as I looked down. She was sitting inches from the bank, just resting there in the dappled shade under some branches. You simply couldn't mistake her in the water. She was built like a bulldozer and was as thick across the back as a breezeblock. 'That'll do!' I said out loud. I put a bucket in the swim adjacent to the snags and went back to my van to load the barrow with all my gear.

When I arrived back she had gone from her resting place, but I could see swirls and tail patterns coming from further into the snags so I knew there were still fish about. I was in no rush to get my rigs in the water because while the fish were still close by I ran the risk of spooking them. I'd blown a few similar opportunities by rushing things in the past so I sat well back from the water and carefully tied a nice fresh rig specifically for this situation.

To get my bait onto my spot I needed to use my baiting pole because it was impossible to cast it there because of the marginal trees. This is something I have done many times before and is pretty much standard practice on Tolpits. The margins are by far the most productive areas on this lake, in fact I've never known another water where such big carp come in as close as they do here. It's truly amazing to watch.

The banks of Tolpits always seemed to be flooded. Here the carp were feeding just below my rod tip.

As the afternoon went on, the weather got hotter and the carp drifted out of the snags and started cruising on the surface out in open water. This was the ideal time for me to get my rig in place so I loaded up my baiting spoon with a few broken boilies and a handful of hemp. I put my rig on top of that in the spoon and floated the whole lot out until I had added all the sections to the 8m pole. Then I started to drift it slowly round to my left-hand margin, under the tree branches until it was directly over the spot. With a twist of the pole, I tipped the contents of the spoon right where I wanted it and with the minimum of disturbance, my trap was set. I set my rod on the buzzer and tightened the line but not so much that it would lift my leadcore off the bottom. The feeling of anticipation was immense and I had a strong feeling that a great chance had presented itself to me here, maybe not until the following morning when the carp were back in the snags, but at some point. I just felt I'd get a chance.

Surprisingly, two hours later, I had a twitchy take and lifted into a small tench. Not what I needed at this stage at all because I would now need to go to the trouble of re-positioning my rig with the pole. I did this but again, two hours later another tench spoiled my plans. I was getting a bit concerned that all this commotion would stop the carp from coming back in, so I had no option but to change my hook bait for something that was less appealing to a tench than a 10mm boilie.

I knew that Plodder was a bit partial to nuts. I remembered that a few of her previous captures had been on tiger nuts, peanuts, and Brazil nuts, so that seemed like a good bet to me. I didn't have any tigers or peanuts with me, but I did have a small packet of Brazils in my food bag for a snack, so I tied a new rig up and put a piece of Brazil on the hair. I've never used them before so when I lowered it into the margin I was surprised to see that they float, straight out of the packet. Amazingly, half a nut sat absolutely perfectly with the hook on the lakebed and the nut just wafting above it. I loaded the spoon with hemp and pellets for a third time and floated it all out again.

My next action was at 10am the next morning. I was looking out at the lake, trying to stay in my bedchair for as long as possible so I didn't spook any carp, when my rod just wrenched round with a violent take. It reminded me a lot of a barbel take but this was even more violent than that. My clutch was screwed up tight as I was fishing close to the snags and couldn't afford to give an inch of line. As I held on, I could feel that horrible pinging of branches on the line and I could hear the fish boiling up on the surface down to my left. With a sudden jerk and a very still, solid feeling on the rod, I knew the fish had gone. My rig was still snagged solid so I waded along the margin feeling my line down and I came to a rather large branch with my hook embedded in it. I pulled the lot out and retrieved all of my tackle but found myself experiencing that horrible feeling once again; could it have been Plodder?

I cursed my luck for what seemed to be about an hour, head in hands, and then shook it in disbelief. Eventually, though, I plucked up enough enthusiasm to tie a fresh rig. With this done, I positioned the Brazil nut hookbait and another spoonful of hemp into the same position. I did actually wonder if it was worth it because the fish would have all spooked out of there with me having waded in to retrieve my tackle. To my relief though, a few hours later I started to see fish in and around the snags, so I went to bed that night still confident of another chance.

At around 4am, I was woken by another violent take which saw the rod bent round to its full test curve, straining under the pressure of the tight clutch. It was still pitch black at this stage and I was standing in the mud, with bare feet, playing a fish that I thought was another tench. It came straight out of the snags and was continuously furrowing across the surface, splashing and rolling in its attempt to get away. Slowly, it began to feel as though it had a bit more power than a tench so I started to think that maybe I'd hooked a small carp. After what I could only describe as a quick but frantic fight, I blindly netted this fish in the darkness, still under the impression that it was nothing special, but as I went to lift the net it dawned on me that it was significantly heavier than anything I had ever lifted from the water before. It could only be one fish - Plodder!

There she was on my unhooking mat; after all these years she was mine. Still in the net, I lowered her into the deep margin in the next swim and secured everything with banksticks. While making a cup of coffee, I found myself mumbling out loud, 'I've got Plodder ... I've got Plodder. I can't believe I've got Plodder.'

The rest is a bit of a blur to be honest. You know what it's like when you're so pumped full of adrenalin that you seem to lose track of large chunks of your life? Somehow, I got another angler round to help me weigh her and man the camera while I struggled to lift all 47lbs 2oz of her. I packed up soon after, very slowly, while basking in my own glory, and went home with that smug feeling of satisfaction. Job done.

The story doesn't end there, though. Having caught my long-term target fish, I concluded that it would be best if I didn't fish for the carp in Tolpits again. I still had plenty of the originals to catch, but after banking Plodder I felt it couldn't really get any better so I took a couple of weeks away from the place.

Finally, I'd done it! At 47lbs 2oz Plodder looked in fine condition.

Then, I turned my attention fully to the big tench that live in there so I set my stall out to catch them using the traditional methods of groundbait, maggot feeders and light rods. I had a fantastic session, catching 26 tench up to 11lbs 4oz. My God! Tolpits was repaying me in style for all the blanks I'd done over the years.

Gently slipping the ancient warrior back. It's funny how you don't feel the cold in these situations.

On my second tench fishing session a week later, the action was slow during the day as the weather had turned really hot. I just sat there watching the water and happened to notice that the carp were cruising on the surface, topping up their tans. Half-heartedly, I started to fire out some mixers that I had in the bottom of my bag and unusually for Tolpits, the fish started to take more and more of them.

Tench were the target on this misty morning.

At 11lbs 4oz, this tench was another great result from a fantastic little water.

Not wanting to miss an opportunity, I quickly broke down one of my tench rods, a 1¾ TC Torrix, and rigged up a makeshift controller set-up. All I had with me was 8lb main line, so it was a bit risky, but I couldn't ignore this chance. I opted to use a lump of crust from my lunch rolls rather than a mixer hookbait, as past experience had taught me that the Tolpits fish were very cute at sussing out the one with the hook attached. The fact that I could bury the hook completely inside a lump of crust was a great advantage.

By now, every mixer I fired in was being gulped down. I'd never seen these fish take baits off the top with such aggression; it was like a fish farm out there. Within a couple of minutes, two fish were heading right for my lump of bread, and were competing for the free mixers as they came. Then I saw a big swirl on the surface and my bread was gone. I lifted the rod and felt immediately that I'd hooked the culprit, but the strange thing was that the fish didn't seem to realise it was hooked. It just sat there, it didn't bolt, it didn't dive, it didn't kite, it literally just sat there like nothing was wrong. My tench rod was bent double as if I was hooked to a solid object, yet the fish I was attached to was barely aware of the pressure I was applying. Slowly, I began to pump the fish toward me, still with nothing but a dead weight hanging on the end. As soon as I got it within 10 yards of me, I saw a flash of grey under the water and knew which fish I'd hooked - it was Plodder again.

What strange emotions I began to experience. I was shaking with excitement about hooking a big Tolpits carp off the top, but also gutted that it was the fish I'd caught only three weeks previously, and I was half-hoping she'd come off, if I'm honest, but they only ever do that when you don't want them to. Anyway, after a bit of a tussle among the lily pads under the rod tip, I got her in the net at the first attempt. I then had to stop for a moment to think carefully about the situation. This fish had never been caught off the surface as far as anyone knew, so it was a real achievement for me but on the flip side, it was a recapture. Not wanting to cause her any undue stress, I unhooked her in the net and let her go with my sincere apologies.

Unfortunately, the mighty Plodder passed away in 2009 after swimming the waters of Tolpits for somewhere in the region of 50 years. What a magnificent creature she was! Thanks for the memories old girl.

Chapter Seven
Horton, Rocks and Boulders

Horton Church Lake. What a venue that is! I longed for a ticket and had my name down for one when they stocked it from Longfield and I remember reading about the captures of those stunning old carp. Jay and me took a walk round one day and we bumped into Steve Mogford. Steve was the only one on the lake at the time, and I'm sure he was fishing in either the Spindly or R.I.P. swim. He told us how tricky it was and that, because the weed was a nightmare, it could take hours to find spots. We had a good chat with Steve and then took a walk around this amazing venue. We looked across the open water and I thought, 'somewhere out there swims Jack, Shoulders, The Lady, Moonscale, The Parrot…' It truly was a dream water, and all this made me want my ticket even more. Sadly, I never did get to have a go, as Horton suffered a fish kill and a lot of the old originals perished. Funnily enough, just after that I was offered my ticket and I declined.

Horton was restocked with a selection of the earlier Mark Simmons strain of carp, and some of the originals had made it through the fish kill; such as Shoulders, The Parrot, The Big Grey, No Name, The Wood Carving, Wallace, The Boxer, and Black Tail, to name a few, and some good commons. Include these that survived with the ones that perished, and you've got an amazing stock of carp that had lived in Horton! While I was fishing at Sutton, I always thought about Horton, and how much I would love to have a go at catching some of those old originals before it was too late. So, in 2005 I decided it was time to have a go.

I had a CEMEX Gold Card, so at the end of the 2004-2005 season, I had a quick reconnaissance trip for a day and maybe a night, with my old mate, Nick Helleur. I was fortunate enough to see Nick catch two originals, The Dumpy Mirror at 28lbs and Black Tail at 33lbs This fired me up even more, but it wasn't until the autumn of that year, that I finally got started.

I saw Nick catch two originals, The Dumpy Mirror, and Black Tail.

Horton Church Lake is 15 acres and made up of three parts. When you first walk on to the lake from the lodge end, there is the main body of water, where the plateau is, and right up at the far end of the lake there are two bays, Dog Bay and Church Bay. There are some 31 swims, all named with appropriate titles from some historic Horton happening. The Plateau, one of the most famous swims having produced at some time or other most of the lake's residents, is exactly as its name describes - a plateau, with shallow depths on top. This area of the lake gets very weedy and the carp just love it. It's always the first swim to go in the draw and produces fish at the start, and throughout the year.

The swims just up from the Plateau and opposite are called the Spindly Tree and the Scooter. They are of different depths with lots of weed, but as we move further down the lake and into deeper water, it does get a lot more barren. The margins are then really good areas, though, as they are fringed with grass-like ribbon weed, and once you get into the bays, then there are shallower depths with bars and obviously more weed.

On my first trip, I was set up in a swim named the Salt Circle. Not a great deal was happening in my area, I hadn't seen any carp and I was itching to move on some fish. I hate just camping, it's not for me. It had started to rain and was now chucking it down, so I had the Armadillo door done up with the top bit open so I was still able to view the lake. As I scanned about I was able to see right into Church Bay, and through the downpour, I had seen what I was looking for; one had jumped, down in Phil's Corner, along the tree line off the Church Bay Steps. I was already packing away my kit within the confines of the bivvy and getting ready to move. As I packed up I kept glancing to the area where I'd seen the fish show, and it seemed that every time I looked, one would stick its head out. I threw everything on the barrow, covered it with a groundsheet, then laid my rolled-up and soaking bivvy on top, and I was ready. I had to make a quick trip to the clubhouse first, though, to pick up my phone that was on charge.

At the club house, top angler, Simon Davy, (lock, stock and two smoking marker floats), was chilling out between his trips to the Yateley Car Park Lake. As it's only 48 on, he would do a 48 at Horton to break it up.
"What you up to?" he said.
" I'm about to have a move," I replied.
"Bloody hell! What, in this weather?"
Then I told him what I'd seen, and from the lodge we were able to see into the Church Bay. Before long, one showed and then another.
"Blimey," he said. "That's getting my taste buds going."
Before he got too interested, I said goodbye, stuck my hood up, and made off with my barrow. I heard him shout out 'good luck' as I went.

It was hard work. I had to push that barrow a fair way and I was saturated when I got there. Not long after I arrived, though, I started to see fish. They were showing all along the tree line of the Church Bay Steps swim. My main concern was to get the rods out sharpish, so I pushed the barrow under the shelter of some trees and got my rods and alarms out. I had already baited my rigs before I moved with Monster Tiger Nut, snowman fashion. I was to fish from Phil's Corner as this allowed me to cast to the tree line where I had been seeing the fish. In this swim, I had to set my rods up at the bottom of a slope and the bivvy up at the top. Without spooking the fish, I flicked out two rods and took shelter as it was still raining, and over the next couple of hours, every now and then, one would show itself, so I was happy that I was still on some fish, at least.

Eventually, the rain stopped and as the afternoon gradually turned to early evening without a single bite, I was wondering why. The fish were not showing either now and I felt that I'd missed an opportunity. Looking back, I think the carp were feeding more into the lake in the silt and they were using the marginal shelf as a ramp as they crashed, to clear out their gills, and to me it had looked as if they were in the margins; it was all a big learning curve. I repositioned my baits for the evening ahead, and put one rod on the tree line, but my left rod I cast just down the tree line along my left margin. I walked down that tree line and threw in a few handfuls of 10 and 15mm Tiger Nut boilies, and that was sorted for the night.

At 7am, I awoke to a blistering take that had me running out and literally sliding down the slippery slope on my stomach, just in time to grab the left-hand rod that was bent right round. Immediately, I gave serious side strain to stop this fish from getting further along the tree line and into whatever dangers might be there. I was able turn the fish, and once out in front of me, only then was I able to get my breathing under control. I was into a Horton carp and it could be any one of them.

I got myself down from the furious adrenalin rush as best I could, and gradually began to feel in control once more. The carp now made a beeline for the other tree line, but I was having none of that. I soon got it back out in front of me and it boiled up on the surface. The first thing I noticed was that it was really dark, and I thought, 'that's an original one, that - don't lose it!' I think that had I given it a bit more, she would have gone in the net, because she was nearly ready, but I didn't rush it. I took my time, and then she found a bit more energy and made off for the tree line again.

Once again, I managed to stop it and as before, she was boiling and ready for the net, only this time I saw what I was playing. As that great big carp lay on its side, the disfigured mouth of the Parrot slowly came over the landing net cord. Oh my God! I had the Parrot! My heart was pounding like a drum. She would be at least 43lbs. 'Gently does it ', I said, as lifted the rod that little bit more to get all of her in the net. I can still see it in slow motion playback. Just at that last split-second, the hook pulled and instantly, she turned and swam out of the net.
"Nooooo!" I screamed, and I even thought I had a quick chance of scooping her up. I should be so lucky. I launched my rod about 40 feet into the air, absolutely devastated. I had so nearly caught one of the originals on my first trip. I went over and over in my head what had happened but it was no good, nothing was going to bring the fish back, and with that I packed up and headed off home.

I still curse at losing that one today, but hey ho, life goes on. I was keener than ever now and wanted some sort of payment, fish wise, so I was soon back at the lake and I plotted up in the swim called One Up. It's one up from the Plateau and it's a good swim that can sometimes fish better than the Plateau, especially if the carp are off the left-hand side of it in the deeper water. On this trip, I had a little plumb about and about halfway across I found a strip of weed and a gravelly bit that just stopped and kind of petered out into silt. Everyone around the lake seemed to be spodding hemp and corn, so I thought I would be a bit different and just fish boilies. The biggest I had was 18mm and I fired out as many as I was able with the catapult.

My first fish was Fantail, one of the oldest in the lake.

It was hard to get the range but the wind was in my favour and I did manage to get a good spread out there. My normal snowman and stringer set-up was then cast out on two rods, one on the back of the weed and the other in the silty bit.

The wind was pushing in a westerly direction, it felt fairly warm and as late afternoon approached, the sky turned a nice red colour. I was just admiring the red sky when the left rod bobbin pulled up to the butt and remained there. I jumped up and just as I got to the rod the line clip pulled and the alarm was singing out its tune. The old adrenalin kicked in as once again I battled with a Horton carp. The fish had gone on a long kite left, thankfully into deeper water, and the more left it went the more I was concerned as between the swims were trees and long ribbon grass. I just had to keep pumping away and winding down until it turned and headed in a better direction, out to my front.

Once they were close, you had the ribbon weed to worry about and some of it was very long. My fish dived into the marginal weed and locked me up for a while but a steady pressure soon had it up and ready for the net and this time she stayed on. Del Smith, the fishery head bailiff, was there and he informed me that I'd just landed Fan Tail, probably the oldest fish in the lake.

She was a cracking old mirror and I just had time to get some shots of her while the sunset was still looking nice. I'd banked my first Horton carp and what a fish to start with! Fan Tail at just over 30lbs! I was made up.

The next morning I was off home, a happy angler, but Horton had one more gift for me before I left, and I banked another carp, a 29lb mirror and one of the stock fish. If she thought that she was sufficient payback for losing the Parrot, though, she could think again! After that trip, I decided to leave Horton alone until the next season started, and spend the colder months fishing a bit on the rivers, and when the conditions were right, I would try my luck locally for the carp.

After my little taster at the Horton carp, I couldn't wait for the new season to come around. The winter slowly dragged on, as it normally does, but after what seemed ages the draw for the new season finally arrived. CEMEX Angling do the draws on their waters a week before the start, and I don't know what it is about me and draws, but in all the years I've fished, occasionally I get an early draw, but nine times out of ten I don't even get on, and the draw for Horton was to be no exception.

It's a horrible feeling when you don't make the draw. I walked away from the the lake, hearing all the excitement from the lads that had made it, buzzing as they

If she thought that was payback, she could think again.

I cast to a showing fish and late evening it pulled away.

anticipated what might be ahead of them, but I have to block it out of my mind until it's my turn. I just hit the gym extra hard as a kind of self-punishment for being crap at draws.

By the time I was able to get on, nearly all the good fish had already been out. The one I really did want was Shoulders, and she'd been out at 45-odd pounds. Nearly all the good swims had been taken, and I ended up in the Scooter, which was not exactly where I wanted to be, but at least I had a good view of the lads over on the Plateau and One Up getting amongst them. It was frustrating but what else can you do? I did manage another stockie mirror, though. It was early evening, I cast to a showing fish, and by late evening, it pulled away - good old chod rig.

As the weeks went by, I managed to catch every trip, but still none of the originals had come my way. In the daytime it was hot and sunny and after the morning feeding spell I thought it was just a waste of time to be sitting behind the rods so, every morning at about 10, I would grab my floater gear and go looking for the fish. Those Horton carp did like a floater, and any fish caught during the day was a nice bonus.

Jim Shelley had got the method off to a tee, and I must say fair play to him as he worked really hard at it and thoroughly deserved what he caught. I was watching him one day, spodding out Chum to the middle of the lake and the carp were going crazy for the mixers. Then he cast out one of those Bolt Machine controllers, with what looked like an orange pop-up as a hook bait. He drew the hook bait in among the fish and I said to myself, 'if that goes, I'll eat my hat.' I turned away for a short while, and when I looked back, he was into a fish. They must have just homed in on his orange hook bait. He did catch a lot off the top, including some of the good ones.

I love my surface fishing. I would be at it until it was time to cast out for the evening and I came close to Shoulders one morning. I was fishing in the Spindly Tree and Ben Hamilton had called in for a brew. He was sitting with me when Shoulders came and took a few mixers and after a while disappeared over toward the Plateau for brunch. Maybe the menu was better there.

I had some good days floater fishing and these days would save me from a blank throughout the summer. I found I was able to get away with 8lb line and hook lengths over there, as the water was deep in the main part of the lake. The fish would tire themselves out going on massive runs and I had no problem at all using the light line. It also let me reach long distances. I climbed a tree one day in the Sick swim, and I was able to see the whole lake, where the carp were in a massive shoal halfway across.

I started to get a few spods of Chum out to the right-hand side of the fish. The mixers drifted down onto the carp, and before long their backs started to glisten as the sun caught them as they rose to take floaters. Then I cast long, past the fish, and slowly retrieved the float until it was sitting right among them. I was now fishing way over the middle of the lake and after a while it seemed that the fish were more on the other bank, and I thought, 'What am I doing? Surely it would be better just to go around the other side?'

I reeled in, grabbed my kit and set off. On my way, I passed a good friend and Horton regular, Dean Duke.
"Bloody hell," he said. "Was that you casting across there?"
"Yeah, sorry mate. Was I coming near you?" I replied.
"No mate, not at all," he said. "I was just laughing at how far out you were floater fishing."
He told me that I'd been three-quarters of the way across the lake, probably some 130-plus yards. He thought it was hilarious.

I had some good days floater fishing, and these days saved me a blank.

Anyway, once I was around the other side, the fish were at a much better range. At least I was able to see what was going on. I'm always messing around with floater set-ups and I've found that what works on some waters doesn't work on others. On the Church Lake, I was trying a few different things and ended up trimming one of the artificial tiger nuts into a little floater-shaped cube, and a long hair seemed to do the trick. With a short hair, they were turning away at the last second, and I don't know why the longer hair was better, but something was making a difference.

On this bank, the marginal ribbon weed was a lot denser and it got tricky when in close on the long hook lengths. It was great to catch them in this manner and they really did love those floaters. On the right day, you could get them preoccupied, and that's what Jim was good at, and why I think his orange pop-up worked so well. They were just eating anything that floated.

Every bite I had, I could have been playing one of the special ones, and with that always in my mind, it was such a buzz. I continued to keep the feed going in and the carp were going up and down, gulping away, and mine was soon sucked in. My float disappeared, and then hit the surface again. Damn! I thought I'd lost it, but in fact, the fish had taken my hook bait and the float under, and then come back up to the surface, I'm sure, to feed some more, until it realised that something was wrong, and then did it take off! There was a huge eruption, the line snaked away and a few fish boiled up as it departed, but the rest all just kept on feeding away obliviously.

This fish used the deep water and tore off on a long deep run, but it was great here because there were no snags for me to worry about. After a while, fish would tire themselves out and then I would gradually coax them back to my margin, where they would mess about for a while in the weed, or kite down the tree line. The close-in part was the problem. Anyway, in the crystal clear water I saw a sandy-coloured mirror twisting and turning away in its bid for freedom. She'd got all tangled up in the weed and for a moment I thought she was going to get off, but I managed to heave the fish and the weed up and she lay there, probably thinking about her next move, and just before she had any sneaky ideas, I netted her.

A couple of lads were watching me play the fish and they told me that I had the Little Leather. That'd do! Not an original but, hey, it's a leather and all of 30lbs. I was very happy and if I'd been sitting on my rods, I wouldn't have been having such a great day. A few quick shots in the baking hot sun and I got her back quickly. The fish fed for another hour or so and I did get another 29lb mirror. These stockies were getting bigger all the time. Many people moaned about the

It's not an original, but hey, it's a leather.

strain that went in, and the fish are fairly similar, but over the years they've all become characters of the lake, are now some 15-odd years old, and many have surpassed the 40lb mark. They're not those horrible football-shaped medicine balls, with fins and a tail stuck on, but they are, and always will be, stockies.

My strategy was firstly to try to get on the fish, and when the weather was right, to spend the days floater fishing. It was a busy lake and most times I would have to wait a night before a favourable swim became free. Captors, for example, which was a good swim because there was a nice feature, a shallower part out a fair way that was kind of near the centre of the main body of the lake. The fish would often move over this area, hence the name Captors. I only fished it once, or maybe twice, in all the time I was on there.

The fish however did move about a lot and some anglers would base their trips around certain swims because they had good form. It's no good being in the Plateau swim when they are all up in Dog Bay. I came up with a plan. I hated the M25 with vengeance, and I still do, so in an attempt to miss the traffic, if that were at all possible, I would leave my house about 10.30pm and get to Horton at around 11.30. Then, I'd park up, unload the car, load the barrow, park it somewhere up by the lodge and go off searching for carp.

The Horton carp loved the mixers.

It was great. Everyone was tucked up asleep and, for me, it was like being back in the army again out on night manoeuvres. Sometimes, I'd do five or six laps of the lake and always find some fish. I didn't care how much time it took, because once I was set up, I could get my head down, and it wasn't as if I had to get up in the morning, was it? I learned a lot on these night manoeuvres. Once, I was sitting in Springate's swim, the one that looks down the length of the lake, and it's surprising what you can hear from there. On the flat calm nights, they would always give themselves away. I would hear a fish and belt round the lake to where one had jumped, and then I'd stay there a while and see if another would go.

One night, I ended up in a swim called The Shoulders and the carp were going ape in there. They were crashing about all night, so I raced off for my gear and set up full of hope. I cast two rods to where the fish were mostly showing, and in this case I fished little pop-ups and attached a PVA stocking ball of small pellets, just a mouthful. The fish kept me awake all night, rolling, and sploshing about, and in the early hours, just before daybreak they vacated the area. I awoke mid-morning without any action, and whatever it was they were feeding on, I couldn't distract them with my offerings, so I packed up and moved.

On many occasions, though, I got it right and was rewarded with some action. I enjoyed getting over in the night like that; it made sense. There were times when I found a swim that I fancied, and then I'd fetch the loaded barrow. Often, Del Smith, the head bailiff, was set up in the Plateau swim with his lovely old dog, Roly. Just where his bivvy was set up, near the path, was a tree root that was really hard to push the barrow over. I swear, and you can ask him, that every time I got to that root, I would tip my barrow over and with a deafening crash, all my gear would fall off and nearly go through the side of his bivvy. The first few times I did it, it must have scared the life out of them. Poor old Roly would do her best guard dog bit, and come out barking, followed by Del.
"What's going on?" he'd say - and this may have been at any time of the night. Later on when I did it, he'd just call out. "Is that you, Jerry?"
"Evening, Del." I'd say. That bloody root! It that seemed no matter how I approached it, it always did me.

That season was passing at a rapid rate and every time I fished, I caught a stockie. Surely, I'd get an original soon? At this rate, I'd never get anywhere near catching Shoulders. Shoulders was a hard one to catch because I believe she was a random feeder. She'd turn up on a baited spot, feed for only a short time and then be off. Ultimately, this would cut down the chances of her getting caught. I watched her one day feeding in the weedy bay along with other fish. She'd only have a little and then leave the weedy bay area. I'd see her do a big circuit and eventually, she'd come back, and just sit in the weed, whereas the others would still be interested in the food. Like I said, if she went around the whole lake doing this, taking a little from each spot, she would be hard to catch. That must have been something that the old carp learned from Longfield. However, she was vulnerable off the top.

It was getting towards the autumn now. I was down for a couple of nights and the lake was quiet, with only me and two others on. I was set up in the Spindly Tree swim opposite the Plateau, and the other two anglers were fishing the Plateau and the One Up swim. To be honest, I really wasn't feeling that confident. I hadn't seen any fish and in this swim, to get to any really good spots, you had to be nigh on poaching the Plateau water. I've never found too much until right on the back of the Plateau, and it always lures you into casting that little bit further, and you shouldn't.

I had two rods with chods on, ready to go, leaning against a tree, and if I saw any fish, the plan was to take a chance and cast to them. It was very weedy in the area, so the chod approach was ideal. Well, those rods remained leaning against the tree. I saw nothing, and spent all night just camping under my umbrella.

The next morning, I packed everything on to my barrow and made my way around to my car. I'd decided to go home and this would be the end of my lucky run. Instead of stopping at my car with my gear, though, I went to see the lads in the other swims to see how they'd got on. It turned out that they had both blanked and not seen a fish, and this got my mind ticking over. If they hadn't seen anything, then the fish must be at the other end of the lake, they had to be. I left my barrow with them to look after and went for a stroll, which soon turned into a fast stride as I made my way up toward the Shoulders swim. I was starting get a glimmer of hope that my hunch might be correct.

As I arrived at the swim, I started to scan across the Dog Bay and straight away one stuck its head out on the other side of the bay, close to the left-hand side of the Slope swim, then another off the trees to the left of Heart Tails. Bloody hell! Where's my gear? I was now full of high spirits and in angling mode again. I rushed back for my gear and as I steamed off with it, the lads said, "Oh, You've found some fish then?" I mumbled something about some bubblers, and was off in a full battle gallop with my kit.

I was knackered by the time I'd got to the Heart Tails swim. It was half a circuit of the lake, but immediately, I saw lots of sheeting-up between Heart Tails and Springates. It seemed that the fish were already hitting the naturals big style. The main bubbling was in front of Heart Tails, so I backed away from the lake and proceeded to tear my barrow apart as I sorted out two rods and a net. I had two spare rods with me, already set up, so all I had to put on was some lighter inline leads to my four feet of lead core. All the time, the bubblers were fizzing away and my heart was pounding with excitement. I decided to use a single pop-up on each rod, the 14mm tiger nut ones made by Lee at Hookers.

I made a cast, going beyond the feeding fish, and gently swung it in while trying not to spook them. This was nail-biting stuff and I didn't want to blow it. All that was going through my mind was that any one of those special carp, like Wallace, The Wood Carving, The Big Grey... they could be down there feeding away, and they probably were. It felt as if I'd been sitting there for ages waiting for something to happen, but it was only about 25 minutes. I was just about to reel in the left-hand rod to re-position it and as I picked it up, the line pulled tight on a good liner, so gently, I placed the rod back on the rest. I was scared in case I had spooked the fish and annoyed that I'd even moved it in the first place, and then the line just began to rip off the spool.

I lifted the rod, but the fish hadn't gone that far and, judging by all the bubbles coming up, was trying to rid the the hook on the bottom. This went on for a while

Scar scrapped hard, and there was no way I was going home now.

with the clutch just clicking slowly. It felt like a heavy fish and it took some effort to get it to come up off the bottom, but one of the Horton bailiffs who was right down the other end of the lake, had seen that I was into a fish and had came round to help. He arrived just in time to grab the net as a big-framed mirror was about ready to land.

We recognised this fish as one called Scar. She had been out at the start at over 40lbs, but wasn't that big now, although over 30, for sure. The hard-fighting Scar weighed 33lbs 8oz, and I was mightily chuffed to have caught her. Scar was carefully put back and there was no way I was going home now. I had to fish at least another night.

I spent the rest of that afternoon chasing bubblers up and down over three different swims, but I eventually settled in Springates for the night because just before dark the fish were still in the area. Just after dark, a very good one crashed with a big belly flop, sending waves to the front of the swim. In close, in front of Springates, the margins dropped away quickly and there was a fair amount of Canadian pondweed. The fish had been bubbling along the back of the weed in the silt, so I placed my baits for the night just beyond it. It was a really dark night and it felt like I was a long way from my rods from where I was lying under the brolly.

I screamed out 'Shoulders!' as loud as I could.

At 4am, one of the rods had a savage liner, and I woke up not knowing where I was or what was going on. I stared at the red LED until it went out, and it was then pitch black again. By this time, I was fully awake so I got up and checked the rod. The line clip had been pulled. It must have been some liner!

I decided to stay up and as it began to get light, fish started to show. Both my rods were baited with only the Hookers tiger nut pop-ups and a small Funnelweb bag of halibut pellets. The fish seemed to be mainly in an area between me and the Slope swim, where I have seen fish on other occasions, and I got sucked into chasing them about. Quickly, I reeled in, hooked on another small bag, and cast to the fish. This went on for a while and it was starting to drive me mad. One would show, then an even better one in another area, and I was getting nowhere. I had to leave the rods alone but just after 7am, a big lump launched itself out, followed by another just to its side. 'That's it,', I said. 'One more cast, and then I'm going back to bed. I can't take it any more'. My lead landed between where the two fish had shown, so I slackened off the line, got back into my sleeping bag, turned my back on the water and tried to shut it all out.

The fish were going mad and all I could hear was the taunting sound of fish crashing out. Surely, one would find it! Just then, the last cast rod gave a few bleeps, and I was out there like a shot. It was a funny old bite, a bit tench-like, and as I picked up the rod, I could feel something on the end but it didn't feel big. It had to be a tench, or perhaps a small grass carp. Whatever it was, I just wound it in gently and at one stage it did take a tiny amount of line, as bigger tench often can, but it was soon in front of me in the deep margins, in the weed. I lifted it off the bottom with ease and as it came up all I could see was a great big, brown flank.

'My god! It's bloody Shoulders!' Before I knew it, he was in the net and I was screaming out, 'Shoulders!', as loud as I could. I was so happy it was unreal. I had caught my dream fish, one that I had always looked at in the press over the years, a fish with so much history and today Shoulders was mine! The weight was certainly irrelevant but for the record, he went 43lbs 8oz. To think I nearly went home on that trip! I was fully prepared to run the course to catch Shoulders, though, and I would have, no matter how long it may have taken. I've always believed you get out what you put in. I did work hard, too, so I told myself I'd earned what I was feeling that day, and I loved the feeling!

Ladders helps me to escort Shoulders to the mat.

Shoulders, the one I dreamed of catching.

After catching my target fish and having such a good run over at Horton, I didn't want to spoil things by going back. Let's just say I was happy with my result. It was still early enough in the year to have a break and fish a few other waters for a change of scenery, and although there were still loads that I dearly wanted to catch at Horton, I'd do it in my own time. I spent the rest of the year on Wellington Country Park mainly, intending to return to Horton maybe at the start of the next season. In March 2007, though, I turned up to fish the Road Lake, found I had the wrong gate key, and with Horton just around the corner, I thought I'd just call in there, have a brew and borrow a key from someone.

I popped into the lodge, made a brew, and then naturally, took a stroll down to the Plateau swim that was empty, amazingly. It was March but as soon as the temperature rises a degree or two those fish would definitely be in the area. I stood in the swim finishing off my coffee and I saw a fish, definitely a carp, and then another rolled. I thought no more of it and instinctively just went and got my gear to set up.

Nothing would stop me from smiling that day.

The weather was bang on for the time of year; unusually warm and it felt very carpy, if there is such a thing. Secret Dan (Dan Caller), was already plotted up in the One Up swim next door. He hadn't had any action so far but had seen the few fish that had rolled when I arrived. I knew roughly where the shallower spots were, so instead of plumbing and spooking the fish away, I just cast a couple of snowman rigs and stringers out to where the fish had shown earlier.

Within a little while I started to receive liners, just subtle ones but it was a good sign that told me the fish were still present. I had a few brews with Dan throughout the day and we chatted about what fish we would love to catch.
I said, "You know what? I haven't caught any commons yet. That's what I'd like, one of those original commons. That'd do!"

I was still getting a few liners and I love it when it's like that - you know you are up for some action - and then one of the liners carried on going. The fish didn't go mental, it just swam off the edge of the plateau and then plummeted into the deeper water. I kept a steady pressure on and just let the fish bob about a bit, all the time trying to steer it away from the plateau. Once in the margins, a few big boils came to the surface as my carp waved its tail deeper down, a few rod lengths out. Dan came and grabbed the net and soon we had a big-framed mirror rolling in it. 'Welcome back to Horton!' I said to myself.

My carp was one of the stockies one known as Pebbles, and she weighed 37lbs 5oz. She was a lovely-looking fish and I was well chuffed with my catch. Dan did me some photos, and back she went. Well, I was glad I'd called in to Horton. It's funny how things happen. Because I didn't have a key for the Road Lake, I had now caught a 37lbs 5oz mirror. Happy days!

I got the rod back out just before it got dark and settled down for the night ahead. As the evening drew in, the temperature dropped and Dan was now getting the liners. I was in my bivvy when I heard a Steve Neville alarm sound out from Dan's swim, so I went to see what was happening, and sure enough, Dan was playing a fish.

"Well done, mate," I said as I stood behind him and watched the action. Dan's fish gave a good scrap, and then it was my turn to hold the net so I crouched at the front of the swim and let Dan and his fish fight it out between them. In the dark, it came up to the surface and Dan steered his fish toward the waiting net. I had a horrible flashback, as a carp with a deformed-looking mouth was just about visible as it went in.
"I know what you've got, mate. It's the Parrot, son. Oi Oi! Well done, mate!"
Neither of us could believe it. As ugly as it is, it was one of the sought after

Pebbles welcomed me back to Horton.

Longfield fish, and one that I hoped to get even with. Dan was well chuffed. The old girl weighed 44lbs 8oz; I got some shots and Dan slid her back. We were having a good little session and we wondered just what else might be out there.

It was a quiet night for me fishing up on the Plateau, but at first light, I heard Dan's alarm once again singing its tune, so I grabbed my coffee and went to give a hand with the net. Dan was into a good fish and as I waited with the net, I noticed the change in the weather. It was considerably colder and the wind was now blowing up the other end of the lake. It was late March and only a few weeks previously it had been freezing, so we must have timed it just right for these few fish to come on the feed. As Dan's fish tired and made its last few attempts to get away, we could see that it was another good mirror. That was the exciting thing about Horton; you just never knew what you might catch, and the lake holds so many prizes.

Dan walked back in the swim and I slid the net under another big fish. "You've got a lump here, Dan." I said.

"Oi, oi! It's the Parrot, mate. Well done!"

He came and looked in the net and there lay one of those prizes I was talking about, a fish called Merlin. What cracking carp! Merlin was so-called because he just appeared one day, as if by magic. She was a fish that was on everyone's list. Dan had a major result. The Parrot and Merlin - what a catch, and what a session! Merlin weighed 42lbs and she was in great condition in all her winter colours. I got some nice shots and back she went. Dan's a great guy and he took it all in his stride, as Dan does, but I could see he was buzzing his head off. Well done, mate, that was historic! I left Dan to himself for a while, to let it all sink in.

Back in my own swim, I looked at the lake and tried to summarise all that had gone on. When I'd arrived the temperatures were definitely on the up, fish were present on and around the plateau and judging by what had been caught, I would imagine it was a fair-sized group of fish. I was receiving lots of liners and I'd caught Pebbles. As evening approached, the temperature fell, the fish dropped off the plateau into deeper water, and Dan started to receive liners and caught two amazing fish.

The wind was now hacking up toward the Sick and Church Bay end of the lake, but regardless of the conditions, I decided to give my swim another 24 hours and see if anything occurred. All the twitches and liners indicating that fish were present had disappeared and the weather was getting worse, with a bit of rain chucked in as well. Dan and I hadn't even seen a fish for over 24 hours and I took it as a sign that our magic trip might be over.

I started to pack all my bits up in the bivvy as I had to be off that day, anyway, and halfway through sorting out all my stuff, my left rod just burst into life. I jumped out and took control of the rod, a bit shocked by the take because I'd written off any further chances of action. This was a massive bonus and I played the fish carefully. I didn't want to make any silly mistakes and lose this one. It was Dan's turn with the net and as my fish rolled in the margins, we both saw the gold flank of a common.

"Brilliant," I said. "A common, just what I wanted."
The next time it came on the top, it was easily ready to net and in she went. What a turn up for the books! How lucky was I? At last, I'd caught a Horton common. It was a lovely fish and weighed 34lbs 12oz. Later, we identified it as one called Sid, as far as I know an original. It's great when your rod goes when you're packing up. It doesn't often happen, but when it does it sure makes me drive home with a big smile on my face, and I bet Dan smiled for weeks. What a great trip!

Merlin in all her winter colours at 42lbs.

At last I had caught a Horton common. Sid at 34lbs 12oz.

I was doing a bit of time here and there on other waters, but I couldn't stop thinking of some of the Horton originals still swimming about the lake. One fish I really did like was Wallace, a cracking linear mirror. It had a slight dip in its back and I'd seen a shot of it from a side-on angle; it looked stunning, and the fish was getting bigger all the time. There was a swim I really fancied that I thought she might just turn up in, the Gate in Dog Bay. I'd baited this spot in the Gate once before for a few weeks, and I'd found a nice bit of gravel on the back of some onion-type weed, about two rod lengths out. I'd been trickling in some bait and made plans to have a go, but before I even managed to get in there, someone - I can't remember who - saw some telltale signs of fish activity, put a rod to the area and caught Wallace. That always played on my mind, and I'm sure Wallace had been out from there before.

Anyway, I turned up on July the 7th and it was the first time since I'd fished in March with Dan. I had plans to fish the area, and it turned out okay really, as a good wind was pushing into the bay. Paul Moulder, who I worked with on Carp Addict magazine, was set up in the Shoulders, a couple of swims down and he had fish all over him. They were rolling about and showing themselves like crazy, and I thought back to when I'd moved in there one night after hearing them going bonkers, and then strangely, received no action. Maybe, on this occasion there would be a different outcome for Paul.

I set up back from the water's edge, flicked out the marker and pulled back through the silt until I felt the tap-tap-tap of gravel, and then the float locked up on the weed. 'That's good,' I thought, 'nothing has changed. I'd been having some really good successes on my syndicate water with a rig that was simply pop-up plastic Enterprise maize, only just popped up, with a shot on the hair just under the maize so that it sits upright on the bottom. I was so confident in this method that all I did was underarm spod out some hemp and corn beyond the weed, and then flick out my rig over the top. The other rod was fished more conventionally with the usual pop-up over boilies, further out in the pond.

After I had got myself sorted, I went and sat with Paul, and watched as the carp played about in front of his swim. The whole time I was there I just kept on about the fact that I was fishing the Wallace spot, she was bound to turn up, and in the end I believed it myself. I was probably driving Paul mad but we sat there until it was time to turn in and as I walked back to my swim, the carp were still at it in front of him. As I drifted off to sleep to the sound of carp jumping, I thought I was bound to be up later on to assist Paul with all the carp he was so going to catch.

Paul Gillings with the incredible Wallace at 43lbs 5oz.

The next thing I knew it was early morning, just getting light, and my rod on the Wallace spot was melting off. As I picked up the rod, it more or less just hooped over and line was demanded. The fish raced off, out toward the other side of Dog Bay at a rapid rate and didn't seem to have any intention of ever slowing down. It fought like a marlin, I kid you not, and I had to slow it down with my finger on the burning spool. At the end of a long run, I managed to turn it and then slowly, I pumped back this powerful fish. It was really aggressive and tore off on another series of long sprints, but it was using all its energy and that soon gave me the upper hand. Once I had it ready for the net I was able to see all the plated scales, and after another quick look, I knew I had just caught Wallace. Well, I was astounded. I secured the landing net and dashed off to tell Paul.
"Paul," I said. "Wake up! I've got Wallace!"
He looked at me and said,"No way. You bloody talked that one on the bank!"
"Honest, mate. Come and have a look."

I got back to my swim well before Paul and as I looked into the net, I realised that something wasn't right. As I stared at the fish, it suddenly morphed into the Woodcarving. Whoops! I'd wanted Wallace so badly that if I'd landed the Parrot that night, I would have seen Wallace in the net. Paul laughed when I told him but, hey, what a fish to catch! I'd always wanted the Woodcarving, as well. It's one of the best-looking carp in the country, but I never thought I'd catch it. It's a tricky one. Anyway, it got better - I had Carp Addict's designer with me to do the photographs, which all turned out fantastic. Thanks mate.

Wallace suddenly morphed into the Woodcarving.

The Woodcarving weighed 34lbs 12oz, a new top weight for her, and my little maize rig did the business. There's something about that rig. Strangely, Paul never got a sniff in that swim, not even a liner, and it was the same when I found them in there. It seems that they like the area but for some reason they just sit mid-water; another Horton puzzle.

My next time at Horton was to be at the draw in June 2008. I thought I'd try my luck because if I was lucky to get a good draw, then a good session could well be on the cards, and that might give me just one more chance at another original. What a bloody laugh! Me, do well at a draw? Not likely. Neither Glen Butler, a mate who was a member of my syndicate lake, or me got a swim on Horton. Typical!

A new member, Niall, came out first, and Tony Moulder, Paul's brother, was second. Tony always seems to do well at the draws. Anyway, I was chatting away and asked Tony what swim he fancied.
"I've only got two nights, because I'm off to work on Monday," he said.
I couldn't believe my ears. The season kicked off on the Saturday and he was only on for two nights? This could well be my way on to the lake.
"So, if you're off on Monday," I said, "and if I was to set up on the Boat Pool, that's just behind Horton, I should be able to jump in your swim when you leave."
"Yeah," he said. Fantastic. What a result! I was chuffed to bits.

It all depended on where the new member chose to go. I was hoping that someone would wise him up and that he'd end up in the Plateau swim. If that were the case, then Tony would go in One Up. I had it all planned out, I hoped. I spoke to Glen and said it might be worth him jumping on the Boat Pool as well, you never know who might pull off. Glen agreed. Tony did end up in One Up and the new guy, Niall, went in the Plateau as I'd thought he would. I couldn't believe it. I would be in One Up two days into the season, that was as good as coming out second in the draw myself!

Glen and me plotted up on the Boat Pool, but it was only camping and waiting, really. Once we were set up we went and sat with the lads on Horton, with sufficient supplies of brandy and coke for a good social with Tony and a few others. Barney (Mick Barnes), was the CEMEX Angling boss at the time and was on the opposite bank. I remember sending him text messages that evening and getting the typical Barney replies, something like, 'yeah, I'm trying to enjoy myself but some noisy twat on the other bank is making lots of racket'. Good old Barney, he was great for CEMEX.

Tony with a 30 on the first morning.

Glen and me left Tony, probably to his relief, and stumbled back to our swims. When I awoke in the morning, it seemed that I'd managed to cast my rods so close in that they were still on the bank. They were in the reeds, and my head hurt. Still, it gave Glen a laugh.

That first morning, Shoulders graced the bank for the first time since I had caught her some eighteen months earlier, and mid-morning, I photographed a fish called Chips, one of the stock fish for Tony at 34lbs 10oz. Things were looking good and I was itching to get the swim now. Later that evening, the magnificent Thorpe Park Common was caught by Niall in the Plateau at 39lbs 9oz. What a fish to open your account with! Glen and me just hung about like a couple of vagrants with another bottle of brandy. We were really enjoying the start to the new season.

Fish were obviously getting around the Plateau area as well as off the side of it, as the next day Tony had another 30, and the lad in the Plateau caught himself a 40 mirror and a 20. The night before Tony was to leave I got chatting to the lad in the Plateau, and astonishingly, he told me that he was thinking of going. I could not believe what I was hearing. He was having a session of a lifetime; a 39, and a 40! Maybe he was so happy with what he'd caught that he thought he'd call it a day. I told Glen to speak to him, and line himself up for the Plateau.

The next morning, Tony didn't have to be off too early, and I was there waiting patiently. It must have been hard for Tony to pull off and I am so glad he didn't try to pull a sicky at work. Eventually, I got plotted up in my new swim. It was worth the wait on the Boat Pool, and not long after I was all set up, Glen moved into the Plateau. What a result for both of us! That was definitely one for the book of Ninja tactics.

As the fish were already in and around the area, my approach was to fish single pop-ups on the chod rig. I had some nice chocolate malt pop-ups that Lee at Hookers had rolled for me; they were yellow, but not a bright yellow. I cast both my rods into the weed off the side of the Plateau, slackened off the lines and all was set. Ash Bradley had moved in one swim down from me, and I had never really met Ash properly, but I must say he's a really nice bloke and we had a right old laugh. At times, the weather was bright and hot, and because of that, more fish were turning up in the area. Ash and me had a muck about with zigs and at one stage we both had fish circling our hook baits that were just on the surface, but no bites materialised.

It was still the start of the new season, the atmosphere was electric, and some very good fish had been caught, all at really good weights. Glen and me were sitting pretty and if we didn't catch, then it would have been damned unlucky.

My old mate Pebbles, destined to be a 40.

Ash shouted, "Jerry you're away." I'd forgoten to turn my alarm on.

Early afternoon, one of my choco malts was picked up and I was into a battle with a heavy carp. The fish just plodded about, using its own weight to keep deep down near the lakebed, and I could only think that I had a big fish on. The ribbon weed gave me a few problems but I soon had a large mirror in the landing net, and I was to discover that I had recaptured Pebbles. I hate recaptures, but they are unavoidable. I weighed her, took a couple of quick snaps to savour the moment, and then slipped her back. She was bigger than when I'd caught her last and this time she was 38lbs 8oz, a fish soon destined to be another 40 in the lake, and a nice one at that.

I got my rod back out to the same area, slackened off the line, and walked halfway between the swims for a chat with Glen. We were chatting away for a while and Glen was having a bit of banter with Ash. Something about him always cooking burgers, so Glen had nicknamed him Ash Burger, or something like that, and Ash came back with Glen Bap. It kept them both happy for a while, which was all that mattered.

Ash was near my rods when he shouted, "Jerry! You're away!" The recast rod was flying and when I'd slackened my line off, I realised that I hadn't turned my alarm on, something I have a habit of doing. To be honest, I think I do it now automatically, unconsciously thinking that if I don't turn it on, I seem to get a take.

Glen was over the moon with this 36-pounder.

Anyway, I was into another very good fish. Ash grabbed the net and the battle was under way. It was identical to the previous one, and it even weeded me up in the same patch of weed, but thankfully, it wasn't Pebbles again. I can't remember what this one was called but it looked close to 40lbs. I wasn't far off, because it went 39lbs 12oz and this was another of the stock fish. Who could ever moan about catching two upper-30 fish in an afternoon? I certainly wouldn't.

Later in the day, Glen decided to entertain us when he hooked a grebe. How on earth did he manage that? In all my angling life, I have never seen this, but Glen found a way. Olli, one of the fishery bailiffs, was quick to come and assist.
"Leave it to me," he said. " I'll sort that."
"Sod your luck, mate. They are ferocious on the bank," we said.
Olli did sort out the grebe, and he received a few jabs from its sharp beak, but the bird was soon back again and diving in front of Glen's swim.

Glen was in fits when he caught that grebe, not because he had caught a bird, but he didn't know how he'd done it. Anyway, just into dark, Glen went and hooked a carp this time. I went to help out, and a short while later, Glen's fish was ready for the net. It was really dark by this time and hard to see what was going on, but Glen did well and he soon had a nice old lump in the bottom of his net. He was over the moon, and so was I. We got all the necessary equipment ready

Between the showers I caught an 11lb tench.

and hoisted the heavy fish to the mat. It was another big carp and weighed in at 36lbs. These stock fish were going to be massive in the future and they were piling the weight on. We got some night shots as Glen smiled his head off. He was one happy angler.

There was no action during the night, well none to our rods, anyway, but at first light Glen caught another one, a 34lb mirror. He was loving Horton. The weather was on a bit of a turn now, it looked like rain would soon be upon us, and I hoped this wouldn't push the fish away from the plateau area. It did start to rain, but just little downpours, then the sun would be out and it'd be red hot again. Between those showers, I caught a massive tench that went 11lbs. I just had to weigh it and get a photo of it. By the way it took off, I thought I was away with a carp.

I'd been fishing the same tactics with the chod, but had started to fire out a few boilies to get the fish searching for food items. It had just stopped raining again when my chod was picked up and a one-toner howled on the right-hand rod. Ash and Glen came to watch as I did battle with the unknown carp on the end. It tried all the usual tricks, like kiting long down the margins and then weeding me up in the ribbed grass, but a little bit of pressure soon had a dark older-looking carp ready for the net. Ash did the business and netted it first go. On looking in the net, I knew it wasn't one of the stockies. 'What have we here, then?' I thought. It wasn't one that I recognised.

Carefully, we got her on the mat and weighed her at 34lbs 12oz. She really was a cracking-looking carp. It had just been raining again but the sun was now out and Ash was doing the photos when Del Smith came walking down the bank to see what was going on. I will never forget what he said. "Well done, Jerry. That's the Big Grey. It took me ten years to catch that one!"

The fish I was holding turned into a precious bit of history and I was so chuffed to have caught such an old carp. These were the ones I was after. The Longfield history fish were a dying breed, they wouldn't be around for ever. Well, I was so made up after that, and I must thank Ash as the shots he took are among the best pictures of a carp that I've ever had. Thanks very much, mate.

It seemed that I'd caught that one just in time as the weather really did come in and it chucked it down. The carp moved further off the back of the Plateau, and an angler over in the Spindly Tree opposite started to get into the fish. I did another night but the next day I packed up. I'd already done two nights on the Boat Pool so I had been on the bank for some five days and it was time to go home. Glen was still buzzing away in the Plateau so I left him to it and he caught a couple more fish before he left. He'd also had a good trip.

It was a great session that I'll never forget, especially the way it all panned out with the draw and all. I had some great fishing at Horton Church Lake, and after having caught five of the originals, I was more than happy to call it a day. I didn't want to spoil my long run of success on the water since losing the Parrot. In all that time, I hadn't blanked once! Long live the Horton originals.

I was so happy to catch this one, a proper old fish.

Chapter Eight
Cleverley Mere and the Amaizing Rig

For a few years now I have been involved in Scott 'Geezer' Grant's charity match, in aid of Great Ormond Street hospital. It's always a great event and it's a good cause that I truly love to be involved in. Every year the usual suspects turn up to fish, including a lot of big names in our sport; Rob Maylin, Lee Jackson, Nigel Sharp, Gary Bayes... to name just a few, and before the paying, anglers make a bid to fish with them and this is one way that funds are raised. It's run like a carp match, where the 'celebrity anglers', as Geezer likes to call them, and their partners fish together as a team. All the fish weights are recorded and the final highest weight makes them the winner.

Rob Maylin is always very keen to keep hold of his title in this competition. He'd won it two years on the trot, with his partner, until the previous one when my partner and I took the title, sadly for Rob...but we won't go into that.

Before the draw for swims, we met in the car park and it was a good chance to meet friends that we didn't get to catch up with during the season. Nigel Sharp, always prepared, already had his kettle going, so I grabbed my cup. Good old Nige. The first thing that comes from Nige's mouth is normally some sort of abuse or piss-take, and I wouldn't expect anything else. He's great, but once we've ribbed each other for a little while, we always move on to the serious stuff. Our angling is something we both live for.

Nigel's fishing partner was with him; a guy called Galvin who I just have to mention is the infamous Phil Harper's son. I didn't know Galvin at the time, but he seemed a nice bloke and as we started chatting about all things carpy, he told me he was fishing on a lake called Cleverley Mere. I knew nothing about the place back then, because it wasn't as well known as as it is today, but

Galvin had some photos with him and after he started flicking through them, I wanted to know more. Some of the fish he was showing me were stunning, but the one that really caught my eye was a mirror called Hendrix. The colours of this fish made it look like a woodcarving, with big plated scales, and at over 40lbs I was sold. I wanted a ticket! Galvin was a bailiff on the water, run by Ben Lofting, so I asked him to put in a good word for me and see if I could get on, and he said he'd would try his best for me.

The whole time I was at that charity event, I kept asking him questions about Cleverley, and looking at his photos. The lake did hold some very big fish. There was one called Ringo that was upper-40, another called Giggsy and a ghostie common, both close to 40, and a few others were getting up there. Wow! They'd kept that quiet! Galvin told me that the lake was about nine acres and split into two ends by a bottleneck, and one end had an island. I hoped I'd get a ticket.

The charity event went well, with lots of banter and a big social on the Saturday night. I have to say a big 'well done' to Scott Grant for such a well-run event. I know he puts a lot into it, as do all the other staff and marshals. They work so hard and have raised a huge amount of money for Great Ormond Street. Nice one, mate!

I kept in touch with Galvin, and one day, Ben Lofting called me and asked if I'd like to go over to the Mere for a walk round. I met up with him and he proudly showed me around the lake, a nice-looking water with a few nice bays. One of the swims took command of the narrow channel and he'd called it the Bowls because it had some craters on the lakebed over toward the reeds on the far side. Ben told me about all the stock and, as you can imagine, I was very relieved when he said I could have a ticket. I rang Galvin with the good news and he was pleased, so a whole new adventure lay before me and I was itching to get started.

I did a bit of homework and found out that a lot of bait was going in, mainly boilies. I had already made up my mind to steer clear of them for a while, and see how I got on, because I'd noticed that it was slow going and not too many fish were getting caught. My first trip to the Mere was late September, and when I arrived there was a nice wind blowing right into the car park end of the lake. There were two swims at this end, the Car Park, and next door, JRs. These two

The wind was pushing into the bank.

swims looked straight up the lake and with the wind pushing into this bank, I thought it would be a good area to start, so I didn't even bother walking round.

I can't remember who'd told me, but someone had said that this end normally only produced the smaller fish, although why that should be was beyond me; it was just crying out 'carp'. The lakebed was mainly clay and gravel in this area, with a few silt pockets here and there, and all along my margins there was some nice weed that went out ten or 15 feet, and then dropped off nicely, making some nice close-in patrol routes for the carp.

Previously, I'd been messing around with a rig that came about while I was fishing on my own syndicate lake, Carthagena. I'd been baiting with boilies throughout the close season, and Cartha carp will trough boilies all day long, they love them, as do most carp. So, at the start I'd managed a few fish just fishing bottom baits, but over the following few weeks as the new season progressed, and the bites became fewer and fewer, this got me thinking.

June, at 28lbs, was among the haul.

I had to change something, so I stopped putting out any more large round baits, and instead, mixed up some hemp, a small amount of corn, some 10mms and barrels, and my hook bait was a barrel tipped with some plastic corn. This was more of a carpet feed and I hoped that they would become engrossed and I would get some more action, because they were definitely shying away from beds of round boilies. Well, the action did return and I had the edge once again, but I wondered if it was just the yellow plastic on the end of my barrel hook bait that was getting me the bites.

On my next trip, I baited with hemp, corn, and nothing that resembled a boilie, with all the 10mms and barrels broken and squashed into little pieces. I had baited the swim for a few days and was going to fish for 48 hours, so this time I fished a size 10 Mugga, with one piece of Enterprise pop-up maize fished lengthways on the hair and popped up only half an inch off the bottom. It looked really good when checked in the margins, and I was sure that it would work. I was fishing to an area of smooth silt behind a weed bed that followed the contours of the margins in about nine feet of water. As soon as night fell,

Sandy - one of 11 takes that session.

the old liners started and at 10pm my first fish was caught. Throughout the night I went on to bank a further four carp, all good fish to just shy of 30lbs. For the time being, my new method was a winner and my only concern was that the size 10 hook was not man enough, as the fish were really fighting hard and I did lose one.

I took out a pack of size 8 Muggas and they looked stronger, but I didn't want to fish a big 8 popped-up so I tied one up with a longer hair and a rig ring to fish the maize blow-back style. I left a gap under the maize and pinched on a small shot. It took a bit of fiddling around until I got the right weight of shot but once placed in a jar of water it looked spot on. The size 8 Mugga lay flat on the bottom, with the maize sitting upright; the curve of the hook, with the ring on the shank, would work perfectly, blow-back fashion. Over the 48 hours, I landed a further six carp on this rig, making 11 carp in the session. Catches like that on the Carthagena syndicate are very rare, so had I stumbled upon something good here?

Anyway, back to Cleverley. So I didn't have all my eggs in one basket, I fished my maize rig on one rod, boilie on another, and one had a tiger nut. That first night I intended to experiment to see what came up trumps. Instead of fishing over hemp, corn, or other particle baits with the maize rig, I made up a tight ball of maggots, using PVA Webcast, about the size of a tangerine, attached this by pushing the hook point through the PVA knot, and found that I was able to cast it a fair distance without it coming off. I put half a PVA foam nugget around the hair, between the hook and the maize, and when I tested one in the margins, the PVA bag of maggots started to dissolve, the plastic maize popped-up the length of the hook link, and the maggots spread in a nice circle around the rig. Then the hook bait foam melted and the rig descended among the maggots, looking very good. The conditions were spot on, too, with the wind still pushing down my end, and the clouds darkening. It felt very carpy, although I hadn't seen any. I woke during the night wondering what was going on, thinking maybe I should have fished up the other end of the lake.

At first light, the maize rig signalled a bite and I was into my first Cleverley carp. It felt small and I soon landed a chunky little mirror of around 13lbs, but it's always nice to get that first one out of the way. All I could think of, though, was what someone had said – 'you only get the small ones down this end.' That played on my mind for a little while before I loaded up the car and made my way to the other end of the lake.

It was quiet, so I had a good look about and eventually settled in a swim called the Field. I climbed to the top of one of the trees and was able to see all that was out to the front of it. There was a lot of weed between the margins and the island, but the margins to the left looked good, and toward the left-hand edge of the island it looked as if the weed dropped away. 'That'll do for tonight', I thought, and set up feeling confident for the night ahead. All the rigs went down nicely on good spots and I thought I was sure to catch.

I woke up in the morning having not heard a fish or received a single bleep to the rods all night. I shinned up the tree for a look and could see that the water was crystal clear, and there wasn't a sign of a carp up this end of the lake. The wind was still blowing nicely down the other end - and where was I? Right on the back of it! I had a bit of a panic attack as I realised my error. What the hell was I doing at this end of the lake? I packed away again as quickly as possible, threw it all on

My first Cleverley carp.

the barrow and this time, instead of putting it in the back of the car again, I barrowed it all the way to the other end, deciding to fetch the car later. As I neared my previous swim, my heart sank as I saw someone set up in there. What an idiot I'd been to listen to what other people thought. I should have just trusted my instincts - a lesson learned. The swim next door, named JRs, was still free, though, so I wheeled my barrow past my old swim. I was bloody shattered! That was a long old tab around the lake, but straight away, I knew I'd made the right decision this time. The wind was churning the lake, which was all coloured up, and as I stood there scanning my new stretch of water, one rolled about 50 yards out. I made a mental note of its position and started ripping my barrow to pieces as I tried to sort a couple of rods out.

Quickly, I set up the net and alarms. I already had two maize rigs ready so it was just a case of making up and tying on the PVA balls of maggots. I aimed the first rod to where the fish had shown, and felt it go down hard. Perfect! It was fairly deep, around 11 feet. I put the next rod a little further out and more to the left, slackened the lines right off, bobbins on the deck, and sat next to the rods on my low chair.

I didn't bother switching on the alarms because it was so windy. I would just watch the bobbins. I looked behind me and my tackle was everywhere. I'd been in such a rush to get those rods out that it was all over the place. It looked as if I'd just walked into the swim and tipped the barrow over.

I sat there for a while. A few more fish showed and it looked spot on for some action. The whole time, I was scanning the water and then glancing down at the bobbins, so when I looked at them and saw the left-hand rod's bobbin tight at the top, with the line bow tight, I was shocked. I stood up, picked up the rod and it took on a curve. I was into a carp!

The fish didn't do too much, just slowly kited and stayed deep down as it went, but I had a good idea that this was a big fish. It continued to be in charge, slowly taking line at will until I was able to get it closer in, and only then did it come to the surface with a big 'boil up' of water. I was able to see the pale flanks of a big mirror and as I was standing on a little jetty. I just jumped straight in the lake dragging the net with me, and played out the rest of the fight waist deep in the lake. She lay on her side, beaten at last, and I steered her into the net, punching the air and giving it, 'Yes!' - so pleased with my catch.

Just as I was bringing the net and rod to the bank Galvin turned up. God knows what it must have looked like, tackle everywhere, and me soaked to the chest about to get out of the lake. I do remember a grin on Galvin's face though. He must have thought I was a nutter!
"What you got, mate?" he said.
"A good mirror," I replied. "Here have a look."
He looked in the net and said, "That's Giggsy, mate. One of the big 'uns, last out at upper-30."

I couldn't believe my luck! I'd caught one of the A team on my first trip! Galvin held the net while I tried to extract my sling, scales and all the bits from the wreckage of my swim, Giggsy weighed in at an all-time best of 40lbs 7oz and I remember thinking, 'only the small ones seem to get caught down this end. Yeah, right on!'

Eventually, I did get set up properly in the swim and over two more nights I caught another four fish, bringing my first session total to six. There couldn't have been a better way to open the account, but more importantly, my method of catching

'Only the small ones get caught down this end.'

them was a definite winner and something I wanted to keep close to my chest. The only person I did tell was Galvin, and he soon started putting the rig to good use. I really liked that end of the lake and the fish did get down there in numbers in certain conditions. I caught a few more from there but it was getting harder and harder to get into that area, as is the norm when a few fish get caught.

I fished around the lake in various swims over the next few trips, and the rig was fantastic. If I could get on carp I would catch fish, and I'm sure a few of the regulars were wondering what I was up to. A few times, anglers came for a chat and I would pray that I didn't get a take while anyone was in my swim. Now, I know it's nothing special. It's only a bit of plastic maize, but my catch rate was getting better all the time and if that was the winning method, it was worth its weight in gold. When I had my rods in, leaning against the bivvy or a tree, I'd always take off the maize and lead shot and replace it with a couple of glugged-up boilies. People would come for a chat and their eyes always ended up looking at my rigs and everyone was piling in boilies with not a great deal to show for it.

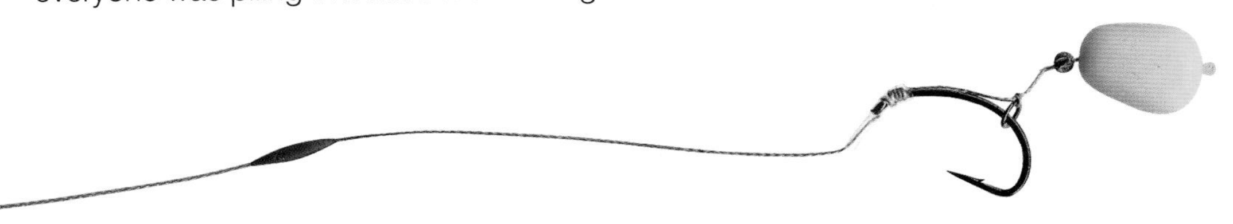

On all lakes, there will be a method, a way to catch them when all is quiet, but most of us tend to sit it out and say, 'oh, they just aren't having it at the moment', which is true in most cases, but fish are either resting or eating, it's really all they can do. Back on Tolpits, it used to go quiet for weeks on end without anything getting caught. One particular night, I was woken by fish crashing tight to the opposite bank, I went round to investigate and they were about two rods lengths out, rolling and topping as if they were on to something big time. I went back to my swim, packed down, and moved round there into a 'no bivvy' swim that wasn't fished much, probably for that reason. I managed to squeeze my umbrella in, a bit twisted here and there, but who gives a damn.

At daybreak, I flicked out a tiny Arsley bomb and pulled back. The water was about 11 feet deep, the bottom felt like thick silt and when I inspected the lead, the swivel had a large bloodworm caught in it. Bingo! That's why it had been so quiet, not because they were 'not having it at the moment'. I'm sure they don't just stop eating. I flicked out two smelly, fishy 14mm bottom baits and slackened the line off fully. The bubbling continued and I kept an eye on my slack line as little tweaks told me they were still about.

I was shattered, having been up for most of the night, and it started to rain early afternoon so I decided to have a bit of a kip. I was awoken by the first run in weeks and as I picked the rod up, the carp was already halfway across the lake. As the big ones do, it hit the surface and from there, all I had to do was guide her back to my margin. I heard something behind me, looked over my shoulder, and saw about six anglers standing there, watching. One guy picked up my net. I had a few lily pads to contend with, in close, but nothing serious. It was without doubt one of the big 'uns and it slowly came in, but once close, held the bottom. I had played it very gently. The lead core appeared through the lily pads, the net went in and I was moments away from seeing my prize when the hook pulled, and all went slack. Gutted, or what! I turned to the lads for some condolences but no one was there, although I'm sure they had been!

Anyway, what could have been, eh? All I'm saying is that sometimes we have to dig a bit deeper and it's what I love about carp fishing. I'd get bored if it was a case of 'yeah, chuck a few boilies over there, mate, in that gully. It's a dead cert that you'll catch all night long.' Thankfully, the carp are not as silly as that! It was obvious that they liked the maggots at Cleverley and were just clearing the area of them, while hoovering up anything else in their path. Any hook bait could have been used, but the maize worked well enough for me not to start messing about with something that was already doing the job.

Up before dawn, watching and waiting.

One October afternoon, I turned up, had a walk around and spoke to one angler who had been on for a couple of nights. He'd had a 20lb common but not much else was happening, so I said good luck to him and carried on. I passed the Tall Tree swim and arrived at the Field from where I could look across toward the island. Between the left-hand edge of it and the bank, there was a channel which went around the island. There was no wind on that part of the water and I noticed some bubbling in the channel area. As I watched for a while, I began to see more and more and that was enough for me. I whipped round, back past matey, to get my gear.

While I was setting up, I saw a fish roll and that was just the evidence I needed! With everything all ready to go, I decided to walk all the way round to take a closer look from the other side. So, back I went again, round past matey, who must have thought I'd forgotten things. From the other side, I was able to line up exactly where I wanted to cast my rigs, and I didn't care what the bottom was like or how deep it was. Another fish showed while I was round there, and I took an excited jog back to my swim. I was worried about one thing, though, because the Bowls swim was occupied and to the right was another little swim that would look perfectly to where the fish were showing. If the angler caught wind of it, he could easily move his rods into that little swim and it would be game over. As I tied up my Funnel Web maggot bags, more

An absolute powerhouse of a common.

fish were showing and I couldn't get a rod out quickly enough. The first rod sailed out there, I feathered it down and it landed with a nice thump on what must have been more clay, and the other rod was put out at the same distance up the channel, but about 15 feet to the left.

After only a short time, I started to get the liners, and it wasn't long before another carp fell foul of the Amaizing Rig. Matey, from down the bank, came along as he had heard the run and he couldn't believe it.
"Blimey!" he said. "You didn't take long."
"Yeah," I said. "I cast to a showing fish."
I had a good hard battle with an absolute powerhouse of a common and opened up my session with a 27-pounder.

It felt so good to be able to catch them like that; I felt as if I could go anywhere and catch carp. The fish were not put off by one of their friends getting caught, and they continued to show and bubble away. I think the guy in the Bowls eventually sussed what was going on and left me to it. Good etiquette, mate! I was soon away with another fish and the bloke next door came and looked, but didn't hang around, and I didn't see him until the next day. I landed another common of 24lbs, and the bites went on until I'd had six takes, and then sometime in the darkness, they did the off.

They fed until darkness, then did the off.

When I'd joined the lake in early September, I'm sure that Galvin was top rod and although I'm not into all that 'top rod' business, I'm trying to get across just how effective my methods were. He'd had something like 24 fish, and although I'd only been a short time on the water, I was not a million miles away. Having said that, he was on the rig and when he was fishing, he was getting among them, too. My targets on Cleverley were Hendrix and Ringo, and I was wondering if I would see either of them in my net before winter set in.

Late October, and I was down for a three-nighter. I'd wanted a chance in the notorious Bowls swim, but it was hardly ever empty, so on this occasion I couldn't believe my luck when I arrived and saw it free. I thought perhaps all the big 'uns had been out or something, and although I didn't need to, I sprinted to the swim with my bucket to secure my plot. No one was going to get there before me, even though there was no one around.

After I'd set up, I breathed a sigh of relief. I was in the Bowls swim, yippee! With three nights ahead, anything could happen. I could see why it was a good swim. Anything that was passing through would have to come past me at some stage, but the channel was wide enough for the fish to live in the area. The far bank had a nice set of reeds that went back a fair way, with good depths for the fish to hide away in, and to the right where the reeds finished, there was a little bit that cut back, and the entrance to this area is supposedly where the craters are. There were good margins under the rod tips, too, and as the channel was wide there were plenty of little spots across it.

I went round and climbed the tree on the reed line so I was able to look down into the reed beds. Before long, I was seeing carp emerging from the reeds and swimming along for a bit and then re-entering further along. On the reed fringe, it dropped away to some good depths and with my glasses on I was able to see what lay below, which was a fair bit of blanket weed, as well as Canadian, but there were some nice sandy and clay-looking clear spots.

These were the areas I was trying to line up from the bank. It was a long walk back to the swim and I must have been backwards and forwards all afternoon that day until I was satisfied with where I wanted to place my baits. I couldn't afford to make many mistakes with the maggots. I could lose a whole bag each time, and they would be all over the place, so the spots I chose had to suit the rig. It wouldn't work the same on a choddy bottom.

I had to find my spots with the marker, walk back round, check it was okay from up the tree, then check that if I cast left or right of it my rig would lie in the clear.

Then I cast just the lead on it, clipped up and tied my rig on. A hell of a lot of mucking about, but I knew it could well be worth it. So, I fished two on the reed line and one toward the crater on a nice smooth area, and with all the traps set, I was buzzing, anticipating some action.

As the night drew in, I imagined the carp were leaving the sanctuary of the reed beds and were out on the prowl for grub. Every now and then I would hear one bosh out and see the ripples as they lapped against my bank. Suddenly, out of nowhere, the right-hand reed rod pulled up tight and immediately I lifted into a fish. I felt it as it tried to get back in the reeds, so I turned its head and then it just came off. Gutted, I reeled in quickly to see what had happened and there was no hook. I'd been bitten off, or cut on a mussel or something. I had most of my hook link and the very end of it was not cut clean but frayed.

I thought I'd been bitten off and I'd heard of this before, when they take it right back and chew with their pharyngeal teeth. I preferred to think that anyway, because it could only mean that they were eating with total confidence; so it was 1-0 to the carp.

I had to get the rod back out quickly as darkness was upon me, so I paced the rod out to a marker and clipped up, tied on the bag of wrigglers and whizzed it back out to the reed line. It landed as well as it could, considering the light, so I left it, knowing that if I kept on trying I would only end up not getting it out at all.

That night seemed to be darker than usual and I could hear the fish as they rolled on the surface out in the channel. At 10pm the other reed rod burst into action, and I was quick to get this fish away from the reed line. Luckily, it didn't fight too hard, and was soon under the rod tip and ready for the net. In the darkness, I pulled the net toward me so I was able to take a look at my capture. It was a very strange-looking mirror, which looked more like a giant shubunkin, with a weird-shaped body like a cut and shut. Anyway, it was a fish at least. I don't think I weighed it, just got a couple of quick snaps and set it free.

The rod was rebaited with a maggot ball and cast back to the general area, as best as I was able. In the middle of the night, that recast rod had me up, once again, playing a fish, and a long, hard battle ended with me landing a nice 27lb powerhouse of a common. This was turning into another good session! To top the already productive night, just before daybreak, the rod in the crater area was off and a slow heavy carp plodded about the channel. I felt as if I was playing the fish for ages. Every time I got it close to the net, it waved its tail from side to side and powered off, away from the net.

She went over 35lbs.

I'd seen that it was another common, but there was no point in rushing it. It was a fit fish but would soon tire; a few more attempts to get away from the net and she gave up and lay on her side as I steered the determined old girl over the net cord.

She was a big-framed, deep carp, and I wasn't surprised when she went over 35lbs. What a great night's fishing! One lost and three banked. I found out later that the common was one known as Cash. I got some good photos of her, as it was now light, followed by a well-earned cup of tea and then back to the bag, absolutely shattered.

During daylight hours there was no action to the rods and I wondered just how many were still left in the bay, so I spent most of that day up and down the trees on the reed line, watching the carp in and out of the reeds. There were still plenty of fish about and I was hoping they'd be out and about later that night and that I would be in for some more action.

Not long into darkness, the action resumed - they were definitely creatures of the night - and I started the evening off with another nice upper-20 common. There really were some spectacular commons in Cleverley. Pleased with my session, I started wondering if any of the other big 'uns would turn up. Surely they had to be somewhere in the area? A few fish woke me in the night, they were crashing out in the channel, not tight to the reeds, so I reeled one rod in and re-baited with a nice ball of maggots. It cast out so nicely, going down with a reassuring thump, and I knew that it would only need to be near fish and I would receive some action. It was a very good rig to cast at showing fish, providing the bottom was firm.

It felt like I had only just drifted off to sleep when the recast rod was away. These sessions are great, and the fact that they don't happen that often helps me to enjoy every minute of them. This fish tried its best to escape from the channel and into the other part of the lake, heading down to the car park end to my right. The rod was bent sideways as I gave it some serious side strain until I felt the fish turn, and I could hear it on the surface. From there, I just had to get her back into the channel, so I kept the side strain on and carefully steered the fish back toward me. In the past, I've played a fish for a while using side strain, and just when I've got them back where I want them, I've changed the rod angle and they've fallen off. This is something I'm always wary of now. Sometimes, the change of angle is enough for this to happen.

This time, though, I had no problems, thankfully, and I soon had this one ready for the waiting net. A nice-sized fish was pulled back in the net, and on inspection, I saw it was a grey-looking mirror with noticeably small pecs. It weighed in at just over 30lbs and Ben told me, later, that it was one known as Melted Pecs. The name suited it because they really did look just like they'd been melted. Nevertheless, it was a cracking carp that I was very pleased to have caught, and this fish made my already mega session even better.

She had little melted pecs.

I got the rod back out and stuck the kettle on. I must have sat there for an hour or so listening to the odd fish, and it was about 3am when I started to feel tired and decided to get back in the bag. You know how it is, though, I had the feeling that as soon as I got comfortable something would happen, and a bleep or a liner would have me racing out of the brolly. I was expectant and on it.

The funny thing is that I was sure there was another angler just to my left in the Gap swim, and I can't quite remember if he was in that one or a bit further along, but I do recall that he was totally oblivious to any of the action. I was once again falling into REM stage, when an almighty carp walloped out, somewhere near the craters. I nearly jumped out of my skin, it was such a big crash, and I was out in an instant with sleeping bag still attached - lucky it wasn't strapped to the bedchair, or I'd have taken that, too! The carp had thrown itself out a little further than where I was fishing so I reeled in, quick-style, attached a new ball of maggots and made a cast to the area. I was happy that it went down okay and was close to, if not bang on, the spot.

I really had to get some sleep now after two nights of action. I was dead beat and drifted off wondering which fish it was that had made such a big noise. I don't like to keep on writing 'and then my rod ripped off again', but it's the truth, that's exactly what happened. I found myself standing there, half asleep, with a heavy old carp on the end. I've done this many a time, as I'm sure many of you have. Somehow, you're playing a fish before you properly wake up. This one was different to the others, though. It took line at will, and a few times it just sat on the bottom as if it was weeded up. A steady pressure eventually got it moving again and the whole time it was keeping itself deep on the lakebed. Slowly, I gained some line, a bit at a time, and then the fish would take some back. Every now and then, it went aggressive and stripped a fair amount of line and I had to just finger the spool to try to slow it down. She was tiring now, and I managed to get her up on the surface. I knew she was beaten and, as she wallowed about on the top, I drew her carefully over the net. My heart was pounding as I wondered what I'd just caught.

I grabbed my torch. I already had everything else ready from the previous action, so I flicked the torch on to the red beam, and shone it into the net. It was a huge mirror. It was Ringo - it had to be. Before me lay a new PB, and one of my main targets in the lake. I was blown away and I couldn't believe it. I got all the bits ready but I'd have to sack her up for a while to get someone over to do the photos. She was heavy as I lifted her to the mat, but I only wanted to confirm it was her on the scales and then get her back into the water quickly. The scales read 48lbs 14oz so I punched the air and gave a little 'Oi Oi!' No one heard though, and I didn't care, because I knew!

A pig in a sack.

I waded out in my chesties, safely sacked her up, and then rang a couple of mates, Neil and Chad, who were fishing on my own syndicate lake. I gave them the news and immediately they grabbed their cameras and started out on the hour-long journey over to Cleverley Mere. Good old boys! That's what good carp angling mates are like.

When they arrived, I relived the last 48 hours of the session, and they listened with great interest. They were happy for me and it was great to have those two there with me to share this capture. The fish had been sacked for about four hours by the time the light was good enough for the shots. It was a beautiful morning but misty, and this was why it took a while to do the photos. A lovely red sunrise came up on the horizon and the mist hovered over the lake. It really was a sight!

When we were ready, I decided to re-weigh the fish, and this time she settled the scales at 48lbs; that was good enough for me. Later, I spoke to Gary Bayes and he informed me that they could lose up to 4oz of fluid per hour in the sack. I wasn't worried about a few ounces, though, and 48lbs was great. We got some really good shots and nice scenics of the dawn, and that was one special morning that I will never forget.

Reeled in, and recast bang on the spot.

Ringo. A new PB.

Neil and Chad made off back to Carthagena, and I was left in a swim that looked as if I had once again just slung stuff all over the place. I rang Galvin to tell him my news and he was happy for me and said that he was on his way over to fish. When he arrived, I told him that I'd had enough. Even though I had another night, I was too shattered, and anyway, I was more than happy with six fish, and one that I'd lost. With two nice 30s and a new PB of 48lbs, it was time to go home.

Galvin jumped in the Bowls after me, and unbelievably, he too went on to catch six fish. He had Giggsy at over 40, and he caught the last one that I wanted, Hendrix, at 40-plus. I then thought that perhaps I should have stayed. All Galvin's fish came naturally to the Amaizing Rig.

Before the winter took hold of the country, I managed one last trip to Cleverley. I was lucky to get back in the Bowls swim again, but the action was slowing down as the water temperature was dropping. I still had a couple of fish, though, topped by a 31lb mirror called Bella that had great big orange pecs. She was to be my last one of the year because after that, it started to get very cold and I decided to call it a day until the New Year.

The winter was a drag, with not much in the way of carp fishing for me. I've done all that before and, to be honest, I don't really enjoy it any more, sitting out in the freezing cold wet weather, generally for nothing. I always keep an eye on the

Great big orange pecs.

weather, though, and if we get a warm spell then I will definitely go. Those little windows can be very productive.

There was one more fish that I wanted from Cleverley, Hendrix, the one that I first saw the picture of at the charity match. So, that was my first port of call after the winter. I had to go to the Nash headquarters for some business and my car was loaded up with my tackle, but I was unsure where I wanted to fish. Hendrix had been out a week or so previously and I was a little doubtful that she'd be out again for a while.

Anyway, after my visit to the Nash camp, I automatically headed off toward Cleverley Mere. It was the very beginning of April and the weather was actually very nice, the sun was out and I felt that spring was on its way. When I pulled up at the Mere no cars were visible and the lake was empty, so without thinking, I went and placed a bottle in the Bowls swim. It seemed a good starting place.

Apart from all the reeds and trees still in their winter colours, I could have been back in autumn. Everything was still the same, apart from the water temperature, which was freezing cold. I climbed up my little overhanging tree that gave me a good view over the bay, and started to scan about the reed beds and the channel. Once my eyes had adjusted, and with my glasses on that never leave my head, I was able to penetrate the depths. The water was gin clear. There was a little breeze, making the channel harder to view but where the reeds gave shelter, I was soon able to focus on a few carp that were lazily sitting among the reed stems. Every now and then, one would poke its nose out, drift off into the channel and I would lose sight of it.

The sun was still shining and as the wind completely stopped for a moment, I couldn't believe my eyes. About 30 yards out, was a big group of fish just sitting under the surface, and there were loads there, probably most of the lake's stock. I wondered if they'd have a floater. You never know; I've had a 30 off the top before in March. I got down, ran back to my car, unloaded my gear, and dragged it to the Bowls swim. Once again, I had everything just spread all over the place as hurriedly, I sorted a floater rod out. Floater fishing was not the sort of thing I was expecting to be doing, but if that's what it takes. I had mixers with me and was soon back round and up that tree with my catapult.

I put a few pouches out about 20 feet to the right of the carp, and relied on the slight breeze to push them onto the fish. I was able to see them a lot more clearly now, and sitting away from the main body of carp was a big fish on its own. I kept my eye on this one for a while and for some reason it didn't join the group. Then I saw the scales on its side. It was Hendrix. There she was, my target fish, so near but so far. She was obviously not getting involved with the group because she had only been out a little while before. As the mixers drifted over, a few carp became interested and they made half-hearted attempts at snuffling one, but Hendrix was on her guard and drifted further from the group; she didn't want to get involved with that lot.

I stayed up the tree for a while and in the end, a few mixers were starting to get taken, but the breeze was moving the fish as they followed the food source, and I was in danger of pushing them out of the area completely. As they were happy to be in the channel, I decided not to pester them any more. My target fish was present so I thought the best thing would be to get back to my swim, sort out all the crap and get everything ready for the evening ahead.

My tactics were to be the same as usual, only this time I had some red maggots for some reason, whereas all the other fish had come to whites. Halfway out across the channel, I found a nice area of soft silt that ran along behind some more of the hard clay, so I decided to spod maggots out there and then cast the usual rig and ball of maggots to the spot. I made a change on my other two rods. I really like the Nash Monster Carp pellets as they break down well in cold temperatures and give off good attracters, so instead of maggots I made the PVA ball up of Tangee Squid pellets.

I remember being really fussy and precise on these two rods, trying to get tight on the reed line, and after a few frustrating attempts I was finally happy. Just before dark, I had a confidence boost as a good fish showed over the maggot rod, and at 10pm, the rod on the red maggots pulled away. I was into a heavy carp that felt a really good fish but sadly it just fell off. I was gutted. I hate losing fish and I hadn't lost many on Cleverley; in fact, that was only my second and my worry was that I had just lost Hendrix. During the night, I was getting liners close in, and they had to be from a fish that was up and down my margin. I received no more action that night, but I hoped the fish would still be in the channel and that the one I'd lost wouldn't push them away.

The next day was pretty much the same as the day before, weather wise, with a slight breeze and sunshine, and at midday I reeled in and went back round to my climbing tree. I really needed to see that Hendrix was still about. The same group of fish was still out in the same area, as if they had been there all night long, but where was Hendrix? Just then, he appeared. 'Thank God', I thought, at least he wasn't the one I'd lost.

I watched from the tree for ages, and noted that the fish were leaving or entering the reeds from two different gaps and just out from both of these were little clear areas, and these were the spots I wanted to get my two rods on. The water along the reeds was a good depth, between six and eight feet in places, perfect for my maize rig.

I was mainly watching Hendrix, trying to suss his mood, and he was definitely grumpy. He didn't like any fish coming near him and he backed away. It was as if he thought the others would get him into trouble. Another angler had turned up, Lloyd, who was a bailiff on the lake. Lloyd went into the little gap beside my swim, fishing the channel, but at least I would have some company. I went back round to say hello and to get the kettle on, and before I knew it the evening was drawing in and it was time to get the rods sorted. I topped up the spodded maggot area and put that rod out, and then took ages getting the reed rods into position. It did take me a while and I thought I may have trashed the swim but I had to get them just right.

Finally, I settled on my low chair, kettle on, and all I could think about was the liners I'd been getting the previous night. It was nearly dark as I flicked out the marker, and it went down nice and hard. As I pulled the lead back, I felt it come up a ledge; the top of it was soft and then, suddenly, the lead locked up. It wasn't far out, so I heaved it in and the lead was tangled in that long stringy grass-like weed. I love fishing near this type of weed and the carp seem to like it, too. I flicked the marker out a few more times to double-check that this ledge did, in fact, run across the front of the swim. It did, and was about six feet in depth, tight to the weed, and this had to be where I'd been receiving the liners. I picked up the rod that had taken me so long to get into position, and reeled it in, made up a new bag of pellets, hooked it on, and under-armed it on to the ledge just behind the weed, then slackened off the line.

Lloyd and me sat by the rods chatting and drinking tea, and I received a little liner off the close rod at about 10pm, so something was about. I just hoped it wasn't pike as it was that time of year. I was just thinking it might have been pike when it absolutely screamed off. It took a long run, started to kite to my left, and I had to wind down quickly to try to prevent it from getting round into the bay that Lloyd was fishing. There was a bush to my left and my line was dangerously close to it. My fish was already around Lloyd's side and this was not good. All I could do was keep side strain on, walk out a little way, and hope she'd come back. I kept the rod dipped under and, slowly, she came my way. Lloyd grabbed the net and waded out - he had brought his waders, luckily. She boiled up a few times on the corner of the bush and then made another attempt at getting back round it. This was nail-biting stuff and I was crapping myself. 'Please don't let me lose this one', I was saying, over and over.

I thought I was hearing things.

It was pitch black, making everything seem that much harder, but I had the fish back at the edge of the bush again, boiling on the top, and Lloyd waded out until I was unable to see him. Then he shouted, "I got it mate." Phew! That was a close one.

"What fish is it, mate?" I asked. Lloyd put his head torch on and looked into the net.
"Er, it's Hendrix, mate." I thought I was hearing things so I asked him again.
"Are you sure?"
"Yes," he said. "Well done. It's Hendrix."
Bloody hell! I was gob-smacked.
"Yes!" I shouted. "You crafty devil. You thought you would stay away from your friends and creep about under my rod tips, did ya?"

Well, I was so pleased to get her after she'd been staying away from the others, and I'd moved that rod. Surely, it was meant to be! For the record, she weighed in at 43lbs 8oz, and she truly is a stunning carp. I didn't sack her up, we did the shots in the dark. Thanks Lloyd. Glad you turned up, mate.

After Hendrix, I was ready to move on. There were others to catch but I knew I'd be doubling up on fish, and I hate that, so that was the end of a very memorable few months on such a quality water, Cleverley Mere. Thanks Ben, for the opportunity, and thanks Galvin.

Looking back on my time on there, I caught everything on the maize rig, and if there was a rig to get me out of trouble, that was the one. There's more about the Amaizing Rig, and later on, you will see just how 'amaizing' it really is.

Chapter Nine
Yateley Car Park Lake - Lessons learned

The first time I laid eyes on the Yateley complex was back in 1993 when Essex Jay and I got tickets. At the time, we were just starting on the Nazeing Meads and we thought we could fish anywhere, as if we had all the time in the world, but those 19 years have gone so quickly.

I can remember the first time we walked on to the complex. The place was famous, the home of so many big fish and nearly all the lakes held old English warriors. As we walked down the causeway between the Car Park and the Pads lakes, the whole place seemed so daunting to us. We passed the Pole Position swim, where a guy called Jeff Pink (Pinky), was in session, chasing the Pads Lake big 'uns, Jumbo and Scale on the Shoulder. We carried on along the path and passed Nigel Sharp on the Car Park, and to be honest, we felt a bit intimidated. We'd read so much about this place and the quality anglers who fished there, that we tried not to make eye contact with them and get out of our depth in conversation. As we made our way to the end of the Car Park Lake, Rob Maylin was in the Chair swim, fishing into Brutes corner. Bloody hell! The place was full of these top anglers.

We walked around the North Lake, the home of the mighty Bazil, and it was no different over there. We felt that we'd bitten off more than we could chew, but looking back I now know that it was just all the carp fishing heroes being there that made us feel like that.

We both really wanted to get stuck straight in and start fishing for Heather and Bazil, but while we were there we popped over the road for a look around the Copse and the Match lakes. For some reason I wasn't that bothered about them, even though they were mega waters. To us, fishing Yateley meant that we'd come a very long way, or so it seemed, and if we were to fish the complex it had to be on the other side of the road. So we made our way back and as we reached the Chair, Rob Maylin stopped us and asked for our tickets because he'd seen us bowling about and wondered who we were.

Anyway, we decided to start on the North Lake and not long after our walk around we did a weekend. Traffic is always bad on a Friday night and we had a long way to go, so by the time we arrived most of the good plots were taken, but the atmosphere was immense.

I was in the Christmas Tree swim and during the night I had frightener when one of my rods ripped off and I caught a huge tench. As I slipped him back, I asked him if he'd seen Bazil lately. Jay had a couple of days off work so he'd got down for a few days and was ringing me to keep me updated. He told me he'd seen the fish named the Snake going up and down his margin all day. At 34lbs, it was the second-biggest in the lake and as with all the carp, very much sought after. The next morning, Jay lost the Snake and he was gutted. He said it had just ploughed through the weed, and that was it. What a shame for him! That would have been unreal, to catch that fish - or any of them - on your second trip. It gave us confidence, though.

The Car Park Lake. The home of so many tales.

We were getting there later and later on the Friday nights, and were unable to get any swims on our next couple of trips, so in the end we called it quits and decided to leave it alone for the time being. All these years later, I so wish that we'd stuck with it. The Car Park, at that time, was mega and I feel sure that between us we'd have caught all those old fish eventually; Heather, Arfur, Single Scale, Dustbin, Big Orange, Little Orange, Chunky, Ugloe, and Pearly Tail, some old commons and the Pineapple mirror. What a line up of fish!

I did go back to do a few sessions on the Car Park at the time when Darrell Peck was doing the business. I really loved it on there and, again, wished I'd stayed on, but I just wanted to be getting runs and catching fish, so, once again, I blew it out.

It was not until September 2008 that I finally decided I'd better get my arse over there because those old warriors wouldn't be around for much longer. Sadly, Chunky, Single, and Ugloe had already departed, so time was running out for me to give it a good go.

The cleverness of the Yateley carp has been well documented over the years and the Car Park is ultra-hard. They are so pressured that they seem to have adapted to it and somehow they know how to avoid anglers' traps, because that's exactly what's going on there. In fact, I wonder if they *are* feeling the pressure any more. They've all lived a long while in their little nine-acre world, so avoiding anglers' baits has become part of everyday life for these fish.

Ever since we fished over at Hainault Park Lake, just after I got out of the army, the Yateley complex has been the Mecca of English carp angling, and out of all of our gang no one had, as far as I knew, caught a Yateley carp. As much as I would have loved to catch any of the fabulous carp from the Car Park Lake, it was always Heather that I really wanted. If I could have caught Heather the Leather, I would have felt that I'd reached a certain pinnacle in my carp fishing life. She was a truly historic carp and probably, at the time, the most creditable fish in the country.

Although you're no longer allowed to climb the trees to view the lake, the temptation is always there, and it's the only way a keen carp angler gets a bird's eye view of his target water. The Car Park is surrounded by great climbing trees, and you can't keep a good man down! Some of the good trees are really high and I've heard the story of an angler who was spotted at the top of one of them by a bailiff that lived in a nearby town. I don't know if that's true, or if it was just a frightener, but talk about being caught red-handed! Anyway, most of the lake can be seen from a good tree in the Bars swim... allegedly. At times, the water is crystal clear and the bar system glows yellow. When the lake is full of weed, a bit of time spent up that tree saves hours of plumbing, or so someone told me, obviously.

The carp were seen all the time around the lake. They were often very mobile and I hardly ever got up a tree without seeing some of the lake's residents. As I said, sadly, a few of the fish had gone, but my dream fish, Heather, was still there at 50lbs-plus, and so was Arfur Tail, who went high-40s to 50lbs, caught at the right time. Next was the Big Orange, best weight high-40s, but was usually around low to mid-40s; Pearly Tail and Baby Orange both would do 40lbs, caught at the right time, and one of my favourite fish of all time, a classic-looking carp, the Dustbin, at low-40s. These were the remainder of the A team, the carp that everyone was there for.

There were some nice old commons to mid-30s to back them up, and Pineapple, a heavily-scaled mirror that I was told came out of someone's fish tank and is now around 20lbs, a clever fish that doesn't seem to get caught too often. So I was potentially fishing for two 50s and four 40s. That's some fish to have in one lake, and I can only imagine what it must have been like to have added Chunky, Single Scale, and Ugloe to that list.

I'm not sure if this was my first session or not, but I think it was. I had set up in the Snags, a swim at the top end of the lake next to Brutes corner. We were only allowed 48 hours each trip, and then you had to be off for 48, and it seemed that every time I had to leave the lake, things were just starting to feel right or if the swim had been quiet for a while, the fish moved into the area.

There were many obvious spots visible around the lake and I remember Terry Hearn saying once, "the spots are the spots." In other words, what Tel is saying is, when they get caught, those blatant spots are where they get caught from. To back this up, I was speaking to Simon Davy, (AKA Lock, stock and two smoking marker floats), one day. Simon is an awesome angler who has caught many good fish and he told me that when he first came on the Car Park, he decided to go about things completely differently to all the other anglers.
"These fish see the same thing day in, day out," he said. "If everyone was fishing pop-ups, then I'd use bottom baits, or a totally different bait and I wouldn't fish any of the known spots. I'd always fish other spots in all the swims and just do the opposite to everyone else. It seemed the obvious way to go."
"So, how did you get on then?" I asked him.
"I blanked," he said, "for a whole year!"

The Chair swim. The swim of mixed emotions.

He is really funny, especially the way he says things, and he cracks me up, but he's a guy who is no fool when it comes to catching big carp. He'd already sacrificed a whole year and I took notice.

Back to my 48 hours in the Snags. Directly in the swim to the left is an island, not that far out. The gap between the swim and the island makes the channel that leads around into Brutes corner, which was a favourite area of Arfur's and she had been caught from there a good few times in the past. Directly to the other side of the island is the Chair swim, from where you can fish a rod into Brutes corner if you wish to, so the channels round the island that lead to Brutes corner can be fished from both swims.

When I had a flick about with the lead, I found some gravel off to one side of the island, but the bit I liked was further down, in thick silt at about six feet or so deep. To the left and right of the swim are snags, hence the name, and these close-in areas also produced fish. Straight out from the swim are three bars that come toward you. They are covered in weed and the fish just love this area, but most of the time it's not really fishable from the Snags, for a few reasons including line lay, and if you went too far, you'd be encroaching on the Works, the swim opposite. To be honest, though, there were plenty of nice spots in the Snags.

On this trip, I had some Vitalin with me that I'd mixed up with pellets and a few bits. My plan was to put out a few balls off the side of the island and fish my maize rig over the top. The weather was perfect and the wind was blowing up nicely into my corner of the lake, so the conditions were spot on. I settled in for the night and at last I started my campaign on the Yateley Car Park. On any other lake on a night with a good autumn wind blowing, I would've been expecting a bite at any time, but this was the Car Park. The night was quiet but just before light I caught a tench.

At mid-morning, I reeled in and went for a walk round to see a mate, Phil Buckley, who had moved into the Chair swim. He'd already caught Heather and was on a mission to get Arfur. When I arrived back in my swim, I noticed some bubbling going on over where I'd caught the tench and assumed that it was more tench getting on the remainder of the Vitalin. I stood there looking and then, as if in slow motion, the Pineapple came out to the wrist. I saw it as clear as day as it showed about 20 feet out from the side of the island, not a million miles away. That sighting gave me a boost of confidence and I hoped that the Pineapple was hanging out with some of his mates. Because I had caught a tench, I decided to have a change of rigs, opted for a snowman and

Brutes Corner. Arfur loves this area.

then cast the rod back on the same area as the previous night, with my other rod fished with the same method just left of it in the channel. I scattered a few boilies over both rods and slackened off both lines ready for the night ahead.

By late afternoon the wind had started to pick up again and a low, dark cloud seemed to make the night come a lot quicker. Once again, I crashed out full of hope. Sometime during the night I heard something jump between me and Phil. It was still windy and I heard it above the wind so it must have been a right lump.

In the morning, as I lay there looking at the rods, I started to get subtle liners on the rod I'd had the tench on. Every now and then the bobbin would just lift slightly and fall back again, so I got up, put my trainers on and made a cuppa. The little liners went on for a while and then the rod just bent round and melted off. I was stunned. Carp on! I leapt at the rod and a powerful fish steamed off across all the bars heading toward the Steps swim. It wasn't stopping for anything until finally, it buried itself in a weed bed. Phil came round and I told him I was just weeded up solid. He said he'd heard that one go in the night and agreed that it was one of the big 'uns.

There was only one option left for me and that was to take to the boat. There are a couple of boats over at the lake and we are allowed to take one out when necessary. They are chained up, but the bailiffs have the keys to the lock-up where the paddles and life jackets are kept, and as long as there are two people to a boat, it's cool. Phil and me made our way out to where the fish was, and I hadn't felt anything on since a little while after I was weeded, but that doesn't mean a thing so I was still hopeful, although I couldn't believe I'd even had a take. Phil rowed as I wound in the line, and as we got nearer, I ended up extracting my rig from the weed. My carp had got free, but strangely, although I was gutted, I wasn't too upset. I could hardly have expected to turn up and just bang one out. It would have been bloody good if I had, though!

I was convinced that it had been one of the A team, so at least I'd had a bite and I knew I could do so again. The 48-hour thing was a bit of a 'mare, and over the next few sessions I saw the same old thing go on over and over again. I was in the Chair swim one day, and you could look down the length of the lake and see all the markers going out to the same old spots. Bait boats were allowed and as one angler left, another would drop in, out would go the marker followed by the boat to drop off the bait. These spots must have had plenty of bait on them but, like I said, these spots would do the fish.

I was really pleased for John to have caught Heather.

I remember someone once, near winter, bringing a black, rotten maggot in on his hook so there must have been a lot out there for him to hook one. In the past, I've never been into bait boats but most anglers used them on the Car Park. Nobody was bothered about branches over their heads so the limbs of the trees in some of the swims were hanging too low for an overhead chuck with a carp rod. I always like to use 13-foot rods, and the boat did save a lot of spodding time and kept the swim quiet, so in the end I joined in on the boat thing.

I spent the couple of months before winter getting to know some of the swims and witnessed the Dustbin on the bank, an incredible fish I would love to catch. I got to know a lot of the regular anglers, who had great nicknames like, ‘Listen 'ere Mate’, ‘The Inflater Man’, and many more. The lake had an atmosphere, it really did. In every swim, I could envisage past captures of the old warriors. I've never had those kind of feelings on any other lake. It really is a special place.

My last trip was sometime in mid-November but the bird life drove me insane, so I gave it a swerve until March. One day, I was up in the tree in the Bars swim, looking down into the margins and out toward where the beginning of the bars started, when I saw what looked like one of the new stock fish. It was up in the water, about three feet under the surface, and I followed it until I lost track of where it went. Well, to see a fish was something to go on at least.
Then, from nowhere, Heather appeared, gliding along and following a similar route. I was amazed to see these fish up and moving about. It was bitterly cold and the water temperature must have been only a couple of degrees from freezing, but it just shows that at times during the winter they are active, and I’ve witnessed this many times on my own lakes,

On my next trip down, John Pack ended his quest to catch Heather and I was there to see her on the bank at 51lbs. What a sight! I prayed that one day I would be the lucky one lifting her for the cameras. I was well pleased for John, though, because he had worked hard for Heather over the years. John's capture ended the season for me, and I was already looking forward to a fresh start on June the 1st.

The draw for swims was due to take place a week before the start, at 2pm in the Yateley car park. I was making good time but as usual the good old M25 let me down and I was stuck in stationary traffic. In the end, I had to ring the head bailiff to ask him if he could hold on a bit longer as I was nearly there. When I eventually drove through the gates, a big group were all waiting patiently and I literally had to chuck my ticket straight into the carrier bag for the draw. As expected, I was more or less last out, something I'm used to now, and there were only two swims left, the Chair or Tray Bins. Tray Bins was an in-between swim that no one ever fishes and I didn't want to squeeze between two anglers and ruin their good draw results, so I chose the Chair.

Once the first 48 hours were over, it was back to the normal procedure with swim choices. It was just a matter of getting down and finding out who was going home, who was staying and so on. At times, though, it did get out of hand as groups of friends would be in touch and tactics were played to get into certain swims. You just had to get wise yourself and regard it as all part of the game.

When I arrived for the start, it was scorching hot but the wind was pushing down toward my end of the lake, which was handy, and at least there would be the wind to cool me down. I hate red-hot swims, and I hoped the carp would also favour the windward end. Down the left-hand margin of the Chair swim, there's a tree that grows out from the bank. A thick branch has grown out over the water, with a big canopy on the end, so I climbed out on this for a better look. I slipped and landed right on my shin and boy, did it hurt!

There was some Canadian weed tight against the margins and from underneath it drifted a big common that I must have disturbed. This had to be *the* big common. It certainly looked well over mid-30 and it would most likely be heavier as the fish had not yet spawned. To see this fish was a great confidence boost and I was now very pleased with my late draw.

After spotting one fish, I was sure that others would not be too far away so I decided my approach would be to have one rod down under that canopy, and the other out off the island at the opposite end to where I was fishing on my my first trip when I lost one. My rigs were in-line leads that I had set up to eject on the take, with the leadcore going around the outside of the lead. For my hook length I was using Nash Bullet braid, because I'd put it against lots of different braids and I found that it was the most supple, and it sank. It was the perfect hook length and I had a bulk spool of it. I still had some of the old original Fangs that I loved, and I used these in size 8, with the hair on a blow-back ring, and black tigers as my hook bait.

I was able to walk down the margins with the rod and reach out from the branch, if need be, to lower my double black tiger nicely under the canopy. Then, with my pole and scoop, I was able to drop off some black tigers over the top. Job done. I was more than happy with that rod, so my other rod was fished in the same style off the island. Everyone had cast out and the new season was under way at last.

A nice wind was still pushing nicely up my end of the lake, and I stayed up until midnight, but there were no socials really because everyone was in their swims, on their rods and wondering if it would be Heather tonight.

At 1am, without a single liner or any other warning, my canopy rod was melting away. I flew out to the rod and I was into a Car Park carp! I grabbed the rod and it bent round hard to the left as the fish fled the area of the canopy and out into the lake, as I'd hoped. I was using braid as main line, something I'd been trying for while because it gives you so much more feeling when you play a fish. Many people say that they hook-pull with braid, but I can only think that it's because they play them too hard. With braid, you can feel every head movement and everything the fish is doing, and at times the fight feels so aggressive that you just have to get used to it.

This fish had not gone too far, and my heart was pounding as I wondered which one I was playing. It had to be one of the remaining mirrors and I so hoped it was. About 20 feet out from where the fish had been hooked, it hit the surface as the lead fell off and then was only at the other side of the canopy. From there it made a few more heavy bids to get into the weed surrounding the area, so I kept leading it back, all the while on the top. Lots of waves came back in the dark to the sound of splashes as it waved its tail on the surface, until it came round to my side of the canopy and into my waiting net.

I looked into the net and there lay a huge mirror. Landing a Yateley carp was something I'd always wanted to do and I was so happy. The feeling was simply unreal. I'd had only a brief look in the net and for all I knew it could have been Heather lying there. I rang my mate Wayne who was on the other bank.
"Wayne," I said. "I've got one. A big mirror!"
Wayne was as happy as me and was soon on his way round. Before he got to me I had a proper look and was sure that I had the Big Orange. Wayne arrived and confirmed that I had caught my first carp from the Car Park, so I let out the shout of 'Big Orange!' and I really enjoyed that.

Over the years, the Big Orange has been up to weights of over 48lbs, but sometimes she gets herself into a bit of a state with some nasty scrapes and scratches. These get infected and she can look a sad sight, and so she was said to be a self-harmer. Who knows what she got up to? There could have been a number of reasons that she got in this state. Maybe she'd suffered from parasites and the constant rubbing and scratching on branches and other sub-surface objects were the cause.

The lads help out with Big Orange.

I punched the air with delight and screamed out her name.

Luckily for me, she was in a reasonable condition and a good weight, too. She went 45lbs 8oz and I punched the air with delight. She wasn't on the bank long. The photos were quickly done and I slid the old girl back.

Wayne stayed in my swim, I got the rod back out on the spot and we chatted away for hours until nearly daybreak. Wayne's a great bloke, such a character and he's the spitting image of Gary Newman. He loved the Car Park and was so full of enthusiasm. Some of the things he did were mad. He'd stay up all night to watch the fish, which is good angling, but then he'd hardly sleep in the day, and after 48 hours he'd have to go to work. He was like a zombie at times. Wayne told me stories about days gone by, of anglers who had fished the Car Park, like Tom Banks who is a very private angler and was fishing in the back bay one night. Apparently, someone saw a flash and he was doing self-takes of the Dustbin. Wayne used to say, "If I get any of the big girls, no one will know a thing about it. There will be a few self-takes, and all anyone will hear is the car park gate shutting as I leave."

One night, I was fishing the Waiting Mans swim and Wayne was in the Gate, over to my left. I got up at about 2am for a leak, and before I returned to the old bag I looked out from the swim and a flash from the left caught my eye. At first I thought it may have been some sort of lightning, then it went again and I then realised where it was coming from. It was from Wayne's swim, the Gate. 'My god', I thought. 'He's got a big 'un and he's doing self-takes, the nutter!' I ran round to see if I was right and as I got there I could see that he had the camera resting on a bucket or something, and was rattling out some self-takes of one of the stockies. I really thought that he'd had one of the A team then.

By the time I got off to sleep after catching the Big Orange, it was daylight and I was shattered but still buzzing to have caught her. I was only able to sleep for a little while, though, as the sun was soon burning into my eyes, so I had no choice other than to get up. Wayne was already reeled in and up and about. I don't think he ever slept. With the hot weather, the carp started to trickle into my area, and the mighty Arfur was in and out of Brutes corner. She was big, with a pre-spawn weight of at least 50lbs and she would come out and hang about just off the side of the canopy.

Out from the Chair swim were the bars, three of them that crossed the area toward the End Works swim. These bars were all tangled together with lots of weed and the fish just loved the area, especially as it was hot, and I had a feeling that they may well spawn in this area. Some parts of the bars were shining an orangey-yellow colour. These were in shallow water and from the Chair I was able to see the black shapes of the carp as they moved across them. I pulled the rod off the island, put some hemp and black tigers out with the bait boat, and then dropped them slightly down the side of the bar. It seemed that most of the fish were crossing the bar and then following it along, using the cover of the darker side.

As it got hotter I was getting more and more tired. Wayne, the android, had been round for a chat and was now opposite, with Mark the bailiff in the Works swim. I'd been watching the Dustbin and two of the stock fish mooching about over the bars and they'd been getting very close to my rod, but tiredness got the better of me in the end and I fell asleep in my chair, head back, dribbling away.

Suddenly, all hell broke loose. One of the rods was screaming, but the take was setting the other rod off. I'd woken with a shock and for a moment couldn't work out which one was going. Then I saw that the line clip had pulled on the bar rod and line was peeling off the spool. I lifted it and looked out to the spot, where a huge bow wave rode across the water as two other carp went their separate ways in a bid to get out of the area. Meanwhile, everything had locked up solid. Wayne had seen the whole thing from up a tree on the other bank and was soon round.

"That might be Dustbin," he said. "I saw them feeding on your bait."
I was getting nowhere with the weeded fish so the boat was summoned. Wayne took the paddles, I kneeled in the front and, as we made our way out past the

After a hectic night and two lost fish, the morning arrived as if nothing had happened.

canopy, Arfur was sitting there looking massive, not really bothered by us as we passed by. Sadly, my fish had got free and must have been well gone. All I got was my rig back, about 20 yards away from where I'd cast it, and a big ball of weed. As we made our way back with the boat, I got another nice view of Arfur as he drifted back into Brutes corner. It's funny, we say 'he' because his name is Arfur, but really it means 'half a' tail, and Arfur is a she. Anyway, once back on dry land, I put the rod back out to where it had been and tried to sit out of the sun. I had put the loss down to one of the stockies, but whatever it was, I was very close to Dustbin making a mistake. I couldn't wait for the evening to bring cooler temperatures.

I got the canopy rod in position and left the other one up on the shallows of the bars for the night. As the evening wore on, I heard some very heavy fish going just behind my canopy. I was hopeful and stayed up until midnight, waiting for action. This was to be my last night as I had to pull off the next afternoon, and a few times I was woken by fish making heavy splashes. At 2am, the canopy rod bent round with the Neville alarm screaming and I was on it quickly, as a big fish, for sure, pulled away hard. It was well out from the canopy and then I felt the lead come off as the fish hit the surface.

I wasn't able to see the fish but I could hear it on the top. It made a good attempt at getting further down the tree line but I gave it some side strain and slowly began to get the upper hand. I estimated it as not far from the other side of the canopy and everything was going okay, then all went solid. I tried to get the fish moving but I could no longer feel a thing and had that sick feeling that it was off, and sure enough it was. My rig was left solid and in the end I had to pull hard to break the little branch it was attached to. Gutted or what! To have caught the Big O and then lose two had really upset me. You don't want to lose fish on the Car Park. To put it into perspective, some lads don't even get a bite all year, some have never had a bite after fishing the place for years, and I had just lost what I would lay money on was one of the A team.

I was so mad that I put my head torch on. I didn't care about spooking the fish now, and what were the chances of another take? I got the boat ready, placed some more bait and the rig in it, sent it down to the spot and dropped the lot off, all with the torch lighting up the canopy. I didn't care and went back to bed raving at myself.

At 5am, that same rod burst into action. I couldn't believe my luck, and this sort of thing just doesn't happen on this lake. This one also felt like a good fish and I believed I was getting a payback from losing the last one. You wouldn't believe it!

I was winning the battle and once again I got caught up in some unseen snag and lost the fish. I was screaming. I've never felt so done in my life. I had just f***ed up big style, and then all the 'what if I'd landed the three I had lost?' started playing on my mind, and I swear it still hurts now.

I didn't know what was going on. I grabbed my landing net pole and waded under the canopy, waved the pole from left to right under the water and I couldn't feel anything that I might have snagged on. Well, I was sick, I can tell you, and what made it even worse was the fact that Arfur was now right down the other end in one of the quiet corners, looking a bit sorry for herself. I lost her, I know I did. She had been in my swim the whole time and I was sure she wasn't going anywhere. God knows what the other one was, and to be honest I would hate to know. That should have been the session of a lifetime. Oh well, life goes on.

On my next trip, I had set up in the Waiting Mans swim and had done the night with not a lot going on. I know that around this time James Davis had just caught the Dustbin from the Island swim at 43lbs. What I would have given to catch that one! Just down from my swim were the snags in the Gate swim, and the fish often get under these snags so you can observe them from the bank. I would often take a little walk down there to have a look, and as I looked this time, I saw two fish, not right in the corner but under some branches before the main corner. They kept moving around and I was soon able to identify Baby Orange and the Pineapple. They would move into the corner and then come back to the same area, and then all the leaves and crap would come off the bottom and hit the surface, accompanied by thousands of tiny bubbles. They were digging holes under there, so I packed up and moved to the Gate swim.

I set up just one rod and with the help of the bait boat I was able to drop off a small amount of hemp and a few black tigers. You couldn't get an accurate cast here as there were branches in the way and even if you did, it might take forever and clear the fish off. Where I had seen the fish, there was a little gap on the outer part of the hangers, just enough to allow me to get my bait a little nearer to where they were. If I'd landed it right on the outer edge then the bait and rig would have just dropped off into the deeper water.

I was sitting there on my low chair, reading my book, and about 20 minutes had passed when I received a take. The rod bent round and I was sitting right on it, so I was quick to grab it. Immediately, I kept it low and gave side to stop the fish getting right under and into the snags. I managed to guide it out and

James Davis with the Car Park Lake's Dustbin.

away from the trees and then it just fell off. Shortly after, lots of tiny bubbles came up as it smashed through the weed on its departure from the area. I just looked up to the skies, laughed and said, 'Come on, give me break, please.' I was sure I had just lost the Pineapple because she has a tiny mouth and I'm sure that's the reason she's hard to hook, and I'd probably had a bad hook hold. I took a walk back round and, sure enough, the Pineapple was nowhere to be seen, but the Baby O was still there and seemed oblivious to anything that had happened.

I repositioned the rod back to the same spot and sat down feeling really unlucky and more than a bit disheartened. Half an hour later, the rod pulled round aggressively and I had to keep the pressure on. This fish was pulling hard, the lead came off and and suddenly the reason for the two losses in the Chair swim became clear. Once the lead is off, the fish rises in the water and in this case, under the outer branches of the overhanging trees. From the bank, I could see the fish on the surface taking me into danger. Once again, I was in a losing situation and all had locked up, so I ended up going out on the boat to retrieve my rig. What a complete balls-up!

A Back Bay battle and not knowing just what's on the other end.

The result. A pretty stock fish.

I'm not even going to go into how I felt, but what I do want to go into is the leads coming off. Back in the Chair swim with the Big O, I managed to get the fish to come round the edge of the canopy. The other two were coming the same way but as they were up in the water they were getting caught up in the branches on the surface.

I was obviously dipping the rod as deep as I was able to, but I was just unable to get the fish to come down and I was unaware of the fact, that is until I saw it for myself in the Gate swim. I'm sure that if the leads had stayed on, then I would have landed those fish and had an amazing season.

Apart from those situations with fish rising under canopies, I have reservations about ditching the lead, full stop, but this is only the way I see it. Previously, on my own syndicate water, I was having some good action but the scraps I was getting were unbelievable; they were going mental. It was summer, the weather was hot and I was concerned because some of the fights were lasting half an hour or so. I was worried as the fish had spawned just a few weeks back, and the last thing they needed was a half-hour battle. To start with, the takes were just like any other, until the lead came off, then they'd go on massive long runs as far as they could go, nearly flat-rodding me. I would have to clamp the spool to stop them, and they were some of the hardest battles I've ever had.

The next night, I decided to keep the leads on to see what difference it made. The fish were well on the bait and I soon got my first bite. It was a nice steady run and normally the lead would pop off and all hell would break loose, but this time because the fish was deeper, it found some weed. It took a bit of pressure to get it moving again, and then it kited as I wound down until it found the next weed bed.

Before long, I had landed my fish, no problem, so the leads were staying on. I once spoke to Darrell Peck about when he fished the Car Park. At the time, the weed was horrendous in the Bars swim and I asked him if he dumped his leads. He told me that he never did and he'd never had any trouble.

There have been loads of times when I've kept my lead on in weedy waters and sometimes, when the fish break free from the weed, I've led them in with them wallowing along behind the ball of weed that has collected all around the lead, but without the lead on. I think you get a direct line straight to the hook and all the pressure is then on your hook hold and I have lost fish like this. Rightly or wrongly, I now keep my leads on.

I've landed plenty in the weed while keeping the leads on.

With the lead staying on, and the fish staying deeper, the fight was nowhere near as long as when I was dumping the leads.

For the rest of the season, I worked hard on the Car Park. I'd been keeping the bait going in all year and I'd had a few takes from the new stock fish - they kept you on the ball! Gaz Fareham caught Heather at 52lbs 3oz and he had a great year, also getting Pearly Tail from the Gate swim. Good angling!

Before I knew it, I was once again in traffic on the M25 and nearly late, as usual, on my way to the draw for the next season. I kept up my good form at draws and came out stone-last again, so I about-turned the car and drove back home. Never mind; I was as keen as mustard this season and on a mission to get even with the Car Park fish.

The weather had not been particularly hot, but 48 hours later when it was my turn to get on the lake, it turned really hot again, just like the previous start. I'd been keeping in touch with a mate, Simon Hartrop, who was in the Chair swim, and on the changeover I planned to jump in behind him. I hoped that with the better weather the carp would be back in the area and I might get my chance to get even.

I was all packed and ready, all my gear was sorted, and the next day I was off to Yateley. I was sitting in the clubhouse on my fishery when I received a text from Jerry Bridger. It read, 'Hi mate, is it true about Heather?' I wondered what he was on about, but it could only mean one thing. I rang Simon immediately.
"What's happening, mate?" I said.
"We're just burying Heather," he replied.
"No way!" I was shocked.
We all knew it would happen sometime, though. That was my whole reason for going on the lake to have a go, before time ran out.

At least I got to see her with John Pack. I was there and had sat on the little stool in one of the swims that had 'Heather Tonight' carved on it. I never caught her but I felt her presence at the lake, and had plenty of exciting nights wondering if I would be lucky. After Heather went, I wasn't able to go back, and then sadly, Pearly Tail and Dustbin were next to join Heather and her other friends, Ugloe, Single and Chunky in what will be the big Car Park in the sky. Thank you, and rest in peace old warriors.

Chapter Ten
A Common Sense

I love to fish for those big old mirror carp. They are distinguished by their unique scale patterns, making them all different, but with common carp, although they are beautiful-looking fish, they can all be pretty much the same... until they get big, that is.

When I fished at Hainault Lake, the big common weighed in at 21lbs and was very much on the list of desirable fish. It hardly ever came out and I think that's what made it so sought after. When she was landed, she was treated with the utmost respect, and word would spread round the lake that, 'the big common's been out.' She was not a massive fish but back then I didn't know of any commons that were over 30lbs, only the ones I'd read about at Redmire and places like that, and to us, they were fish that only came along in our dreams.

Yes, there is something about big commons and even if the lake doesn't hold one, then someone would create an imaginary one. You must have heard it, 'I saw her two years ago, sitting in the weed. 50lbs, all day long.' I've heard this story time and time again over the years, and it's nearly always a massive common rather than a mirror; why is that? It could be because that's what people want it to be. For some reason, our dreams of big carp are always about commons, a Dick Walker legacy perhaps, and I love these stories. For anglers like me, who are always chasing their dreams, these tales are what keep us going, because in some cases, that huge common may just be true.

Over the last seven years or so, until now – 2011 – I've had a run of some great catches of big commons and I want to share them with you. I seem to have a knack for winkling out those incredible carp, although I honestly don't know what it is. It could be coincidence, maybe it's just luck, or is it a 'common sense?'

Chapter Eleven
The Long Common

Running your own fishery is every angler's dream and I've been fortunate enough to have it come true for me, but believe me, getting a lake up and running is hard work. The rewards at the end of the day are well worth it, but you do have to make sacrifices. As for me, well, my own angling went on the back burner for over two years. I really wanted to get back to my fishing, though, and I needed a challenge, which I found in the shape of a 40-plus common that lived in a local club lake I was lucky enough to have a ticket for. I'd had my eye on this fish for years, and what a carp it was - a real stunner and more than enough to get the old juices flowing again.

The lake in question is not much more than two acres in size, very deep at one end (20 feet plus), crystal clear, tree-lined, and with some major snaggy areas in the corners. In mid-April, I started walking it, and soon realised that I hadn't been on a water like this in years. I could see carp everywhere in the crystal clear margins, swimming backwards and forwards from snag to snag. It raised the heartbeat just watching them and I could have sat there all day.

In one corner, there was the biggest set of snags you could ever wish for, similar to the ones at Tolpits, and as the weather warmed, the carp would sit high in the water absorbing the sun's rays. There I would be, perched in a tree watching them. I saw some good fish, lots of 20s and quite a few 30s, both mirrors and commons.

On my first trip, I decided to fish the swim next to these snags. I noticed the route they took in and out of the area and after a little cast about, I found one nice gravel patch where the water was five to six feet deep. A good spot for an ambush, I thought.

Bait-wise I decided to use the new, at the time, Dynamite Halibut boilies, which I really like in conjunction with the halibut pellet. I fished a bottom bait in a PVA bag with pellet cast to the gravel area, with a few pouches of boilies. My other rod was fished in the margins to the left, in a more silty area. About an hour after casting out, I started noticing a few feeding bubbles around the gravel spot. It was early evening and the fish must have been leaving the safety of the snags to have a quiet munch - and so it was 'bleep' then bang, I was away. The fish headed straight back toward the snags, as I knew it would, but fishing this particular gravel area gave me a fair bit of time to apply the pressure and turn it around. After a good scrap, I steered a nice common into the net, my first carp from the lake. Fantastic! A cracking common of 27lbs.

I was the only one fishing the lake that night, and as I'm not keen on sacking fish, I had to let her go with no photos. A shame, being my first one from the lake, but the memory's there. Anyway, by the morning I'd let another three 20s go - commons of 20lbs, 21lbs and 23lbs. What a great start. Four 20s on my first session and I was buzzing! I started to realise it wasn't going to be so easy to single out the big common though. For all the time I'd spent walking the banks, I was yet to see her.

Over the next few trips, I fished the same swim and had some nice carp up to 25lbs, including a few mirrors, which seemed that much harder to catch. Things were going really well and the fishing was just great when I was there, in my own little world, which was just what I needed.

On one trip, I spoke to a member who'd caught the big common from a certain swim at the end of April. I noted this info and decided I'd have to give the swim a try in the near future, but I was still doing well on my little spot near the snags and it's hard to pull away from an area when you're catching. I should have moved earlier though. Before long, the big one came out at 43lbs from the very swim I'd been told about. It was a lesson learned. Still, never mind. Blimey - I'd only been fishing the lake for a few weeks, and I still had the big girl to look forward to, whenever, if ever. I was enjoying my fishing and that's what it's was all about.

I started to work my way around the lake, fishing all the swims. I caught a 28lb common and a pretty, fully-scaled mirror of 22lbs. It was now mid-May and the weather was getting hot. I started paying a bit of attention to an area that no one else seemed to bother with. It was a corner of the lake near the entrance, and nearly everyone bangs the gate and walks straight past it.

I realised it wasn't going to be that easy to single out the big common.

I was in my own little world, this was just what I needed.

Slack lines in the crystal clear water were the way forward.

One of only two fully-scaled carp the lake holds.

A little willow just up from the corner always seemed to hold some fish so I spent a few days watching them, and then one day there she was, the big 'un. She came gliding along, tight to the margins with a few of her mates. I had found her at last, but judging by the way the carp were behaving, I think other things were on their minds, like spawning. Anyway, I still had a go. I fished one rod from the corner tight along the margin and I laid on the bank for hours, watching and waiting. I caught a small common. You always do, it's in the script!

I decided to do the night in the swim and managed another couple of small commons. Then the next day she was back again, the big common. I was sure to catch her today, I thought, as I lay along the bank watching, heart pounding. She drifted through, stopped over a few pellets right near my hookbait and began feeding. This was it, surely a take was imminent? Then, out of nowhere came a couple of small commons. The ignorant little sods smashed along the side of her and she was gone, along with my chance. With that, I decided to leave the fish alone for a while and let them have their time. I would be back in the autumn.

My first session back was the bank holiday at the end of August. I decided to go over on the Monday because I knew it would be busy and thought that people would be starting to pack up and leave. It was banged-out when I got there with only one swim left. I spoke to one of the anglers and he said only a couple of fish had been caught all weekend and the bloke that had been in the empty swim had copped the hump and gone home because of the lack of action. The swim that was now free was one I really liked and had caught a few fish from, but really I'd fancied trying other areas of the lake. However, without any other options, I made my way round to the vacant peg.

I'd only been in the swim for a short time and already I could see signs of fish out in the middle. They were very discreet, just the odd fin breaking the surface now and then, and it was obvious that lots of pressure, with almost everyone fishing the margins, had pushed them out to the middle of the lake. I watched for a while, trying to get a picture of what was going on and thinking about what I needed to do to catch.

The bloke on the bank to my left had just cast his rods short, and he was the guy that had caught, so that left me with some scope to go for the fish I'd been watching earlier. Two pop-ups were tied on and, as gently as possible, I cast them to the middle. Fish were still showing and after about an hour I had a ripper on the right-hand rod. This fish stayed deep and all the way in it hugged the bottom. It was a real job getting her up in the water, but eventually the fish was in the margins, a nice, dark mid-20 common with a huge tail that would account for its scrapping abilities.

That afternoon, until late evening, I had another three takes. I lost one of them and landed a couple of 20s. A great afternoon's fishing to begin stage two of my campaign. Anglers began leaving the lake and with the lessening of pressure the fish were spreading out a bit, getting back to their normal routine, so I pulled one rod back from the middle. During the night I had a fish on both rods, including a 25lb mirror from the one I'd put at close range. From my swim, the snaggy corner was to the left, so I reeled in and went over for a quick look and, as usual, there were lots of fish hanging around the snags. Every now and then, they would leave in twos and threes, follow the snaggy tree-lined bank, and move from one part of the lake to another. It was like a busy roadway.

Just further down from the snaggy corner was another swim. I stood there for a while and saw the same groups of fish moving backwards and forwards. From here, you could only ever fish the margins because if you went out too far you would encroach into another swim's water - the one I was in. Among these fish, I saw a deep-bodied carp, one known as the Football Common. It was one of the lake's characters and a fish I would have liked to catch, so I stood there watching.

A nice, dark mid-20 common.

It's great when it's crystal clear and you hide yourself away and just watch - better then anything on TV! Suddenly, the Football Common was back again and I had to have a go at catching her.

On one side there was part of a willow tree, which hung down into the water fairly close in. It was a good ambush area and I began to wonder if I could hit it from my swim, so I headed back. Looking across, I could see that it was possible, it was a tricky cast but nothing too hard, so I went back round with a handful of boilies and stood well back out of view. One at a time, I fed baits into the ambush zone, plonking the boilies just off the hangers; now to get that rod on the spot. A slight crosswind was making it a bit tricky, as two casts were on the right line but both dropped a bit short. You know when you feather it down, worried about landing in the trees and completely trashing the swim, blowing your chances. Third cast - hit or bust. Out it went, and landed bang on, within inches of the hanging branches. Well happy!

I doubt if anyone had ever fished this area in this way before and the line lay and angles were just perfect. I spend a lot of time trying to fish areas from different swims, laying the line toward the swim instead of coming away, and it makes a difference for sure.

The rod was only out for ten minutes and then it was off to a fast take and I had to give line immediately. The fish headed out into the middle of the lake away from danger, but on the surface the whole way. It was now three-quarters of the way across the lake, thrashing around on the surface, and I had to get some control over this fish because from way out there it could have gone in any direction and caused me all manner of grief.

Eventually, I started to tame the beast, and what a scrapper it was, right to the very end. Near the net, I could see that it was the Football Common. What a result! Not the best-looking fish in the lake but certainly one of the characters. Over the years it had obviously had many hard battles and because of this had suffered some mouth damage. From the fight it gave me, I'm not surprised. Poor old girl, a real veteran warrior. She weighed 31lb 8oz and I slipped her back to fight another hard battle another day.

My plan was working out really well so the rod was cast straight back out. I fished through the night and by the next morning I had landed 11 carp and lost one. Nine 20s, one 30 and a double. What a great little session! I ended up fishing many different areas from that swim, using the water to the max. This was all well and good, but was I going to catch the big 'un like that? I didn't think so.

A very rare mid-30 mirror.

The Football Common powered off to the middle of the lake.

As it was now heading towards autumn and I was prepared to go right through the winter until the spring, I decided to freshen up my baiting approach. I felt that The Source would be a good choice for my winter bait, so I started to put a bit in, cutting back on the halibut.

The fish were really feeding hard now on the natural larders, and some days went by with plenty of sheeting up in the silt but no takes whatsoever. I've seen it so many times. I was still catching but didn't seem to be getting any closer to the big 'un. I hadn't seen her for ages, and I really wanted to find her because I knew it wouldn't be long before she came out. No matter how much you would like it, though, you can't be on the lake all the time. It drives me insane when I'm not there. Every time my mobile phone rings, I'm thinking: 'Yep, she's been out' - and then it happened. I was sitting at home in my garden with my missus on our wedding anniversary, a glass of cold wine in my hand, when my mate Dicky turned up with an 'I've just caught a 40lb common' look on his face; and so it was!

My heart sank straight away. 'It might not come out until next spring now,' I was thinking, but Dicky and me had been fishing a fair bit together over at the lake, and he's a good mate and a very capable angler who fully deserved to catch her - the bastard! I went back to the lake with a still-grinning Dicky to do the photos. I'd seen the Sutton Big Common on the bank at 41lbs to Jason Barber, and I'd also been fortunate enough to have caught that fish myself, albeit at a lower weight. It's an awesome common, but when Dicky unwrapped this one, my God, it was impressive! So well proportioned and the nicest common I had ever seen. She looked great in the photos. It took a week or so before I could get my head back on and continue with my dream quest.

Dicky had caught her from high up on the marginal shelf and I thought she could still be in the same area of that bank, but might have dropped down into the deeper margin. It was now October and I am always hopeful but, in truth, I thought my chance had gone. I'd been fishing the deep margin spot as regularly as I could, and although it was a really tricky place to place a bait, but once in position I always felt confident. I used a scoop on a long pole to drop bait on the outer hangers, an area that you couldn't reach from anywhere else on the lake. It seemed so perfect. I was catching the odd fish and keeping a nice bit of bait going in.

I turned up for a two-nighter in mid-October and went through the assault course of getting my bait on the spot before settling down for the night, and at 11pm I was away. It felt like a good fish but I soon had her controlled under the rod tip. It went through my mind; is it her? Could this be it? No, it was a nice 26lb common — well appreciated and all that, but...

I eventually managed to coax her up in the water.

And now, at last, one lay in my net.

I now had to get my rod back on the spot in the dark and I must admit I was close to just chucking it in the margins until the morning, but I made the effort, got the pole out, and surprisingly got my bait in position without a hitch. Blooming miracle! A cup of tea and it was back to the old bag.

At 4am all hell broke loose. Before I really knew what was happening I found myself standing there playing a fish, my heart pounding from the adrenalin rush. After a few powerful lunges, wrapping the rod round nearly double to my right, the fish was soon under my rod tip. I finally steadied my breathing and got control of my heart rate. The battle was now deep down in the margins, with the fish plodding backwards and forwards, and me unable to lift it off the bottom. I eventually managed to coax her up in the water and after about three boils on the surface, I slid the net under the fish. All I could think of was how glad I was to have made the effort to put the rod back on the spot.

I grabbed my torch and had a quick look in the landing net. It was a good common, as long as my landing net was wide. I started getting my bits together - scales, weigh sling, mat etc, but as I was doing so I kept having to have another look, still not really knowing what I'd caught. I lifted the net a bit so I could see the fish properly and it finally dawned on me. It was her, the big girl. I couldn't believe it. A dream come true! I was punching the air, giving it 'Yes! Yes!' and all that. I had been dreaming for years about huge commons and now, at last, one lay in my net.

Dicky works nights and would be on his way home around now, perfect for a quick text to him, and to everyone else I knew! Before long, Dicky arrived and we weighed her. She went 43lb 8oz on the scales. Blooming superb!

With the photos done, which came out very well thanks to Chad and Dicky, we put her back. I packed up shortly afterwards and went home to tell the tale of the Long Common to anyone who would listen, even my dog Thomas, who I've never forgiven for not seeming suitably impressed. Man's best friend indeed!

Chapter Twelve
A Brace of Forties - Wellington

After catching Shoulders at Horton Church Lake, I decided to pull off for a while and fish around a few places and it was at this time that Gary Bayes suggested I should join the Nash team. Gary's a good mate and a genius when it comes to bait, so it didn't take me long to make my decision and it turned out to be the best thing I ever did. My first time out with my new Nash bait was my first session on Wellington Country Park. My mate, Ian Poole, had taken me over to Welly for a guest session the previous year. He'd put in a good word for me with Andy Pye, the fishery manager, and I was lucky to get a ticket. Good old Ian.

At the time, Wellington was really making an impression in the carp world with some big fish getting caught. There were many upper-30s and about eight that would do 40lbs, so you can see why I was so interested in the place. When I arrived, I stashed my gear in a swim named the Hole in the Bush. It was popular because it had an island to fish to, and the channel between the Hole in the Bush and the island was a good ambush place because the carp would be using it as they made their way from one end of the lake to the other.

My swim was on a spit of land and when I walked down to my right, I came to Bramble Bay, so I walked down to have a look. The bay was completely coloured up, all murky and yellow, whereas the rest of the lake was nice and clear. The carp were completely having it in this area, they were going mad, and this is not a small bay; it's at least four acres. As I stood there, a big lump smashed out along the other bank of the bay, with a huge splash, just off one of the marginal bushes. I was already making my way back to my barrow.

As I pushed my gear around the bay, I was looking as I went and all the way round the bay I only saw a few places to fish from, so I decided that I would park my barrow up, keep it there as a base camp and go off stalking. The perfect place I found to leave my gear was in a swim called Lorries, on a point and facing into the bay. It also covered a channel that went into the bay, and you could even swing your rods around into the main lake from there. It was the perfect swim and if the fish decided to leave the bay I would still have a chance at picking them up as they left. It was looking like we might get some rain so I set up the bivvy and got everything tucked away just in case. I looked across the Bramble Bay, and noticed that the weed was top to bottom, and a big mound of it had already been raked in and piled up in the front of the swim. Later, I found out that it was Ian Poole who'd been raking.

Armed with a rod and all the other bits I needed to stalk with, and the now empty barrow to transport it, I set off on a slow walk around the lake. I was looking for signs of fish actually feeding and although it was already evident that they were, or had been, I wanted to drop a bait as near to feeding fish as I possibly could. I was using a 2oz inline lead, about 4 feet of leadcore and with my new Scopex Squid bait I fished a snowman on a blow-back ring to a size 8 Fang, and to this I attached a small Webcast ball of oily halibut pellets. I left my gear and searched out all the margins, leaving a few pellets here and there, and just kept walking round until I found something to have a go at, but most of the fish I saw were out a bit further in the middle area of the bay. It was already late afternoon, and suddenly, the sky turned jet-black and I would be in for a soaking unless I got back to my base camp, so I wrapped everything up and got back sharpish.

A liitle bit of weed never hurt anybody.

The rain held off but the sky was still black as I started to get sorted out for the night ahead, trying to find a couple of spots. The weed was thick, as I expected, but eventually I did find two little clear-ish areas. One of these was a channel in the weed that led into a clear spot with weed all around it, so my plan was to fish one rod at the beginning of the channel, and one in the clearing. I spodded out some hemp and small pellets, with some 10mm Scopex Squids mixed in, and then cast two snowman rigs to the spots and fired out some 15mms for good measure.

I was just tidying up my swim when one of the fishery bailiffs turned up. Kenny was a nice old bloke and we had something in common, as we'd both served in the army. We chatted away for a while and then he asked if I minded him stalking around the bay.
"Of course not," I said. "Feel free."

The nights now were rapidly drawing in and the odd fish had rolled not a million miles away from my clear area that was surrounded by weed. Apart from the small channel that led to the clearing, I bet there was a maze of little tunnels under the water that linked up all over the place. At eight o'clock, it was pitch black. I was getting a brew on the go and I had a couple of liners on the left rod. The latching light went out, lit up again, the bobbin pulled up to the top and the line snapped out of the clip. I picked up the rod and it hooped over instantly as the fish took a short amount of line and weeded me up. As I stood there with the rod bent, holding the pressure, I heard a voice.
"There's plenty of fish in the bay, Jerry. You should be in for some action tonight!" Kenny was walking past my swim after his little trip around the bay.
"I've actually got one on now," I said.
He couldn't see me properly as he was going past, but now he came and stood by my side as I tried my best to coax the fish out of the weed, or even to get it to break away from the main bed,so that I could bring back the weed and the fish with it.

The fish did break away and still had some weed over its head as it slowly came back to me, and then about 20 feet from my bank, it broke free and went off on a couple of short runs until it was once again weeded up, and I had to repeat the process. The water was shallow in front of my swim and to be fair I really should have had my waders on in order to net it. Luckily for me, though, Kenny was there, and he went out in his wellies with the net, and the next time it came close enough, he scooped up my first Wellington Country Park fish. I grabbed a head torch and we both looked in the net at this massive common.

I couldn't believe it! My first night and I'd gone and caught a right lump; I was buzzing. I got my mat and bits ready, slipped my waders on and Kenny helped me to lift it out and on to the mat. Another angler, Rick Golder, came round to see what was going on, and we hoisted her onto the scales. She went over 40lbs and we settled at 40lbs 8oz. Well, the last thing I'd expected was to catch a 40lb common on my first night. I was so made up. Rick took a few photos for me, then I waded out with my prize carp into the safety of the deeper water, another quick return shot and she was gone. It wasn't even 9pm.

Kenny produced two bottles of Budweiser from somewhere and he drank a beer with me and then made his way off home. I flicked the rod back out as near to my spot as possible and sat on my bedchair for a while in a daze, thinking about what had just happened and how lucky I was. Before I eventually went to sleep that night, I decided to wear just my boxers. That way, if I had any more action I would be able to walk out into the lake without having to fuss about getting into my waders. During the night, the threatened rain eventually arrived with a vengeance. It was lashing it down, and occasionally, I woke, turned over, snuggled back into my pillow, and drifted back into the land of monster carp.

At first light, the right-hand rod was bellowing out a tone that went right through me and instantly had me out, and still half asleep, bent into a carp. The only thing they were able to do was bury themselves into the weed, but fortunately, a lot of it was floating, which was good because the fish would dive into it and just sit there. I was then able to wind the bundle of fish and weed gently back. It was still raining and I was out about ten feet or so in my boxers. I'd forgotten the dog walkers, nothing will stop them from being out, and just as I thought about them, I heard the sound of a woman and her rottweiler who'd been round the day before. She had to come right past my swim. My boxers were wet now, totally see-through and clinging to my privates, and as I turned just at the wrong time, she looked at me, and I said, "Morning." I wasn't sure if she smiled or laughed, but anyway, back to the fish.

I managed to get the carp most of the way back without too much of a problem. I could feel it still on and, every now and then, it would kick its tail and send up a vortex behind the weed it was wrapped up in. I had to walk back a bit to get the net from the bank, and as the fish came nearer, I was able to see a good-sized mirror just behind the weed. I had to get the net right under all the weed to net it, and the first time I just netted the weed and was furious with myself, so I waded out to above my waist and this time, on the second attempt, I scooped the lot up.

I couldn't believe it! A 40-pound common within hours of being there.

By this time, more dog owners were walking about and I was standing there more or less naked, with a fish in the net, but unable to do anything. Thankfully, Rick was able to see from his swim and came round to help out, so I quickly put my waders on and a jacket while Rick held the net. I took over from Rick, had a look, and there lay another chunk of a fish. I removed all the weed and Rick gave me a hand to carry it to the mat. We unrolled the net. I unhooked him carefully and Rick recognised the fish as the Dark One. I double-checked that the scales were zeroed to my weigh sling, and using a weighing pole, we lifted it and the scales read 41lbs. What a night's fishing that was! A brace of 40s. Only in my wildest dreams did I imagine that would happen, but it had, it was real and I was on cloud nine.

Once again, the photos were done and back went my second 40 of the trip. This place was unreal and from then on, I renamed Wellington 'Jurassic Park', because it was just that full of monsters. I still had another 24 hours of my session left so naturally, I put the rods back out, got myself dried off and put a bit more bait in. The carp were still about and the conditions were spot on. It was still overcast and windy, and every now and then a fine drizzle would blow in with the wind. I just kept thinking about my catch. I'd already caught Shoulders from Horton earlier; what a season I was having!

Lost for words. The Dark One at 41lbs.

Later in the afternoon, I had another take and landed a chunky 33lb mirror. They seemed to love the Scopex and this just boosted my confidence sky high since I had only just joined Nash. Things in the bay seemed to be quietening down. The colour of the water was slowly turning back to normal, and I had seen a few fish show as if they were trickling out through the channel and back into the main lake. I was soon able to see the dark colours of the weed more clearly, so I flicked out a rig to one of the gaps in the weed that the fish would have to pass as they left. I still had some spod mix left, which I put over that rod. My last night was soon upon me, but I was more than happy with my catch and ready to get off in the morning to go home to celebrate.

At first light, the same as the previous day, I was up and bent into a fish, as another big carp took me through the weed beds. This one, though, took me further out into the middle of the lake where it was even shallower, and was rocking about in the weed making a big disturbance. It was lashing it down with rain and somehow, while I was playing this one, I managed to get under my umbrella and put on the waders and a waterproof jacket. With that done, I was ready to finish the battle, but as with the others, when they got caught up in the weed it was just a case of praying that they didn't fall off, and guiding them back. A few times, it broke free and steamed off but I was soon able to get the net under another nice carp.

This one capped off an amazing session.

The rain stopped and the sun came out, and just as I was wading back with the fish an angler turned up with his gear, so he helped me to weigh and photograph this one. It was very yellow and went 35lbs. It had capped off an amazing session for me, and I was ready for the off. I was nearly packed up when suddenly, the channel rod was flying away, and I thought, 'this place is unreal'. I ended up catching a nice 20 as a little leaving present.

When everything was on the barrow, I stood there in the swim for a while. All the colour had dropped out of the water completely now and it had returned to its normal state. I reflected on the trip and all the carnage that had gone on, and now looking at the bay, it was all still with no wind, the sun was out and it was as if nothing had happened. In all my time at Wellington, I only did about ten trips. I have to say, it's an amazing water and a credit to Andy Pye, who runs it. It really is a Jurassic Park.

One freezing cold February I did a trip with Nick Helleur. We were flying around the lake looking for fish, and ended up catching a few from the same swim (Lorries), fishing into the bay. Nick had them up to 27lbs, and then I saw a big fish jump in the main lake so we moved further along the bank and fished out toward an island.

We flew around the lake like nutters. One of Nick's fish, a 27lb mirror.

A strong wind blew up so we sat in Nick's bivvy drinking tea, and then at midnight, the wind dropped leaving a crisp, freezing cold night. As I returned to my bivvy, I looked up to the heavens and saw an amazing shooting star whiz across the sky. I made a small wish asking for a big fish in the night, and at 1am, I was up doing battle. Nick got up to man the net, and as it was shallow, he got his waders on and waded out a bit.

I walked back up the bank, drawing the fish toward the waiting net and Nick scooped it first time. Until then, the fish we'd caught were, by Welly standards, the smaller ones.
"It's not a bad one, mate," Nick said. "Looks like a 30."
"That good?" I said.
As he dragged the net and fish back, he kept looking into the mesh, and each time he spoke the fish was getting bigger.
"I don't know," he said. "Could be an upper-30."

Finally, on the bank, this fish kept growing and I found that I'd got myself another Wellington 40-pounder, at 41lbs. My shooting star wish had come true and I'd banked a true winter 40.

My shooting star wish had come true.

A winter favourite. My ever-reliable, orange Esterblend pop-ups.

Ian nodded his head with approval.

My last ever session on Wellington was in late March, and another amazing one. I fished the swim called the Hole in the Bush, out at long range as I'd seen some fish show off some overhanging bushes on the island. It was a fair chuck, over 100 yards, and to make things worse a strong wind was blowing down the channel left to right. As it was, I was still using my winter favourite, 12-14mm orange Esterblend pop-ups, the same as I'd used for years and had caught the winter 40 on. There was still weed out by the island so I was using the chod rig; the fish were already present so the last thing I wanted to do was scare them off by chucking a marker rod at them.

Ian Poole had just finished a session and was on his way home, but he called in for a chat. As we sat and talked, a few fish showed in the same area and I tried desperately to get a hook bait in there. I lined up a cast and waited. When a gust of wind dies out, there's always that little interval before it blows back up again, and that's when I launched my chod. After a few attempts, I timed it just right, whacked the rod hard and the rig sailed out, landing right on target. I turned to look at Ian and he was nodding his head in approval.
"That hit the spot," I said.
I was winding up the slack and had undone the clutch to pull some line off the spool, when it started to spin in my hands and I was in. The fish must have taken the bait, as soon as it hit the bottom. A good scrap followed as the fish went on long kites left and right, as they do on long lines. It's always horrible when a strong wind is blowing and the old line sings away.

Ian manned the net and I had my first fish of the trip, a nice-looking mirror of 35lbs, in all its winter colours. What a start to the session! Little did I know just what lay ahead of me. I kept on fishing long to the island and caught another five fish from there, all on the Esterblend, my old faithful. I even caught a 36lb ghostie! During the session, I'd also been putting in a lot of Scopex Squid. Down to my right, there was another island and I'd found an area off the side of it that was thick silt so I'd put out five kilos as soon as I arrived, the fish had got on it and I started to get a few bites from there.

Ian 'Ting Tong' Macmillan, had moved next door to me, and I have to tell you this little story. Ian has a really bad case of OCD and everything has to be immaculate. He told me that when he finishes a session he even strips the line off his spools and cleans it. That's mental, it really is, but each to their own and I really like Ian, he's a right character. I noticed he had a dustpan and brush in his bivvy, and I'm sure someone told me that, nowadays, he has an electric Hoover. Well, I used to love talking to him outside his bivvy and every time he looked away, I'd flick things into it.

A 35lb winter mirror caught on the drop.

He'd look back, spot the bits straight away, and expel them from his disinfected dome. I loved it, and as I walked away, I just couldn't help but turn my toes in and flick a nice bit of crap through his door, as if by mistake. Poor sod, he'd get in a right mess about it.

Anyway, I had a take from the silty spot off the island and this fish was a powerhouse, giving me a right old scrap. My rods were up on the bank and the swim dropped into the water so the best way to play them was to get in the lake and wade out, otherwise if they ran you left or right down the margins, you were bound to catch your line on the margin trees and bushes. So I was in the water playing my fish but my landing net was on the far side of my other rods, leaning against a tree, so to save me having to climb over my lines, Ian offered to go and get his net for me. He brought back the net and I put it down by my side, but this fish was nowhere near ready and was on yet another powerful run heading left towards Ian's rods.
"You'd better go dip your rods, mate," I said, looking back at Ian. "It's on its way to your swim."
He didn't seem that bothered, until his alarms started to scream away as my fish ploughed through his set-up.

I even caught a 36lb 'spookie'.

All I could see was a lot of scales down either flank. The Big Linear at 39lbs 14oz.

"Noooo!" I heard him cry, as he ran back to his rods.
"You're gonna have to loosen your clutches!" I shouted, "so I can get the fish back." I was getting no response from Ian. I don't know what he was doing, probably lying on the floor crying.

I was gaining on the fish, and it was all made that much harder now I had a few of Ian's lines attached, but I managed to net it. 'Phew! That was a close one and I was lucky to get it in,' I thought, as I looked in the net. All I could see was a lot of scales down either flank and I knew I had another special fish. Ian was taking ages, even though I had sorted out his lines and had let them go. God knows what he was doing next door, but eventually he turned up to help me out with my fish. I'd bitten my line, lifted the net to undo the arms and, under hardly any weight on the landing net handle, the thing just snapped at the spreader block. Well, you can imagine. Ian let out another loud cry of "Nooo!"
"Sorry, mate," I said. "Not very strong those handles are they?"
Ian ran around a bit on the spot, and he then helped me out with my fish.

What a beauty! It was a known fish called the Big Linear, and she weighed just shy of 40lbs – 39lbs 14oz. Wellington had once again given me one of her prizes, and that fish ended a fabulous session, with 11 fish caught that included five over 30lbs in March. What a great trip! Ian was great fun and I do love him really, even if he does think I look like David Dickinson. I said my goodbyes to Ian, left him my landing net, and it was farewell to Wellington Country Park, where some of my most prolific carp fishing memories were made.

One of the five over 30lbs.

Chapter Thirteen
The Black Common - Croxley

Croxley Hall was another lake I'd heard about, and it just so happened that an old mate of mine, Toby Cook, from way back at the Lagoons, was running the water. I managed to get in touch with Toby and he told me that there might be a place and if so, he would let me know. One of my mates, Stuart Court from Tolpits, already had a ticket and he'd been keeping me updated about the place. It seemed there were some very good fish to be caught. From what I could gather, there was one big mirror that was upper-30, and I think it had gone 40 before, but the real jewel of the lake was a common that was over 40lbs and, without any doubt, it was one of the nicest common carp I had ever seen. The only one that comes close to it is the Cotton Farm fish at Lee Jackson's water in Kent. This fish is to me, and this is only my view, probably the best-looking common in the country. It's a dark chocolate colour and one that I would just love to have a photo of. The stock in the lake was in favour of commons and was definitely a venue for anglers to catch a PB common. There were also fair few more that were good 30s and I think a couple at the right time had scraped 40lbs. So I was just waiting for the call. Toby was true to his word and one day he called me up and said I could have a ticket. Well, I was overjoyed and wasted no time in sending off my money.

I had an idea of what it looked like, because I'd been checking out the website where they have a view of every swim. The lake is 10 acres, and gets a lot of Canadian weed during the summer. It's a long rectangular shape and at one end, the banks narrow and then open up to form a nice bay. The lake has many features, including bars that get very shallow on top in places, and the fishery management had placed some kind of tray system on top in order to grow some Norfolk reeds, something to be aware of in the dark when playing a fish that's kiting. There were plateaux and silt, and I was champing to get started on this cracking carp lake.

My first session was at the beginning of April. It had been a cold winter and I knew that a few fish had been caught on maggots, but I'd already decided to avoid them because I thought the fish would now be hungry for some proper grub. I left my barrow at the lake entrance and took a walk round. It was a nice day and the sun was out but it was short-lived; only weeks before we'd had ice and severe frosts. I had done a few laps but not much had taken my fancy, so I ended up stopping for a chat with a guy in a swim called No Carp. There's always a 'no carp' swim, whether it's called 'no carp bay', 'no carp point' or simply just 'no carp', and generally they are good swims. This guy told me that he hadn't caught any fish, and as we chatted, I saw a great big mirror come out, right to the wrist. I used my bionic right eye to measure the distance and mark the spot with a tree on the other bank. It had to be that big mirror, the one they called Elvis - I'm not joking, that's what it was called. To see that one was a good sign and it just so happened that the bloke in the swim was off later on. I asked him if it was okay to move in when he left. "Of course," he said. So I went to fetch my barrow and spent the day in a swim next door.

I used my time to organise my tackle for the night ahead. I had planned to use my favourite method, the snowman, which consisted of a Scopex Squid bottom bait and one of my winter favourites, a small 10mm Orange Esterblend for the top. To this I attached a small PVA Webcast ball of little pellets and broken boilies. I only wanted a mouthful for the fish and I hoped they would just suck up the whole lot.

I got in the No Carp swim with just enough time to find my spots, and the first thing I did was to whiz out a marker to where that mirror had shown earlier. I over-cast it to get a good pull back across the area, and found a lot of silt at first, but as I pulled the lead back through it, at just about where I thought I'd seen that fish, I felt a tap-tap-tap. I let the marker up and it was about eight feet deep and looked bang-on. This was to be my left-hand rod without a doubt. Out in front of the swim was a plateau at about 50-odd yards. It was shallow on top, so over the back seemed a good choice for a bait, but as I plumbed up and over the feature, I actually preferred the near side of the plateau, the bit my side of it, as it dropped off into a nice silty food trap. Most people probably fished over the top, so I thought I'd do the opposite.

With both rods set, I was now fishing my new water. Croxley is in the Colne Valley and only walking distance from Tolpits. It's a beautiful, well-maintained private water set on a lovely estate, and there's another lake called Cressacres, that nowadays, you have to fish first before you can get on to Croxley. I can tell you it's well worth the wait.

As darkness fell, the fish started to show. I could hear the sound of them as they flopped about around the lake, and big ripples, visible only from the reflection of the moonlight, gave away their whereabouts. I crashed out that night hopeful that something would happen and then, without any liners or bleeps, the rod that was this side of the plateau was one-toning it. With just a mouthful for them to feed on, one had just sucked in the little parcel that I'd left them in the silt, and was now steaming off toward the other end of the lake to my right.

It was ripping a lot of line from my spool and all I could do was let it go. For a while, I kept a finger on the spool to check its speed a bit, and then I remembered those bloody trays on top of the bars. If the fish took me near them or even around one, it'd be game over for sure. It was pitch black and I was certain there was one of them down that way somewhere. My other worry was that one of the rules is no leaders or leadcore, and with all the gravel about, I would imagine a fair few fish get lost.

Not wanting the fish to go any further, I clamped down on the spool and with that, it changed its route and came left and back out in front of my swim. Thankfully, it had missed any of the trays, and it felt like a heavy fish. Every now and then, it was rolling on the surface some 40 yards out and sending back big ripples. I'd been playing the fish from higher up on the bank but to land it I had to drop down to the water's edge.

I love those mornings, waking up with nature. It's a big part of it for me.

I did so, got the net ready and I now had it under the rod tip. As it kicked hard with its tail to dive deeper, it was sending up vortexes to the surface and it really was hanging on but I was only moments away from catching my first Croxley carp. It was just a matter of getting her up to the surface and then she'd be ready. Suddenly, I was playing nothing. My line was hanging from the rod tip, and my fish was gone. I had been cut off by something and I never felt a thing. It's worse when you've had them on a long time, as I had. It was a good fish for sure, and I doubt I would have lost it with leadcore on, but hey, rules are rules. I re-tackled and cast it out, but it took me ages to get back to sleep after that.

It was a bright morning, I felt that spring was on its way and was looking around enjoying the view. Some parts of the lake had mist over the surface and it was a pleasure to be there. I love those mornings and waking up with nature is such a big part of it for me, something that normal people miss out on. Just before 8am, the bobbin on the rod cast to where I'd seen the fish the previous day, started to pull up and the alarm let out a series of bleeps. My first reaction was to look to the spot where the rod was and I could see two coots bobbing up and down over the spot where my hookbait was. That was the last thing I wanted. They had the whole lake and they had to come and pick on me!

I turned the alarm off, slackened the line and reset the bobbin, made myself a brew and sat there on my bedchair enjoying my first cuppa of the day. I was in deep thought about the fish I'd lost during the night, thinking about what could have been... if only this, if only that... you now how it is. In the background, I became aware of a sound. It would have been only for seconds, but seemed a lot longer. I glanced to my left and saw that the spool on the 'cooted' rod was spinning. Instantly, I looked out to the spot where the two coots had been and they were practically running across the water away from my rod, freaked out by whatever was below. It's always a shock when the alarm isn't on, but I love it. I tend to do it a lot, too. It's like I'm tempting fate.

I took control of the rod – well, to be honest, the fish was in control as it continued to take line - and I was crapping myself. Because of what had happened the

night before, I felt as though I would just be getting cut off all the time. As soon as I started playing the fish, I noticed that an angler on the opposite bank had reeled in and was on his way round. Shortly after, he arrived behind me.
"All right, mate?" he said. "My name's Rob. I thought I'd come and give you a hand."
I was pleased about that, as I would be able to play out the fish from the higher bit of bank without stepping down and risking another cutting off.
"Cheers, mate," I said, and I told him of my misfortune during the night.

In the daylight, I could now see what looked like a couple of submerged poles, a few feet out, that had some mussels attached and I was sure that they were the explanation for my lost fish. I was making progress and had this fish in the danger zone of the margins. Rob got down with the net and in the crystal clear water, I saw a good-sized common go past. Rob turned and looked at me.
"Bloody hell, mate! Do you know what you've got on here?"
Having been a member for a while, Rob knew the fish well and he had just seen something that had got him excited'
"Well, I saw it was a common," I replied.
"I'm not saying anything," he said. "I'll wait until you land it."
Now all sorts were going through my mind. Just what fish was it? As it boiled on the top, I walked backwards and Rob scooped it into the net.
"I can't believe it," he said. "You've got the Blind Eye Common!"
"Oh yeah?" I said. "What's the story with this fish then?"
"Well, apart from the fact that it hardly ever comes out, and this is the first time in a good few years, it's one of the originals," said Rob, "and last out it was over 36lbs. I didn't say anything because from where I was when it went in the net, it looked like a nice common, but that was all I knew until I saw it."

On the bank, it truly was a stunning fish, a nice bronze; and it did have a blind eye that was a yellow colour. We pushed a bank stick through the top of the scales so we could both take the weight and they settled at 38lbs 8oz. I was so happy and this certainly made up for the loss in the night.

Rob did me some good shots and I slid the blind-eyed carp back to keep out of the way for another few years. I thanked Rob very much for his help and he wandered back off to his swim. What must he have thought? I turn up for my first trip and catch one of the lake's gems. Sometimes that's how it goes, though, if your name's on it and all that. Over at Croxley there's a 48-hour rule, I had another night to go and before I packed up in the morning, I caught another nice common of 33lbs. I was really liking this place and couldn't wait to get back.

The Blind Eye Common. A rare visitor to the bank.

One thing I learned quickly about Croxley was that it was one of the best surface waters I have ever fished. It was probably due to the weed that year. In places it was top-to-bottom Canadian and the carp loved it; they seemed to feel safe to feed in and around it on the surface. I absolutely love surface fishing and zigs so I was keen to not miss out. The carp at Croxley were so up for a floater it was unreal. I'd be up early and start to get the mixers out just after daybreak, while the mist would be still clinging to the wate. The kettle would be on, and within only a short time, big sets of shoulders would start to break the surface, and I would say to myself, 'today is gonna be another good'un'. What a way to start the day! Perfect.

I had some amazing floater sessions but one stands out. I was in a swim called the Feathers. It was really weedy, and on daybreak I got them scoffing down the mixers and some really good fish were among them. I soon started the day with a chunky 33lb common that was hard work as it weeded me straight away, and as it was out about 40 yards, it took a while to get it back. So I wasn't going to give the next one I hooked the chance to dive, and the plan was to get it back in close as quickly as possible. The carp were going up and down in a line devouring the floaters and, as I watched excitedly, I knew a bite was imminent. A big fish chomped its way to my hook bait and, as it took it in, I struck and wound down, not giving the fish the chance to get going. Before the fish and I knew it, I had it two rod lengths out, as planned.

I'd get the mixers out and get them going before the sun came up.

The fish was in my territory now but it was aware of the situation. It bored down to the bottom, and buried itself in thick weed. I kept the pressure on and thousands of bubbles were frothing on the surface as my carp dug deeper. All I could do was stand there with the rod bent over and hope that it would eventually move off, but no, this fish was having none of it. I tried different line angles but all to no avail.

Another angler had come along to fish and stayed for a while to see if I would get this one in. While he was there, I got the fish moving from its dug-in position. It came to the surface with a big boil-up and then powered back to the lake bed, but this time only about 15 feet from the bank. I was in my shorts so I waded out and the margins dropped off sharply so I was soon up to my chest, but now the fish was right under the rod tip and I was having no luck. I tried everything, and I even had my small bolt machine surface float just out of the water, so the fish wasn't that far below, but no matter what I tried I just couldn't budge it.

I'd had it weeded up for ages and as a last resort, I pointed the rod so that the tip would be pointing at where I thought the fish was, and then backed off a bit. With a straight rod, I started to pull gently and immediately I got it moving. The angler watching applauded.
"Well done," he said."
"I've done this before," I told him, "and it's worked, but normally as a last resort."

I played it for a while thinking I'd won the battle, and guess what, it buried itself in the weed again. This was getting a bit silly now. My friend on the bank decided he'd had enough, wished me luck, and wandered off to find a swim. When he'd gone, I thought I'd try the old straight pull again, only this time as I got the fish moving, the line snapped. To be honest, I thought the line had done well to have lasted that long. It was a 10lb mono that someone had given me, a prototype without a label and it really was tough. I wish I had some today. Anyway, I was gutted but I praise the fish in situations like that, and the carp was victorious, but I had a feeling that it was a big old lump.

During that long battle I'd asked the watching angler to fire a few mixers out and the whole time I was playing that fish, carp were still slurping away. I soon had a new hook length tied up and I was once again in with another chance. A breeze had started to blow up, making it a little harder as I now had to keep casting to drift the hook bait through the swim. My perseverance paid off, though, and I hooked another good fish that I tried the same tactics on - getting it close in quickly - and this time it worked. Triumphantly, I landed a big-framed common that went 37lbs, and that made me feel a whole lot better after the lost one.

On the take, I tried to get them in close as quickly as possible. My tactics worked with this upper-30.

As the wind was now blowing too hard for me to surface fish, I set up a zig and fished it just under the surface. For a hook bait, I like to trim up a Scopex Squid pop-up because they are a similar colour to a mixer and work really well. I fished both rods like this. The fish were evidently still up in the layers and it was a good way to fish; both rods were on the alarms so I could relax and have cuppa. When the fish takes the hookbait, there's a massive eruption over the rod followed by the alarm screaming. It was great and I caught plenty this way. I even fished the zigs at night. I never had much action but at first light one would rip off without fail. Those times were really enjoyable and I was fishing for big fish. It was such a buzz.

Most of my trips that spring were focused on floater fishing, providing the weather was favourable. The weed was savage and a lot of swims were unfishable, so I chose to set up where I thought each day would bring some floater action. A lot of fish were held up in the weed between Nick's and the Long Bar swims, so I spent the afternoon floater fishing between the two, but as the evening drew in, I had to think about getting the rods set for the night ahead. By this time, the fish had taken a bit of a hammering on the surface so I started to drop the zigs at night and fish on the bottom over bait. I was still in a floater swim, though, and finding spots was tricky, especially if I was still floater fishing when it was nearly dark, and not giving myself enough time to get sorted.

On one occasion, I just about had time to find a couple of clear holes in the weed and spod out some hemp and corn, and to each spot I cast my trusty maize rig with plastic pop-up maize. With the rods all set, I continued to watch the fish finishing off the floaters that I had been firing out, and a few times I nearly reeled a rod back in and started on the surface again. It was a muggy, sticky night and the carp became active as the hot daytime temperature dropped a few degrees. The mozzies were loving it. It was one of those evenings when the tiny black midges just would not leave you alone, and those things are nasty little sods - they draw blood!

I was just thinking about how I was ever going to get any peace that night, what with all the insect activity, when I received a take on the right-hand rod. The fish instantly shot off and went under a weed bed, and I was sure it wasn't a carp but a Baron Greenback (tench), and it was weeded solid. I put the rod down and loosened the clutch, and every now and then it would take some line. Then I'd pick the rod up and it would more or less end up back in the same weed bed, and I was unable to budge it. This went on for a while until I got really tired and needed some sleep. The floater fishing really does take it out of you when you're at it for hours on end. I decided to get my head down and I hoped that the tench would shake itself off, or every so often, I might get up and try and get it in. Yeah, that was a solid plan. Lights out.

I focused most of my attention on zigs and floater fishing.

The start of another fine day at Croxley Hall.

Time to get those mixers out.

It seemed that I'd only been asleep for a little while when my left-hand rod was off. I jumped up to deal with it, and a tap-tap, on the rod tip was confirmation that I was playing another Baron. My method of the plastic over hemp and corn can obviously attract some unwelcome visitors, and it's something I have to put up with, but all the good fish I've caught on this method easily outweigh having to get up for the odd tench.

I got this one in sharpish, because the last thing I wanted was two weeded-up tench. Then, I picked up the other rod and this time, I managed to extract it from its weedy refuge. So now, I had two rods on the bank. It was about 2am and there was no way I was getting them back on the spots; it was hard enough in the daylight. I leaned them against my brolly and got my head down.

It must have been about 5.30am when I awoke for some reason. A bit of cloud cover had moved in, a fine rain was spraying the side of my sleeping bag, and as I lay there, I was staring at my rods and thinking, 'what the hell am I doing here?' I had two redundant rods leaning against my umbrella, so I wasn't even fishing, and it was looking like it'd be a washout for any floater fishing later on. With that, I jumped out of the old bag and grabbed one of the rods. I took aim at the left-hand area, sent out my plastic hook bait and as the lead hit the water I stopped the line with the tip of my finger and felt it down, thinking 'Yeah, you'll be lucky, son'. Thump, it went. Bloody hell, that'll do! I couldn't be sure if I'd fluked it and landed on my spot, but it was staying there. The rain was picking up and I was getting wet so I quickly attached the bobbin and slackened off the line. I left the other rod and got under the cover of my sleeping bag.

The next thing I knew, the recast rod was pulling around and I was really annoyed by now. Those bloody tench are a right nuisance, so I jumped out, and to be honest, gave it a bit of stick. Before long, it was weeded up a couple of rod lengths out, and still thinking I was playing a Baron that was buried in the weed, I heaved away until it was under the rod tip. I was cursing away to myself the whole time and then suddenly, the Baron kicked hard with its tail, shook off the weed that was smothering it and turned into a huge and very dark common. Wow! For a moment, it just lay there allowing me to get a good look at it. I knew which fish it was, but I ignored the thought.

As she had come in so easily, she was now up for a battle and she powered off, spraying water as she went while I held on for dear life. Her powerful charge soon came to a halt as she found a large clump of weed and I kept the pressure on, so, little by little, I was able to get the fish and the weed moving. As it neared the net, I jumped in for the last bit and scooped the whole lot up. She went mental in the mesh and she was not a happy lady. I took a look at my catch, and there lay the most beautiful fish I had ever seen - it was the big girl, the Black Common.

I was speechless. I just couldn't believe my luck. A lad from down the other end had seen that I was into a fish and came round to help out. This was such an unexpected end to a crap night's fishing. I bit the line, we carried her to the mat and weigh sling and once she was revealed, she looked even more stunning. The scales read four ounces over the magical 40lbs mark, and it really did hit home then, that the weight of a fish is so immaterial, when they look like that. I held, what must be the nicest common in England, posed for the photos, then waded in with her to let her go, and gave her a kiss goodbye for the pleasure of having caught such a great carp. After catching that fish, I decided to stay away for a while because I'd had a great spring and early summer and caught some amazing fish.

The Black Common. The best-looking common I have ever seen.

The following spring, though, the thought of floater and zig fishing had me wanting to get back for another go and maybe a chance to hear Elvis singing on the end of my line. It was early April when I got down and my mate, Stuart Court, who I fished Tolpits with, was down for a few days. He was set up in Nick's swim so I had a walk round for a chat. As I made my way around the lake to get to him, I had to pass the bay at the end of the lake. Two swims can fish this area; one is the End Point, which covers the entrance into the bay and has a side gap so that you can fish into it, and as you go past the End Point, there's another day-only swim called the Snags. The wind was blowing gently into the bay and it looked really good, but as I walked round I didn't see a single carp.

Stuart's the most laid-back man I know. He cracks me up, and he always seems the same, nothing fazes him. I first met Stu at Tolpits and we had plenty of sessions together on there, so it was always good to catch up with him. Nowadays, Stuart fishes for carp during the spring but then turns his attention to the other species, tench in the summer, and then barbel and perch later on. I know he has caught three different 17lb barbel from three separate rivers and it's fair to say that he's a pretty good specimen angler.

We chatted for a while and I told him I was thinking of fishing near to the End Point swim so I was able to keep an eye on the bay as I was sure they would at some stage turn up in there. I went and got my gear and wheeled it round to a swim called the Grassy, which was just down from the bay, and throughout the afternoon I didn't even get the rods out as I never saw a fish. I must have walked round to Stuart about six times, and each time I passed the bay it was devoid of fish, but it just looked so good. Where the hell were they? I was sure they'd be there. The wind was still blowing in nicely. It was perfect.

I made my last walk round to Stuart as it was now getting later in the day, and if they weren't about, then I'd have to go up to the other end for a search about. I went round but nothing had changed, there were still no fish in the bay. I spoke to Stu for a bit and then made my way back to get my gear and then go looking. As I got to the day-only Snag swim, I looked toward the entrance to the bay and there they were; loads of them, big black shapes all following each other into the bay. 'About bloody time', I thought. I knew they'd turn up eventually, but I was starting to doubt if they ever would.

They were travelling just under the surface and I knew from a previous cast about that the water was about eight feet deep in that part of the bay. I flew back to my gear to grab my zig rod and everything else I would need, but I still had to tie a hook length up. It's horrible when the fish are all there and you just can't seem to tie one quickly enough. I've done well in the past with just a simple cork insert for a hook bait, so this was what I threaded on the hair, on a hook length of just over seven feet.

I flicked the rod out to the left, hoping to intercept them as they came through, and fish were still funnelling in, so I laid the rod down on the floor and set the clutch. The line was a bit tight so I slackened it a bit, it must have tightened up with the undertow, and then sat back a bit from the rod on my low chair. The carp were coming right by me and down my right margin, very close in. I even thought perhaps I should be setting up another rod for on the bottom, in case they dropped for a mooch about.
Just then, Clive Arrowsmith turned up and stood behind me watching the fish.
"Jerry," he said, "your rod tip just slightly pulled round.
"Did it?" I said. "That's weird."

As soon as I'd cast it out, the line had tightened up a bit, but just then it pulled again, and this time I picked up the rod and wound down. It was solid in the weed. I held the rod high but there was no movement on the end, just solid, but I was sure there must have been a fish on, or I would have got the rig back. As soon as I'd cast out, a fish must have taken the hook bait instantly, and dived straight down into the weed without any indication whatsoever, apart from when the line had tightened a bit. I heaved as much as I dared for a while and tried a few different line angles, but there was no movement. Clive had seen enough, wished me luck and went off to look for a swim.

After Clive had left, I gave a more concerted effort to get this fish on the move. I heaved with a high side strain and, little by little, I got the dead weight moving and it was coming my way but still on the bottom. The water was crystal clear and as the heavy weight was by now nearly in my margins and only a little way out, I looked down to where the line was pointing. With my glasses on, I could see the lakebed, and then I saw a huge carp, just sitting there on the bottom. As I watched, it suddenly kicked its tail and swam off. Damn! I didn't say that, and you can imagine what I really said. My heart sank, and I thought, 'Oh well, let's get this rod in.'
As I lifted the rod, it seemed that I still had a lot of weed on the end, so I gave it a harder pull to get it up to the surface and then the weed ball pulled back, and pulled the rod over, and than took a bit of line. I still had a fish on - talk about instantly raise your spirits! The one I had seen must have been following its buddy that was on the end of my line. That was unreal. This fish hadn't gone too far, but I needed to get the weed off that was wrapped around my lead. I shouted across to Stuart to come and give a hand. He just looked across in his laid-back manner, and slowly stood up.
"I've got one on," I said. "Come and give us a hand."
As I said that, I looked down and caught a glimpse of the fish I had on. It was just sitting there on the bottom and it looked a right lump.

I looked back to Stu. He was reeling in his rods ready to come round, but slowly, so I shouted some more encouragement at him to get him moving but he was still strolling along the bank.
"Quick, mate," I said. "Hurry!"
He broke into a slight jog, which by his standards showed that he was hurrying all right.
When he arrived, I passed him my glasses and said, "Quick, have a look at that! I need the weed off that lead."
He saw the big fish sitting there. I walked back a bit and he was then able to strip the mass of weed off. At that stage, the fish decided he was going to start a fight, and from then on, I had a big scrap - all in the margins. It was a dodgy affair. I had

the snags to worry about, not too far away, and the light hook length meant I was only able to give it so much.

Stuart got the net ready as the big common came up to the surface, and I walked back so that he would be able to net it, so from then on my view was blocked.
"You got it, mate?" I asked him. "You got it?"
He stood up and pulled the net closer.
"Yep," he said. "I got it. Looks a good fish, mate."
He looked in the net and then said, "I think it's the big 'un again."
"No, surely not. It can't be!"
I took a look and unmistakably, there she lay in all her beauty. Now, I hate recaptures and this fish was a hard one to catch so what were the chances of me catching it again? I was saddened by that. The only way I was able to shed some joy to the catch was the fact that it was to be my new zig PB, so I weighed and photographed her one more time; she weighed an ounce under 40lbs.

The capture of that great fish again really finished it for me over at Croxley Hall. I dare not even consider staying on. If I were to catch her again, the initial capture would become less and less special, and I didn't want that - no way.

I hate recaptures. It was time to move on.

Chapter Fourteen
Cotton Farm and a Missed Opportunity

I had always fancied a go on Lee Jackson's Cotton Farm, so by the time my ticket turned up, I was already planning a campaign. Cotton Farm is probably the strangest lake I have ever fished. It's right in middle of lots of brand new office blocks that literally surround the whole lake, and at the car park end there's the Wharf, which is perfect for a pub lunch or celebratory drink if you were lucky enough to catch a special fish.

Talking of special fish, there are a few, but one that really caught my attention over the years was Cotton's big common, a truly stunning fish and one that I would love to have on my CV. I think the best weight she has done is 48lbs-odd and it looked as though she was going to make the magical 50lbs. Apart from the big girl, there was another common that does occasionally go 40lbs, and some of the other fish were absolutely stunning, with really nice-looking mirrors and commons over 30lbs.

I was starting on Cotton at a good time to be in with a chance at the big girl. It was early April and already feeling like spring. Cotton Farm has the weirdest algae-type weed, and it's a type that I've never seen before. As soon as the sun is shining this stuff will start to multiply quick-time and it can soon cover large areas. It was like a goo that would stick to everything, and it was only early spring so God knows how bad it would be later in the summer. I'd heard all sorts of horror stories, mind.

The lake is rectangular, with a well-maintained pathway that runs all the way around it, and the ground staff are always busy with the surrounding gardens. Hoards of office workers walk around the pathway during their lunch breaks, and in one corner of the lake there's a raised area with a rail around it, so it's a very good viewing platform for spotting the fish. On many occasions I'd be standing there looking, and then suddenly be surrounded by about 30 office people having a fag break, all smoking away as fast as they could. Obviously, they only had a short time and some of them would chain smoke two as fast as they were able. I used to feel a bit out of place standing there in my fishing clothes, surrounded by all the suits and chatter, and they could chat for England. Then they would chirp their way back in a big cloud of smoke and all would settle down again.

After 5pm, the office staff went home and the lake became quiet. At night, the whole place was lit up by the orange-coloured floodlights that were all around the pathways and offices, Cotton Farm was so different to anywhere I had fished, and I wondered why they called it a farm.

There were two very convenient swims right next to the pub, and as you looked down from that end of the lake, the right-hand side had a shallow ledge that extended 30 yards or so, and then dropped off into deeper water. I think this area may have been back-filled at some stage as there were a few bits of iron and metal sticking up that could cause problems if a fish were to take you anywhere near them, but I never actually saw anyone have any trouble with them.

I'd be keeping an eye on that shallow bank when it warmed up later, but the area that I really liked the look of was at the very end of the lake where there was a reed-fringed bank. I'd waded out into these reeds, peered off the end of them and I could see a nice depth that dropped away into about eight feet and more. I liked this area, because I felt that the fish would be frequenting the margin on a regular basis. There were no night swims on this bank and the only swim along it that we could fish was at the end, below the viewing platform that I mentioned earlier, and fortunately, it was closed for some sort of repair.

The last swim on the left-hand side of the bank was perfect for putting a couple of rods over to the reedy bank, and it was easy to bait up. I could just walk round there with a bucket and throw my bait in, the tried and tested Scopex Squid Plus, which I would use anywhere with the utmost confidence. I scattered it all the way along that bank so the carp would come across it, and concentrated it more in the two areas where I intended to cast my rods. There was weed in places so I decided to use chods on both rods, and pulled the stop up about three feet so that my hook bait would settle nicely on top of any weed that was there.

On my first session, that gooey weed was floating about and was building up in my margin, so I had to fish with the rods up high to be able to keep the lines out of it as much as I could. There were a few massive boulders in my swim and these were in a few of the swims around the lake. They were handy to climb up on, though, for a better view. The track that went past my swim went up a steep slope, and along my margins to the left there was a huge willow that hung over the lake. Along the track on the right was little gap with another steep slope that led down to the big trunk of the willow. I was able to slide down it and I say 'slide' because it really was steep, and sometimes slippery where the water sprinklers had soaked the ground. Once down by this big trunk, I could see perfectly under the big canopy of the willow, and the carp were always under there. It was nice to watch them, and I'm sure they always knew I was there.

On my first night, the wind was pushing nicely down my end of the lake against the reeds. I cast my two chods with the lead landing tight to them, feeling it down and as the lead swung in, I knew I'd be fishing a few feet from the base of the drop-off, just where I wanted it. As darkness fell on my first evening on Cotton, the wind dropped, the lake became quiet and still, and I experienced the way the lake was all lit up. It wasn't something I was used to, but all lakes are different and Cotton is unique in its own way.

The Cotton goo was building up in my swim.

As I drifted off, I heard a few fish top at my end of the lake, and I wondered where the big common was that night, but at 4am I was awoken to my left-hand rod's bobbin pulling up to the clip. I jumped off my bed chair and lifted the rod high and as I did so, I felt the fish powering off along the reed-lined margin, going right. I didn't want to catch my other line, because I was sure there were clumps of that gooey weed clinging along its length. Luckily, the fish travelled past my other rod and was now coming round to my right, safely away from any danger. This was good and I hoped that if I had any more fish they would all travel in the same direction.

Just to the right of the main part of my swim, there was a beach-like spot that looked out to the middle of the lake and it was very shallow in close, so I had to wade out a bit but I landed my first Cotton Farm fish, a nice long mirror, without any trouble. I weighed and sacked him up, as daylight was only a short while away, waded back out through the shallow beach area to deeper water and put my fish out on a long cord, tied securely to a bank stick.

Then, I then tied on a new hook bait and recast the rod to the same area as before, clipped on the bobbin and slackened it off the same as the other rod. The bobbins were both on long chains and off the floor, sitting upright. The rods were set high, and that slack bobbin was the only loose line, as the clutches were tight.

I was really knackered that morning so I got back into the bag. I was happy to be off the mark with a 24lb 8oz in the sack, and it didn't take me long to get off to sleep, but it seemed that I had only been dozing for a short while when I was alerted to a single bleep. I looked at the rod, it was the recast one, and the latching light was on. The bobbin had just moved from the upright position to just lying back toward me, and I just assumed it was either a liner or the rod was settling down after just being cast out. I was sure that if it was a take, I would receive some more indication and so I drifted back off to sleep while looking at the rod.

I was up a little while later, as soon as it was light, to get someone to photograph my fish, and I looked at the rod that had bleeped, but the line was still slack and angled to where I had recast it. My only concern was that maybe it was not close enough to the reeds, so I decided to recast quickly as it was light and still time for an early morning bite.

I picked up the rod, took up the slack and as I wound, the line was pulling out of the water and was now pointing to the big willow that overhung down to my left

The scene of my disaster. Gutted!

'Oh my god!' I thought, and that single bleep came rushing back to me. I had mucked up.

The line went right under the canopy and was tight, probably caught on the roots of the willow. I placed the rod back on the alarm and made my way up to the track to the gap that led under the canopy. As I slid down the slope to the willow trunk, I looked into the clear water and straight away I saw three fish. They normally swim off immediately to the outer area canopy when someone goes down there, but they were just sort of hanging about. As my eyes became more adjusted, I could see just what these fish were; there was a mirror and a common approaching high 20s, and a huge common that looked like the big girl, and what a sight she was! She looked every bit an upper-40 to me, if not 50lbs. By now, I had forgotten about my situation, thinking that whatever had picked me up was long gone, and that my line was just left tethered in the branches of the willow.

At first, I thought that these fish were not aware of my presence. Every now and then, the big one looked as though it was having a feed on the bottom. I could see it opening and shutting its mouth on the gravel, and was even thinking of grabbing my stalking rod, as there is a little stalking gap to the left of the willow.

Every now and then, the two other fish would come along by the side of the big one and then they'd turn away and the big one would try to follow them but always come back to the same place. This happened a few times and I started to wonder what was going on, and then it dawned on me that she could be something to do with my incident.

I waited until the fish was head-on so I was able to get a good look at her, and as I strained my eyes, I was able to see my chod rig hanging out of her mouth. I don't think I've ever been so gutted and annoyed with myself in any fishing situation in my whole life. This could have been the chance to catch a fish of a lifetime and I'd ended up in this mess. The other two fish were its friends, they were waiting for their mate, and they'd stayed in the area the whole time. When I'd thought she was feeding, she was really trying to shed the hook on the gravel. It makes you realise sometimes just how close these fish can be.

Anyway, I had a big problem. I whizzed round to the other bank where one of the regulars, Dave, was fishing. I had to wake him to come round and give me a hand, and as we went back, I told him what had happened and what I had seen under the willow. I wanted some confirmation that I had, in fact, seen what I thought I had. We slid down the slope and Dave looked for a while. Then he said,

Another view of the willow.

"Yeah, I can see your rig, and she looks massive!"
I thought the best thing to do would be to get the waders on and make my way down the bank with the rod, and take the line up as I went. The water was deep along that bank and Dave was keeping me updated as to what the fish was doing. I was hoping I might just be able to untangle the line and then I could still be in with a chance of playing the fish back out and landing her.

As I made my way toward the tree canopy, Dave said, "She knows you're coming. She's getting agitated," and as I got closer, "She's shaking her head now." Then, he said, "She's off, mate. She just shook out the rig and swam off." Oh well, I wasn't too bothered about losing her. I didn't think I deserved her, to be honest, but the important thing was that she got away safely, and that was my main concern. What a night, and what could have been! Obviously, she'd just picked up the bait and kited left under the safety of the willow and all I'd known about it was the tiny drop on the bobbin and a single bleep. It was a lesson learned and something I would try to be on top of in the future.

I got some nice photos of my long mirror and slipped it safely back. I still had another night to go and although I had lost my target fish on my first night, there were still lots more fish I would love to catch, so the session continued.

A long mirror. I was happy to be off the mark.

A stunning, dark mahogany common of 30lbs.

The next night I caught a couple of cracking commons, with a beautiful dark mahogany one at just over 30lbs, and another at 28. I was gutted to have blown the chance at the big one, but I hoped if I stuck with my area, she might well turn up again on a later trip. So the plan now was to keep the bait going in and to fish this swim as much as possible.

As the weather was getting warmer, the weed was becoming more of a problem, and it constantly took my lines out, but I'd been putting a fair amount of bait along the reedy line margin and each trip I was getting action and everything was working well. The carp I was catching were really nice and a lovely strain, and I hoped to catch a few of the known characters along the way. I was managing to get back into my chosen swim each trip, but I didn't think it would last too much longer. I never had any trouble with the fish kiting toward the willow; they always came to the right and I had to manoeuvre the rod over the now high Norfolk reeds in order to land them in the beach area.

As it was getting really warm, I messed about with zigs for a while, and felt confident on them but they never really materialised to anything. I knew the fish were still visiting my end of the lake but they were also getting caught along the shallow bank, so maybe it was time for me to start having a move about.
I was always keeping my eye on the rest of the lake but my swim was producing fish, and I'd already hooked the big one, so I was hopeful she would turn up in the area again.

One night in my usual swim, I hooked into a good fish and had some trouble landing it. It was very tricky when I got them in close now. This fish had gone around my other rod and was sitting in weed in front of the Norfolk reeds, and I could tell it was a good fish, so I just waded in and landed it. I was soaked but the carp was safely in the net so I was happy. My fish was a cracking one, and I later found out it was one of the A team and called White Tips - because the tips of her fins were white - and she weighed in at just over 30lbs. I sacked her up but only briefly, as it was nearly light, and when we took the photos, she looked even better in the daylight.

On my next trip, the swim was taken so I started to flit about the lake. I'd had a good time in that area, though, and I'd known that I wouldn't be able to keep it for long, and I was happy with what I'd managed to catch. It was a nice sunny day and the wind was blowing down to the reedy end but I decided to set up in the first swim at the beginning of the shallow side. To the left of the swim it was very shallow and I was able see the carp milling about.

I caught some really nice fish from the reed line margin.

I just loved how dark all the carp were.

The White Tips mirror. One of the A team.

Stalked from the shallows.

This was a great chance for a bit of stalking and the big boulders were great to climb up on, allowing me to see everything. While I watched, the fish just kept creeping in and out, feeding on my broken boilies. Then, out of nowhere, the big girl turned up. I'd been waiting for this moment and I was so sure I'd be catching her. On a few occasions, I had her right on my hook bait and she was picking up bits of boilie here and there. My heart was pounding but she kept on disappearing until, in the end, I lost track of her. Once again, I'd come very close. Maybe, the third time we met she'd be in the bottom of my net.

The sun was hot but the wind was still blowing, otherwise I think it would have been roasting, and I was fishing with a single boilie and a little bag of halibut pellets attached to the hook, just a little mouthful. My rod was lying on the reeds with slack lines and a set clutch as two good fish crept back in, and then a smaller one joined them. I was straining my eyes, but from my vantage point they couldn't see me, otherwise they wouldn't be coming in and feeding. A few clicks of the spool alerted me to the rod and then it was flying, and I saw a couple of the fish bolt off. I jumped down to the rod as it was pulling round where it lay on the reeds. I had to stop the fish getting out to a little island, as there were all sorts of dangers around that area. I played it hard to get it back and was soon rewarded with a nice old-looking mirror that went 22lbs.

I wondered how old this one was.

The shallows was a good stalking area.

I was amazed at how these large fish got into such an area.

Stuart Holman with the big girl at 45-plus.

All things considered, I was really happy with this capture. It's such a good way of fishing and it sometimes gives you opportunities, like when the big' un had turned up.

In the same swim during the night, it was all very quiet, so I hoped the next day would bring some more stalking chances. The morning brought another hot day, but no fish turned up where they were the day before. I walked along to where the reeds went out into the lake a little way and had created a corner. I was able to climb up a small part of a tree and peer into this corner, and as I did so, I was amazed at how the fish had got right into this small area. No one would ever have known and I'd never have seen these fish otherwise. I had stumbled onto something, and the fish I was looking at were of a good size. It was painful trying to stay up this bit of the tree, in fact it bloody hurt like hell, but I watched for as long as I was able to, until they eventually moved away. They only went a short distance, but far enough for me to drop a little parcel into where they'd been. They were close to the reeds when they came in, so I just laid the slack line down the front of them, and this time I stayed down from that tree, even though the tension was killing me!

Nothing happened for ages and I so much wanted to get back up that killer tree to have a look, but eventually my patience paid off and the reel was spinning away. A similar battle to the day before followed, and I was mightily pleased when a cracking mirror flopped into my net. A few of the lads were about to help out and this one weighed over 28lbs. It was a cracker and I was chuffed to bits. We got some nice shots and I waded out to slip her back. Later, I checked that little spot but strangely, I never saw them in there again.

I don't remember fishing Cotton much after that. They were on the verge of spawning, so I kept out of the way for a while. The big one came out at a spawned-out weight, as you would expect, and I kind of drifted away from Cotton. Sadly, the next season she passed away and that meant the big Cotton Farm fish was never to grace my net. Everyone was very sad, but in her time she made a lot of anglers happy so we thank her for that. RIP, old girl. You did your time. That ended my experience on the Farm. With the queen of the lake gone, there were plenty of other nice fish to go for, but I decided to move on.

Chapter Fifteen
Greenacres and The Compulsive Angler

It was Rich Wilby, who first took me to Greenacres when we went up there to do some filming for Nash TV, and a bit of photography. I'd never been there but I'd heard the lads at Nash talk about it when they'd been before to do the same sort of thing. Greenacres is in Peterborough, owned by Dave Mennie, and when Richard introduced me to Dave, I could tell right away that he was an all-right guy. I knew we would get on well because we had plenty in common; after all, we both had lakes to run and could share our experiences and knowledge.

Dave was in the early stages of building his dream home, right next to another nice-looking lake that would be right outside his back door, more or less. Further down the track lay Greenacres, a seven-acre lake, and although Dave had been stocking it with some really nice fish of a very good strain, there were also the original ones, still very much unknown, plus those that had already been caught. So far, the best was a beautiful common that, at its best weight the year before, was 43lbs. Dave informed me that he'd seen other big fish, too, one them being a big mirror that hadn't yet been banked. So it was all very exciting to be given the chance to have a go.

The lake is rectangular, and if you look down its length, on the right there is an island a little way along, and as the water passes both sides it makes two channels that join to create a bay behind the island. This is a safe area for the fish and, as all the fishing is done from the left-hand bank, and either end of the lake, the far end is called the dam wall. It looked very weedy around the island and from what I could see there was a lot of Canadian just under the surface, making it a very rich-looking water.

Even though the weed was up, it was still only the first week in April and was bloody cold. The strong wind that blew down to the dam wall end made it feel as though it was February. For my first night, I decided to set up in a swim that looked out toward the island, where I'd be in a good position to see a fair proportion of the lake. If I saw any fish I'd move on them - that was my plan, anyway.

Rich went in one of the swims down to my right, we both started to get on with setting up and it soon became apparent just how bad the weed was. It was very hard to find any spots in front of me, but I did eventually find two areas that, although weedy, were presentable with chods. So that's how I approached this area; White Amber chod hook baits, and a scattering of the White Strawberry Amber Attract all around the two areas. I've caught many fish in swims like this and the weed hadn't bothered me at all. I popped next door to see how Rich was getting on but he wasn't there when I checked. I thought perhaps he was with Dave so I went and sat on my rods and took in the atmosphere, wondering if we'd be lucky enough to catch.

An hour or so later, Rich came to my swim and told that me he'd just caught one. He'd been fishing with just one rod on the first bit of bank as you come on to the lake, and had thrown some bait in just off an overhanging tree. After he'd set up his gear, he went back with a rod and flicked it onto the spot. Dave was in his little spot looking after the fish in the net when we arrived, and Rich had caught himself a nice, old-looking mirror of 25lbs. A good bit of Ninja angling to Rich. Well-in, mate! His spot went quiet after that and Dave said he had an area going at the back of the bay behind the island. There was a ladder leaning against a tree and he told us he was able to see the fish drifting in and out of the weed beds from up there. "Why not come and have a stalk," he said, "before it gets too late? It would make good filming." Never one to turn down such an opportunity, I was away to get my stalking rod and bits, pronto.

Rich grabbed his camera gear and we made our way round to Dave's tree at the back of the island. "Climb up, mate, and have a look-see if anything's there." Slowly, I made my way to the top of the ladder and Dave was right. There was a fantastic view of the bay. As my eyes focused, I was able to see everything in the tap-clear water, and there was a lot of weed but plenty of clear channels, and as I looked, the carp started to become more visible. They were following a weed bed and then getting to a certain part that made them go through a gap and into a clear bit of the lake bed. It was a perfect ambush spot, because I watched them all following the same route, and they ended up coming through the gap and into the same clear spot. There were a lot of fish about and only a few bigger ones, mainly doubles and low 20s, but like Dave said, they'd make some great footage.

A good bit of Ninja angling.

Rich set up his camera, while I got a rod ready with a chod rig and a white hook bait. Rich told me when the camera was rolling and I crept into position, dragging the net with me. I kept back from the water's edge, and kneeling, I only had to cast about 20 feet, but there was a little branch hanging over which made the underarm flick a bit tricky. I fluffed the first one, always the way when the camera is rolling, but the second cast landed okay and I thought it would have been great to have had an underwater camera out there to see the rig land and how the fish reacted. I laid the rod on the floor, slackened the line off, and not long after a fish must have made an attempt to pick up my rig as a massive bow wave cleaved the shallow water, indicating a fish leaving the area. I only had to wait a little longer until the next fish came through the gap, the rod tip pulled round and I was away. I could tell it wasn't a big fish, but all the same it was very enjoyable and a cracking little mirror of about 14lbs made a good bit of footage.

The night was drawing in, so we made our way back to get the rods out. It was a quiet, cold night; nothing happened fish-wise and Rich was the same next door. Dave came for a walk round mid-morning so I reeled in and went with him. We made our way down to the dam wall and the icy wind was blowing so hard into this bank, that as soon as I got to the middle swim I had to pull my hood up to block it out.

Dave let me go and stalk one for the camera.

I could tell that it wasn't a big fish, but a stunner all the same.

We stood there for a while and were just about to go back when a fish rolled about 15 feet from the bank. I really didn't expect them to be on this cold wind, we were only just out of March, but I noted where the fish had shown and was already off to fetch a rod.

I arrived back with two rods, a low chair, a net and a few bits of end tackle. Still with the white chods on, I flicked out my right rod to where the fish had shown earlier, and just threw a few white baits around it. I did the same with the other rod close-in to the left, then sat back on my low chair, did my coat up to the neck with the hood up, and waited.

After about 20 minutes, I had a little liner on the right-hand rod and then a fish rolled. I stood up, looking toward where my rod was cast and realised that the fish was right on top of it. As I sat down, the line flicked again, the bobbin started to rise and this time the liner continued as the rod tip pulled round. As I picked up the rod, it bent right round and the fish moved off along the dam wall, slowly clicking line off my spool as it went. Further down the dam wall was a willow tree with some of the branches submerged and the fish was definitely heading that way. I gave it a bit of pressure to stop it going any further in that direction and then it turned and headed out into the lake, as I sighed with relief.

The liner developed into a take and I landed this unknown mid-30 common.

This fish felt a good one but was more plodding about heavily, rather than going crazy, so maybe it still hadn't properly woken up from its winter rest. The margins in this area are nice and deep and I now had it under the rod tip, still plodding as she slowly came up, and then a gold flash of a common rolled on the surface and I netted myself a stunning Greenacres carp. Now, that would have made a good bit of filming!

While I was playing the fish, I could see Rich at the other end of the lake in his swim. Eventually, he noticed that I was into one, made his way round to congratulate me and then he rang Dave to come and have a look. Dave soon turned up and as I lifted out the fish to the unhooking mat, I knew it was well over 30lbs. I unfolded the net and there lay one of the nicest commons I had ever seen. It was just perfect, in mint condition and without a blemish. It had a sloping head and overslung mouth, and I was chuffed to bits to have caught such a lovely fish.

This cracker of a carp weighed over 35lbs and what made it even better was the fact that Dave said he didn't recognise it, so it was an unknown mid-30 common. It had probably came from the River Nene years before, and that meant it was more than likely a Leney, as that was how most of the Leneys in Peterborough got into the lakes; the River Nene is only a hundred or so yards away from the lake. What a result! On the strength of that, I went and packed down all my gear to make a move to the dam wall because I was sure there were other fish about in the area. Rich also decided to make a move, which I thought was a wise choice, as we hadn't seen much at that end.

Rich set up at the end of the bank just before the dam wall, so he had the corner of the lake to his left, which was the beginning of the dam wall end. If he fished to his front, he would be fishing at least down the end where I'd caught mine earlier, and we might both be in with a chance. I set up camp and put one rod back on the same spot from where I'd taken the common. After a bit of a flick about with the marker I found a nice hard area of about 10 feet deep in the middle of the lake. There was a little weed around, but I hoped that if fish were following the wind down, then they might just be taking a beeline straight down the centre. I put a good few White Ambers out around the area to stop any fish in their tracks and to get them searching about, and then cast out my white hook bait among them. All was done, it was now just down to Mr Carp.

During the afternoon, I caught two more fish. They were both mirrors and a couple of Dave's stockfish, beautifully coloured, stunning carp in immaculate condition. The future for Greenacres looked very good.

It was much more comfortable in the shelter of my good old Titan. The evening of our last night soon arrived and I was very happy with how my day had been, and more than happy with my mid-30 common. It truly was a nice carp. The wind was still blowing as I drifted off to sleep and I don't think I would have heard any fish jump unless they were a few feet from the bank. Suddenly, the longer rod was melting off. On autopilot, it seemed that I was out there before I had woken up and a heavy weight was demanding line. I checked my watch, which showed 1am. It was pitch black, and because I had only a T-shirt where a coat should have been, I was freezing cold while playing the fish.

The carp found some weed, and for a while it just sat there as if deciding on its next move. This gave me a little breather and time to wake up properly and concentrate on what I was doing. I could feel some movement on the end as I kept a steady pressure on and the line felt like it was squeaking, as it pulled back through the weed, and then she was off again.

I was a bit concerned because it seemed like she'd gone a long way down the lake and I didn't want her to get too far. The fish stopped again and I thought she may have found more weed, but as I heaved back, the heavy weight started to move, so I began to pump, reeling down and then lifting the rod high again. I carried on like this for a while, but I still wasn't sure where or how far out she was. It started to rain and that, coupled with the wind, made it uncomfortable to be standing outside, playing a fish. This one was giving all the signs of a good 'un, though, so I ignored the weather and got stuck in.

After a while, I saw a carp break the surface and felt that I now had her beaten. She rolled a few more times and then I stretched the landing net handle out as far as I could. I had the rod up high and she was on the top, splashing about. It's always horrible, this bit, because it seems to be when they can most easily fall off. I was in luck, though, and in she went, begrudgingly. 'Phew!' I let out a sigh of relief and just stood there for a while to compose myself, knowing that my fish was safely netted.

I secured the net on a scaffold pole, quickly grabbed my coat, had a leak, and got my torch. I shone it into the net and there was a huge and very wide common. Past experience told me that I'd probably just landed the big common, and I looked up to the skies and punched my fist in the air, as if someone up there was watching, I felt like a young lad at Christmas. The fish was okay so I bit off my line and sorted out the weigh sling and a sack. Then I undid the arms of my net, rolled it up, checked her pecs were tucked in and then lifted her out. She was heavy all right, and I was glad everything I needed was right there by the water's edge.

The face says it all. Another unknown fish at 41lbs.

The scales steadied at just over 41lbs. Was I having a good trip at Greenacres, or what? Very carefully, I placed her into a large sack and lowered her gently into the deep margin. I had a long cord that I tied to the scaffold pole and she was fine there. The next thing to do was to wake up Rich. He was sound asleep and I had to call him three times.
"Rich! I've got the big common!" No reply. "Rich!" I said it again. The third time, he woke and looked at me as if to say, 'what do you want?' He hadn't a clue where he was, or who I was.
Then he said, "Jezza, you what? You got the big common?"
"Yeah, mate" I said. "It's 41lb!"
He was awake now, and he couldn't believe it.
"Well done, Jezza," he kept saying. "I'll get Dave round in the morning."
I left him to crash back out but I didn't sleep for the rest of the night; I was still full of adrenalin.

In the morning, Dave came round with his dad and I was anxious to get the fish photographed and back to her watery home. Dave was a bit surprised by the fish's weight. He had expected her to be heavier than she was, but was by no means gutted that she was down, it's just that we know our carp, and Dave knew the weight that she should have been. Rich set up the camera to film it, and we got everything ready; two mats, water, medi kit if it was needed, and I carefully pulled in the cord. She gave a bit of a thrash about as the sack came up to the surface and when she'd finished, I once again checked the pecs and then lifted her to the mat.

Everyone was waiting to see her so I unzipped the sack and removed it. Dave's first words were, "That's not the big common mate."
I hadn't known any better. I'd thought there was only one big common in the lake.
"No," Dave went on. "Definitely not the big one."
"So which one is it, then?" I asked.
"Dunno. I've never seen it before," was his reply.
So now, there were two even happier people. Me, because I'd had an uncaught, unknown 40lb common, and Dave, because his lake now has two 40lb commons in it. Everyone's a winner. Rich got some footage and when we looked back at it, we could hear the wind blowing and it looked like winter, but we got some great shots and it was a pleasure to see her kick off hard as I returned her. I had a fantastic session on an amazing water and I loved Greenacres, but who wouldn't?

We packed down later, I went round to thank Dave, and he said that I was welcome back at any time. Well, I had a DVD, The Compulsive Angler, to start filming in the coming year. It was an idea that I'd had for years, and I wanted to get a camera to follow me around all spring and into summer to see what we came up with. I asked Dave if it was possible to come back later and maybe do the underwater bits behind the island. It would be great footage to see them picking up rigs and so on. Dave agreed, so I thanked him greatly for my session of a lifetime and said I would keep in touch. I also thanked Rich for taking me, and we went our separate ways. The journey home seemed to be really quick because I was thinking about my DVD and having another go back at Greenacres.

A true angling legend!

My main objective for that spring was my DVD, and everything was planned. The guy to be filming it, Kevin Law, was experienced in filming fishing projects. I'd met Kev while doing a bit for the CEMEX Angling DVD, 'The Ultimate Quarry', and back then I'd mentioned that I had an idea, and he said he'd do it. The DVD was to start at my home at Carthagena Lock where I live in a lock house, and in the opening scene, the camera catches up with me having a quick go for the chub, more or less in my back garden.

I have an area outside my kitchen door where some huge chub congregate. They sit under a willow and people come to feed them all day long in the spring and summer, but no one can fish for them as they are in a section above the weir pool. It's a special little area and some of the country's finest anglers have been and had a go, including carp fishing legend, Chris Yates, and many have caught their PB fish there.

It's hardly ever fished because I don't want it spoiled, but as the fish are there, to an angler like me it's like waving a carrot at a donkey. To be honest, these days I probably fish it maybe a couple of times a year, and I do because I can!

It's not even easy fishing. It used to be, years ago when I first moved in, but these fish know straight away when they are being angled for and I've witnessed some of the greats blank there. Matt Hayes has become a good friend over the years and he is mad about his chub, as many will know, but Matt now lives in Norway with his family, so when he's in the UK he often comes and has a go. Matt has beaten his PB twice now, with big chub over 7½lbs.

Matt Hayes enjoying a session on my weir pool.

After watching the fish on the monitors for weeks, it was time to try to catch one.

Anyway, back to the DVD. Opening scene: me, the compulsive angler, fishing for chub. My good mate, Neil, was to be my partner in the making of it, and he's also a wizard behind the scenes. We set up an underwater camera in Carthagena syndicate lake, in an area that the carp just love in the spring and we had a two-man bivvy, with the monitor and DVR in it, and a couple of low chairs. Neil's an electrician and he was able to run a power cable up to the bivvy, so we could sit there and watch the baited spot when the fish turned up. It was brilliant and the fish arrived every day to feed, so we ended up with some good footage.

It was great to watch the fish that I've known for years in their natural environment.

Kev setting up the camera, ready for any action.

Once we had enough footage, I was going to try to catch a big linear for the camera. It was scoffing every day, but this was all being filmed in an open lake that was being fished, and although the fish were there all day, at night they disappeared. I was expecting her to turn up on the morning I fished and I had a take at 5am, so sure I was playing her, but instead I caught a very welcome 34lb common. Afterwards, I wondered why she hadn't turned up, and then I got the text. A mate, Tony Moulder, had caught her right up at the other end of the lake, just shy of 40lbs. The fish were free to feed where they liked and she was one hungry carp.

Kevin Nash rang me one day to tell me that Tim Paisley was fishing on his Church Pool and asked if I fancied 48 hours on there, as he doesn't like just one angler fishing there on their own. Well, you don't turn down a trip to the Church Pool! There are two lakes at Kev's place. He's been nurturing them for a long time now and they really are little bit of paradise set in beautiful surroundings. Kev has grown fish on to large proportions and over the last few years, he opened the top lake (Church Pool) to just the main consultants for tackle development, and filming, to start with. Now, though, he's let his main customers and close friends on there and the lake is something very special. It has become very hard over recent years, and I've seen some good anglers go without a catch. Anyway, I thought this would be a good opportunity to take along my cameraman, Kev Law; we might just get some footage for the DVD.

I was playing what I expected to be the linear...

...however, Tony had already caught her at 39lbs 12oz.

We arrived just in time to witness Tim Paisley land his PB.

When I arrived at the lake, a few of the lads were running round to Tim Paisley's swim.
"What's going on?" I asked.
"Tim's just landed the big fully scaled," they said.
'Wow!' I thought, 'here's a good bit for the DVD.'
"Quick, Kev, get round there with the camera!" We both shot round there to witness Tim with his new UK best, a 41lb fully scaled, and what a carp! It's absolutely stunning and one that I'd love to catch one day. We got some good footage of Tim with his fish, and this made a good little piece to go in the DVD. Kev and me set up on the opposite bank, and I wasted no time getting the rods out, the clock was ticking. The spot I fancied was around to my right as there was a big weed bed that I was able to fish against, and my tactics were a white hook bait, chod fashion, with a few whites scattered around it. You don't say!

As the day ticked away, I got up to walk down the bank a bit to see if there were any signs of feeding fish near my banker rod. If not, I was going to reel in and recast it for the night. As I walked, I saw a good fish roll right over my rod, so I went back to it and not long after, it bent round with a take. As I lifted into it, it absolutely flew off, straight into the big weed bed.

I tried for at least 20 minutes to extract the fish, but I was getting nowhere. We had a boat that we were allowed to use in this situation, and it was the same as at Yateley Car Park Lake, as long as it was done properly, with a bailiff, we were allowed to go out to rescue the fish, while wearing a life jacket, obviously.

It was really windy and Kev the cameraman had to ditch his camera and come out with me. There was no way I would be able to do it on my own. Kev rowed us out to where the fish was weeded up, but every time we got to where the line went down in the weed, the wind blew us off again. Tim saw that we were out in the boat and took some snaps of us as we were literally struggling to get to where we wanted to be. In the end poor old Kev was near enough rowing on the spot to keep me over the line, and I managed to trace it through a few weed beds, until I was sure I was over the fish. Then, suddenly, it nearly pulled the rod tip down to the water as it powered off on another aggressive run. This time, though, we were able to follow it a bit and I stopped it from getting too deep in the weed, but to be honest, it was really hard in that wind. We were all over the place and I really thought that it would be a matter of seconds before it fell off.

I was keeping the pressure on because it was, once again, buried in the weed, and then there was a sudden big jolt on the line, it went slack, and a big ball of weed rose to the surface. Damn!
"It's off," I shouted, and Tim shouted back.
"Bad luck!" he said, and made his way back to his swim.
I wound down on the ball of weed to pull it off my line and as I did so, the rod pulled round and tore off again. Deep joy! It was still game on, and now I could see the fish - a tan-coloured mirror was just below the surface. I gave Kev some manoeuvre orders and, bless him, he was rowing like a man possessed. I was never so pleased to see a carp in the net. It was an epic battle that Kev won't forget I'm sure! After all our efforts, I was delighted when I lifted the big mirror on the scales and they read 40lbs and ounces. Well, I thought, that's a wrap, but little did I know what was in store for me.

In the early hours of the following morning, I had another take. Kev was there quickly with the camera and this time it was nice and calm. It had been raining all night, the weather was all over the place, and we got some great footage as I played out another big mirror, from the bank this time. I was blown away when I netted it, because it looked like another fish of over 40lbs - and it was, at 41lbs. You couldn't make this up! I was so glad that I'd asked Kev to come along. Who would have dreamed I'd get a brace of 40s?

Second 40, and so glad that I'd asked Kev to come along.

My third 40 in just as many hours. Unbelievable!

Later that day, the sun came out and it was getting quite hot. I noticed a few fish had come up in the water and I was just considering changing one of the rods to a zig, when that rod absolutely took off. As I picked it up, it was stripping line as the fish was trying to get round the island. At that moment, Kevin Nash turned up which was great, as I would now have him in the video as well. Kev stood next to me as I played this battler and it was really good to have Kevin there, it made the capture even better. As the fish came in close, we got some great footage of the fish coming to the net in the clear water with the sun shining. Kev landed my third fish, and I suspected that I had another big one. I was right. It went 40lbs 8oz - unbelievable! I said that Church was a very special place and it truly is. I'd like to thank Kevin Nash for letting me into this little world of his. After that one, I decided to call it a day. We'd got some great filming done and we couldn't have asked for any more. It was perfect.

We finished the filming later at Carthagena, as the fish were about to spawn, and our next port of call was back to Greenacres. We hired a big van to get everything in for the trip, and we had a generator for our power supply, plus all the fishing gear, including Neil's because he was going to fish the nights, all our food and water, camera gear, a boat ... you name it, we had it.

They started to spawn at Carthagena, so we moved on.

Looking for those Leneys.

I had spoken to Dave the day before and he'd told me that the fish at his water always spawned later than most and they were not looking anything like it yet, so with that knowledge we set off. It did take a lot of organising but we were finally en route.

We arrived in one piece, and spoke to Dave for a while about how his new home was coming along. He told us it was fantastic, and that it was going to be a beautiful house. We then headed up to the lake for a look round and to find the fish. We didn't have to look far. As we passed the bay behind the island, we were able to hear them thrashing around spawning their heads off - they were at it big time. This was really bad timing and a costly mistake, but all was not lost. Dave had told us of the lake next door, which he has the lease on and runs as a syndicate. It's a mad lake, with lily pads and peninsulas, gravel bars and islands. Six acres of beauty, and to top that, it's full of old English Donald Leney carp. As we had already planned for me to try to catch a Leney for the DVD, we just jumped on there, as the carp didn't look anything like spawning.

It turned out to be a good few days, and although it was red hot, I managed to get a stunning 24lb Leney off the top in another epic battle, but it all made good filming. So we had to plan another return visit to Greenacres later on, and we settled for a date in August.

A proper ol' Leney.

August was soon upon us and once again, we set off with a loaded van. We decided this time to get a night's fishing without the cameraman, so we would have time to settle in and get sorted, plus me and Neil told him he was a bit of a Jonah and would bring us bad luck. Poor old Kev. All the plans to do the underwater bit were now shelved as the water level had dropped considerably since the spring, and Dave said it was now very shallow and weedy in the bay behind the island. So the plan was to get some rod action, film the actual takes, do a spot of floater fishing as well, and if all went according to plan, I wanted to try to catch another Leney from the lake next door.

I set up my camp once again on the dam wall. The wind was pushing down that end, it looked really nice and I had a good view down the whole lake. Once we had set up, Neil and me set off for a walk round the Leney lake. It was a nice day so we had a chance maybe to suss out a few spots to fish and to get some scenic shots.

The Leney lake is a maze. It has so many interesting bays, and it has three peninsulas that run out to the same end of the lake. Between each peninsula is a channel and these are like little lakes, so a good way to see a lot of the water is to keep walking up and down these long strips of land. On our travels, we saw plenty of fish moving up and down the clear channels in the weed. The lake is shallow in a lot of areas and it's the sort of place you could

The view from the Dam swim.

really get into. You would be able to bait little spots and know that other anglers would not interfere with them.

We'd done a circuit of the lake, and as we came to the end of the bank that ran parallel with the river Nene, I stopped as I saw the tail of a carp waving completely out of the water as it fed. Neil had the camera with him so he managed to get some footage while I snapped away with my digital. This fish was really having a good munch and was totally oblivious to anything. I wished I'd brought my rod along. I could see another couple of fish behind this one, and it looked like those two were feeding on all the leftovers that were drifting along as the one in front was excavating. We watched for a while and I made a mental note to check this area when we finished on Greenacres.

Back at our swims that evening, we had a bit of a relaxed social with a few red wines, and set about getting the rods out for the night. I was using exactly the same tactics as I had done earlier when I fished the same swim, and Neil was in where Rich Wilby had been.

At first light, I caught a 22lb common. We had a smaller camera that Kev had loaned us and Neil had become quite familiar with how to use it, so I promoted him to second cameraman throughout the project. Neil got some footage of my common, and later Kev arrived. He'd had to set up near the beginning of the dam wall because there was no room up where I was, and if he pitched up near me, all his kit would be in shot if I were lucky enough to get any more fish.

As Kev was setting up his base camp, my longer rod burst into action, so Kev had now lost the label of 'Jonah' and was quick off the mark with the camera rolling. Not long after his arrival, we were filming action, and that was just what we wanted. After a good scrap, I landed a nice-looking 25lb mirror. It was one of Dave's stockfish and I thought we'd got off to a good start with a couple of fish caught already.

The weed was well up at this end, compared to when I'd fished here in early April, but it looked great and there were lovely clear strips running between the weed, out about 60 yards or so. I was keeping an eye on an area between two weed beds as there was a lot of sheeting up going on. The sun was getting hot, so I decided to give the swim a rest, bait a few spots for later, and spend the rest of the day floater fishing. I paid particular attention to the side of the weed beds and I found it presentable with a chod, so I gave the area a liberal scattering of the old white specials.

Kev lost the title of 'Jonah'...

...and I landed a nice-looking 25lb mirror to get us started.

At the top end of the lake, it was flat calm on the back of the wind, and considerably hotter. I could see the weed just under the surface and it took me no time at all to get a few fish feeding on the top, but they were not really interested. They would have a few and then drift off over to the denser weed, disappear for a while, and then turn up again on the mixers. This went on for a while and every time it looked good to make a cast, they'd drift off again. I played about for an hour or so and we were all hot, and then luckily for us, the sky turned black and it looked as though we were in for a storm. The threatening sky looming over us ended the surface fishing and I said, "Let's go back now, and get the rods out."

I tied on fresh hook baits, the long rod was clipped up ready to go and went out nicely, the other rod was just a flick in the margin where I had caught that stunning 35lb common, and I even put a third rod left, over to the reed line along the left bank. This was all done in the nick of time and then the skies opened up. Before he left for the shelter of his bivvy, Kev set up the little 110 camera that Neil uses, and positioned it inside my bivvy door aiming at my bobbins - and then he pegged it.

It chucked it down for about 20 minutes, and then the sun came out and was nice and warm again. Kev came back, and I set up my low chair to the right of my rods and sat there to watch the water. As I scanned my swim, Kev was fiddling about changing the batteries in the 110, before placing the camera back on the cushion that was in the doorway of my bivvy and flicking on 'record'.

Shortly after he had done that, I saw more bubbling near my middle rod, and then a good fish head-and-shouldered. On film you can hear me say, "I've just seen a good one stick its head out. I might be in for a bit of action soon." About 30 seconds went by, the bobbin flew to the top and pulled the line clip - all of this is on camera - and I knocked one of the other rods off the rest as I picked up the middle one. The fish bulldozed into the weed bed as I held the rod high, and my line was pointing straight into an enormous bulk of weed.

As I kept the pressure on, thousands of tiny bubbles were fizzing to the surface as the fish twisted and turned in the weed, and suddenly, it broke the surface behind where my line was going. It seemed that my line went in and under the weed to where the fish was now on the top, so I wound down a bit, heaved gently, my line pinged out of the weed, and I made a direct contact with the fish. As I did that, the fish made another dive leaving a big wake behind it as it went, but I was lucky because it dived away from the weed and into more manageable water. From there on, the fight was mainly just heavy, and taking a bit of line here and there until the fish came closer, and when it rolled on the top a few yards out, I knew it was a chunk.

One showed near the spot and I said, "I should be in for some action soon".

Kev was at my shoulder, filming the whole time. I was pumped with adrenalin and excitement, and all that was going through my mind was, 'please don't come off', but it rolled again, nearly beaten, and then into the net she went. I turned and punched the air at the camera; this was so unreal, to get it all on tape. We cut filming for a bit to get a few things sorted. Neil came and said, "well done" - he'd known it was big when it rolled. Neil then rang Dave to come and have a look. We knew that he would like to see his fish, as I do on my lake. I still didn't know which fish it was, but I had my suspicions. We got everything ready, plenty of water, cameras and mats, and then Dave turned up with another mate, Steve Broad from Angling Times. I gave Steve my camera, as I knew it would be in good hands.

With the camera rolling, we lifted her to the mat and revealed this awesome fish. Dave said, "Well done, mate! That's the other big one." I'd thought it was. I was so happy; I could have swum three laps of the lake. This was a major result and to get it on film, the bite and all, was just brilliant. She weighed in at a spawned-out 41lbs, my fifth 40 of the season, and my twentieth UK 40. The wine would certainly be flowing later. We did all the necessary filming, and I slipped her back. I was a very happy man indeed, and Neil called me a jammy bastard.

Up she went and weighed in at 41lbs.

Greenaces was always kind to me. Two gems in two trips.

That evening, the wine did flow, and Dave came over for a beer. We all met at the beginning of the dam wall, and at midnight, I had a one-toner that we filmed. We called it 'midnight madness' because it was. I landed a nice 20lb common, and then hit my much needed bed to dream of Greenacres' monsters.

The next morning, as I was so pleased with what we had achieved so far, and there was no way we could better what had already done, we decided to pack up on Greenacres, and spend the last night next door on the Leney lake.

We spent most of the day trying a bit more surface fishing and stalking, and Kev went out in the boat to get some different angles. It was really knackering stuff to be lugging everything around all day, and Neil was flying around like a madman, helping to get everything at each swim we filmed in. He was really good and it wouldn't have been possible without him, so, Neil, I owe you a big 'thanks', mate! We decided that Neil would have a night on Greenacres with Dave, while Kev and me did the night on the Leney. I told them that I would try to catch one to finish off this bit of filming.

Kev and me had dragged all the kit up the long peninsular, because I fancied this area, and I was just casting out the rod for the night when a guy turned up who I'd seen earlier when we first arrived, and it seemed I was in his swim. I knew he'd been baiting up but I thought he had fished already when I was on the other lake. I didn't know where he had baited. So, rather than get into any bad feeling, and being the very nice bloke that I am, I said I'd move. To be honest, moving was the last thing I wanted, I was ready to hit the sack. We carried everything back to the van and Kev's car and I was really ready to call it a day and just crash by the van, but suddenly, I had a brainwave.
"I know where we can go, Kev," I said. "Follow me."

I pulled the van up at the spot where I'd seen the fish feeding with its tail out of the water, and as I walked into the swim, I was bloody amazed. I even looked up to the skies to see if someone was looking down through the clouds, winking at me, smiling and saying, 'go on son!' That same fish was still there, tail out and waving away without a care in the world. I couldn't believe it! Kev was highly amused when I showed him, and he set up in the back of the van, while I opted for an 'under the stars' night. Right in front of the swim was a big bank of floating blanket weed, and this could cause me some problems because, to get to the area that this fish seemed to like, I had to fish over it and then play the fish back through the weed. Oh well, I'd had worse.

Waiting for the chance to cast out.

As I watched, the fish occasionally stopped and straightened up, moved a few feet and then started to feed again, so I waited a while until she did so and then delicately flicked out my chod. I think she became aware of my cast and moved away to the left, and I was a bit concerned in case she moved off, but just as darkness began to engulf us, she returned with her tail out. She was so interested in that area that nothing was going to deter her.

Not long after dark, Kev crashed in the van and I could no longer see if the fish was still there, although I had a few little liners. It seemed that I'd only just got in the bag when the bobbin began its climb and the Stevie Neville sang its tune. I jumped to the rod as the fish tore off in the shallow water, making a big eruption as it went, found the nearest weed, and dived straight into it. I was able to bring the fish back slowly, and all the time, I was aware of its tail kicking away in the weed.

Without too much trouble, I got it all the way back to the big raft of floating weed, and surprisingly, it just came back in one great mass. Somehow, I netted the lot and began pulling big clumps of weed out of the net. All this time, Kev was unaware of what was going on. There was so much weed in the net that, for a while, I began to wonder if there was a fish there at all, and then I felt it.

Once she had moved, the chod was flicked out.

A brilliant end to a session, with this strange-shaped Leney.

I removed most of the weed to reveal a very old-looking common that seemed every bit of 30lbs.

Neil was on the other lake but not that far away from where I was fishing, and he had heard the take. We had walkie-talkies, and the whole time I was playing it, he kept buzzing me.
"How big is it?" he asked, when I answered the first time. I hadn't even landed it at that stage. Then he called me again.
"Bloody hell, give me a chance, mate!" I said.
I got a sack ready, quickly weighed her, and she went 31lbs of old-looking Leney common carp. Just then, Kev made an appearance.
"What's going on?" he wanted to know. I told him the news and we were both delighted because this capture just about wrapped up the filming.

In the morning, when I got the fish out, we could see that it was jet black, and had a sort of dropped tail, which looked a bit weird but I loved this fish. It must have been very old and I felt so privileged to have caught her. We let her go on camera, and I was in the water with her when one of the rods tore off. I scrambled out to get the offending rod and shortly afterwards, landed a high-double mirror.

What a trip this had turned out to be! I turned to Kev and Neil and said, "That, my friends, is a wrap. Let's get the **** out of here!" We called to say thanks to Dave for his hospitality, Kev went back with plenty of stuff to edit, and on the drive home, I felt as if I'd won the lottery. Bloody superb!

Chapter Sixteen
Church Pool. The Super Bug

It was late February 2011 and freezing cold when we arrived at Church Pool. I was with my good mate, Jerry Bridger, the editor of Crafty Carper magazine, and we were down to try to winkle out some fish in these wintry conditions.

I set up camp in the swim in front of the lodge because I thought that the big weed bed down to the right of the swim might still be there, lying on the bottom, and I hoped that some fish would not be too far away. Jerry went on the bank opposite me so that between us we'd be covering a fair proportion of the lake. I've already spoken about Church Pool in the Greenacres chapter, and as I said, it's an incredible water. I don't get to fish it much but when I do, I like to put in maximum effort as the rewards can arrive in very heavy packages. On recent trips, apart from when I was filming and had that unbelievable catch of three 40s, I've been lucky on Church; it's one of those waters I just seem to click with.

A few years back, we were filming for a terminal tackle DVD and the line-up of anglers was absolutely top class. We had Gary Bayes, ex-British record holder, Jon McAllister, a carp catching machine, Dave Levy, who with minimum time on the bank always pulls them out, and me, addicted to carping. We were spread around the lake and it was my first time on, as well as Jon's, I think, and I knew the lake held huge fish so I wanted to make the most of this opportunity to catch one, but the whole of the first day went by without anyone getting so much as a liner.

While thinking about Church before the off, I'd wondered if anyone had tried maggots, because the fish were getting mostly boilies. I just wanted to get the fish feeding and I'd found a nice smooth area in a channel in the weed where the reflection of the trees in the water marked the spot nicely for recasting, so I spodded a gallon of maggots to this and fished a snowman over it. Just before dark, I saw one fish roll and that was it, all day.

I awoke early next morning expecting a few fish to have been out but no one had caught a thing. The sun was nice and bright and as the temperature warmed up a bit, Jon McAllister was away and landed a nice mirror of 32lbs. It seemed that, as this was early spring and the water temperatures were still low, the fish had started to move into the shallower corner of the lake to enjoy the sun.

First encounter at Church Pool.

Nothing else was caught all day, but later, just as Dave and Jon came round to my swim for a chat, I received a savage liner on the rod over the maggots. We all looked at the rod, and then this time it just melted off. To cut the story short, the fish weeded itself up big style and Kevin told me to use the boat to rescue it. After a dogged battle from the boat, Alan Blair from Nash netted a nice-sized mirror for me and I was so chuffed to get one, as things had been looking a bit doubtful. My fish weighed in at 39lbs 12oz - and it was a leather! Well, that was enough for me. I had achieved what I'd come for and I was smiling from ear to ear. I had one night left to fish, and I hoped that there were some maggots still out there as I recast to the little smooth spot. There was no more action that day for anyone and I had to go home the next day because I had commitments, but the other lads were staying for one more night.

During the night, the same rod burst into life, and a heavy fish that seemed to be hugging the lakebed slowly clicked line from my spool. As I stood there with the rod high, I saw a red light come bouncing around the lake from the opposite side. It was the nocturnal Jonny Mac on his way to help.
"Well done," he said. "Feel like a good one?"
"It's heavy," I told him.
I kept the pressure on, lifted it from the bottom, and from then on the fight was more in my favour. I soon had it close enough to net, and it boiled on the top a few times, then went into the net, and as I pulled the net back, I was aware of its size. It was definitely a big fish.

Jon's a great bloke to have on the bank with you. He's so genuinely pleased for you and only too willing to help out. We got a sack ready and popped her on the scales - 46lbs of big old mirror carp. 'Thank you very much', I thought, and we sacked her up for the few hours until daylight. I really wasn't expecting that; what a good trip it had turned out to be, when it had looked as if nothing would happen.

We got some good photos in the morning, and then I had to get off home. So, my first trip at Church Pool had been very kind to me, but I have had it hard. I was on there in November of that same year and had a three-day blank - and I worked hard! I moved every day but just couldn't buy a bite.

Anyway, on this trip with Jerry Bridger, we just hoped for a take. The weed bed was still very much evident but I found a couple of nice spots to fish. One was just on the nearside of the weed bed and the other further left of it. I fished my old favourite Amber Attract, snowman-style and just scattered a few baits in the general area.

What a chunk of a carp. 'Thank you very much'.

Not too long after I'd cast out, I had a take on the rod at the back of the weed. It was a proper take and I lifted into it as Jerry Bridger came running round. The fish weeded me for a short while and then it was off. It was one of those things, and I thought, 'Well, if that's the sort of action we can expect to look forward to, then great! We are in for a treat.'

I couldn't have been more wrong. Over the next few days, we merrily blanked away, and it was getting colder and colder. I remember taking the water temperature and it wasn't far off freezing. This wasn't good. We'd hoped for a better trip and by our third day, we were a bit despondent.

I went for a little walk to the end bank on my right, and climbed one of the little curly-whirly-type willows that are planted around the lake. The cold wind was blowing into my face and it was really uncomfortable in the tree, as I kept swapping my foot over to rest the other. As I checked out all that I was able to see from my perch, I concentrated on the marginal area, and then as if I was seeing things, a big brown carp went swimming by. I wasn't sure if I'd imagined it and then I saw another go past, and the longer I looked, the more carp I was seeing. They were mid-water and cruising about as if it were summer. Had I not climbed the tree, I would never have known they were there, and the first thing that came into my mind was zigs.

I reeled in my rods and went round to the spot where the tree was. I'd estimated the water to be about eight feet deep in this area, so I made up a four-foot zig with black foam and a little sliver of yellow at the top of it. I shinned back up the willow and after my eyes became adjusted, I could see the fish again, going back and forth, picked a spot to cast my zig to, and waited until they were far enough away, then got down quickly from the tree, and flicked out my rod.

Merrily blanking.

The sight of those fish will remain with me forever.

The area was not more than 15 feet from the bank, so I stayed back out of the way expecting some quick action, but nothing happened. I so wanted to get up that tree again but that would have risked spooking the fish, as they would surely see me. In the end, I just had to get up and have a look, and back in that uncomfortable position, I was scanning for my hook bait.

Once my eyes became accustomed to looking through the water, I was able to see it and two big fish were heading directly for it. I was ready to jump out of the tree but I had to stay and watch, so I called Bridger to let him know what was going down. I was so sure I'd be getting one. He didn't answer his phone, though, and I found out later that he was charging it.

I watched as a huge carp approached my hook bait, but it just went right up to it, and the hook and bait more or less dragged down its side as it swam past. No sooner had one passed than another carp turned up and did the same thing. It was as if they were homing in to check it out, but not one of them would take it. I was up that tree in agony for nearly an hour and I would say that at least 20 times a carp went directly to the zig as if it was going for it, but never did. This was fascinating to watch and really opened my eyes to zig fishing. Was this going on all the time when we are zigging? These fish were totally aware of the rig as soon as it was cast out, they were just going round in a circuit and coming back to it every time.

Eventually, I had to get down but Jerry came round and he got up the tree and saw the same thing. I thought that maybe the yellow bit was putting them off from taking it, so I made up two more hook lengths with just black foam, and decided to fish through the night with the zigs. Carp were certainly not feeding on the bottom where I had been fishing. All the fish that I was seeing from up in the tree were big and some were at least 40-pounders, if not the odd 50 and it was a sight that I can still see in my head as clear as day. I will never forget that. Before dark, I reeled in the zig and replaced it with another rod with just the black hook bait, and a little further down in another gap, I cast out the other rod with the same set-up.

Darkness was soon upon us and it was freezing cold as the February temperatures plummeted. I sat there in the bivvy and wondered if I'd done the right thing. It was shit or bust, really. I had nothing else to try. It had been dark for a few hours and at 8pm, one of the zig rods was off. A few bleeps alerted me and it was almost as if the fish didn't know what was happening, and then it took off. I leapt to it quickly, delighted that I had actually got one on at last! Jerry came round to help with the net which was good as it was pitch black and I would be able to walk back away from the water. That really helps to land a fish on a long hook length. Having someone to help makes it so much easier. It was nerve racking playing the fish because you just don't know what you have on. It could have been the Power Station that goes 50-plus and rucks like hell, so I was expecting the rod to be nearly pulled from my grasp and a big, powerful fish to steam across the lake. This didn't happen, though. The fish gave a little tussle, and then just flopped about on the surface. I walked back, and into the net it went.

It had been dark for a few hours, and then one of the zig rods was away.

Second fish of the night. Another cracking mid-20.

The following morning, and another zig-caught stunner.

Jerry looked into the net and there lay a nicely-proportioned, mid-20 mirror; a lovely-looking carp and quite heavily scaled. 'Great,' I thought. 'I've caught one at last and on black foam, at night,' and I must say that was a first for me. I have tried zigs at night but never had much luck with the method. I recast to the same area, now confident that maybe I would be in with a chance of another, and sure enough at midnight, the other rod in the gap further down was tearing off with a zig-fooled carp on the end.

The ensuing fight was similar to the last fish. It didn't go mad, as I thought it would, but it was a little more difficult to land this one, as I was now on my own. I had to raise the rod as high as I could to get the fish in the net, but there lay another nice-looking mirror of a similar weight to the last one. I was amazed really, because during the day all I had seen were big fish, but I wasn't ungrateful by any means. I was over the moon even to get a bite, let alone to have caught two stunning 20s. I hadn't seen fish like these in the Church before, though. It was as if they were brand new and I wondered if perhaps there had been a stocking of some sort. This last fish weighed 26lbs and like the other, it looked immaculate. Just on daybreak, I had another take, and this one weeded me up for a while as it tore up and down the margins on a long hook length. Jerry came round just in time to net it for me, and in the clear water we saw, another cracking fish of mid to upper-20 slip into the net.

"I've never seen these fish before," I said to Jerry. "They're like something that Viv Shears would stock - very nice fish."
This one was just shy of 28lbs and made a very productive end to that otherwise painfully cold and uneventful trip. In the daylight, the fish were even more stunning. All of them were beautiful shades of brown with golden scale markings, so we got some nice shots and back they went. I wondered just what else might live in this amazing water.

After we'd packed up, I went down to the office to speak to the lads and showed them the pictures of the ones I'd caught. I asked them if there had been a stocking as these fish all looked similar. They recognised one of them that had been caught the year before at 20lbs-odd, but not the rest of them. "No," they said. "There hasn't been a stocking, these are the babies coming through."

In fact, I do remember Kevin saying that they were breeding. He was a bit concerned because a lot of thought had gone into Church Pool regarding the stocking levels and growth rates, something that he monitors all the time, but with new fish coming through it changes the balance.

Anyway, I went home that cold morning very happy, and the whole zig thing was really playing on my mind. It was something that I'd be doing a lot more.

Matt Hayes normally comes to Carthagena in February for his end-of-season chub trip. He's been coming now for three or four years, and it's always a pleasure to have him over. We often spend a lot of time chatting about all things fishing, and we were sitting in my clubhouse at my fishery having a brew when I told him about my successes on the black foam zig.

The carp are hunted day and night on the lakebed with our various types of rigs and baits, but the one place they never seem to get fished for is between the lakebed and the surface. The vast majority of anglers I know never even give zigs a go and, to be honest, I'm pretty happy about this as it leaves that style of fishing a little edge to anglers like me.

I really do believe that it's the most underrated approach to carp angling. People reading this will be thinking, 'Okay then. Why is he making a big thing out of it and telling everyone?' I'll tell you why, it's because most reading this won't even bother. They can't see past boilies, and that's fine by me.

Fish spend the vast majority of their time sitting in different depths of the lake, and not just on the bottom, so when they see a black object in their path, or any colour really, to them it's a possible food item. On the lakebed they swim around all day sorting through all the weed beds and silt, looking for food sources, so the bit of black foam to them, is some kind of beetle, or spider. A vast number of insects and other things must fall out of the trees in the wind, and sink into the water. They are all edible and safe to eat for the carp, and this I'm sure is what they think when they take your foam hook bait.

I was chatting with Matt with all this rolling around in my head. As you may know, Matt is a terrific all-round fisherman and has excelled in catching so many different species, but I was interested in his fly fishing. I believed that if I could simulate some sort of bug or insect that actually does hatch from the lakebed, that the fish are absolutely crazy about, and then get this to float with a hook, then I was on to something very big indeed. Matt said that when he got home, he'd tie me up some bits and pieces and bring them over when he was down next.

Matt's next trip to my place was at the end of the coarse fishing season in March. He'd brought a small bag containing some little zig beetles and they were great. I just knew they'd look natural in the water, because they had legs and looked just like the real thing. My only worry was the hooks, because they were fly hooks and

I wondered if they would be strong enough. There was only one way to find out, and I was eager to see how the carp would respond to them.

My next planned trip was, once again, to Kevin Nash's Church Pool. Normally, I wouldn't get another chance on there until later in the year, maybe the autumn if I was lucky, but we had a session planned. I'd wanted to take Neil over there so we could get a few days angling together as we hadn't had a chance since the DVD, and another friend, Charlie, who had done my billboard advertising. It would be a nice little trip and someone would surely be lucky enough to get a good one.

It was now late March, and I hoped the carp would be well up for it. Without any question, my plan of attack was to fish zigs, and to try out my new wonder bugs. I arrived at the lake the day before Neil and Charlie, as they weren't due until the next afternoon. The sun was out, the lake looked beautiful, and there was only one other angler on - a good friend of mine, Gary Newman from Angler's Mail. Gary had one more day left of his session and would be off the next day when Neil and Charlie arrived. He'd been on a few days already and had caught one, and what a fish to catch! He'd had the carp of a lifetime, a 40lb common and he was well made up about it. He's a really nice bloke and I was chuffed for Gary. I'd first met him at Tolpits over 11 years before - how time flies!

Church Lake is rectangular with an island at each end, and I fancied the end just down from where I'd caught the three fish on my last trip in February. A narrow channel formed between the bank and the island and this is where I set up camp. The shallower part of the lake was down to my right, and if the fish were moving into the shallows, they might well choose this channel to get to my area. A big weed bed was to my left and this spot does normally hold a lot of fish. I hoped that, as it warmed up, they would be moving out of the weed bed, through the channel and past me to get to the warmth of the shallows. I would be placing my zigs somewhere along that channel.

I climbed one of the little willows to scan the area for signs of fish, and I didn't have to wait too long. Just off the corner of the island I saw two carp, only just under the surface and cruising through into the shallows. I looked more to the left and saw another large-looking fish that seemed as though it had come from the weedy corner, but this one was deeper at about four feet off the bottom, in eight feet of water. I think they like to stay in the deeper water as they go through the channel and once they are through, they come up, just like the other two that I'd seen. I tied up one rod at a depth of four feet, and the other was set at seven. I wanted this one just under the surface, off the corner of the island.

Church Pool. A very special place.

I flicked out both rods, left and right, and didn't bother with the alarms for the time being. I laid them on the grassy bank upside down and resting on the reel handles, and set the clutches so that my rods would not be dragged in. I felt really tired, I must have had a late night the night before, I can't remember, but it was so peaceful over there and I felt really relaxed. I set up my brolly and bed chair, lay back in the shade, and started to drift off. I kept waking up with a start, thinking that one of my rods was going, but I'd see that everything was okay, and then drift back off again.

The next time I woke, the island rod was off like a train and line was clicking off the spool. 'Bloody hell,' I thought, 'better grab that!' It was a bit of a shock. I hadn't expected a bite so soon, and this was to be my first take on the beetles. I played the fish as gently as I possibly could. I didn't want to straighten one of those hooks. The fish ploughed into one of the weed beds, but with a steady bend in the rod, I was able to get it moving, and once it was out of the weed and in the channel, I soon had it ready for the net. I extended my arm as far as possible to allow for the long hook length, and a nice mirror carp slowly came over the arms of my landing net. I was just so happy that it had taken the beetle. It hadn't been out long and I guess the first fish that saw it took it instantly. This was what I'd been hoping for, and now I had the proof - a lovely 24lbs 8oz mirror to start the session. I wondered whether the really big fish would see it the same way.

I guess the first fish that saw it, took it instantly.

A lovely 24lb 8oz mirror to start the session

Gary kindly came round to take some shots for me.
"You didn't take long to catch that one!" he said.
I told him of my bug hook baits and he seemed to like them; well they worked, that was for sure. As the afternoon went on, no more action came my way, so after the last trip's nighttime trio, I was sticking with the zigs. I reeled them in just to double-check they weren't tangled or caught up, and placed them back where they were. I was sure the fish would still be using the channel as they mooched around the lake.

I crashed out that night full of hope and I was confident in my approach. During the night, I was woken a few times by some very big carp that were crashing in the channel and off the left-hand side of the island. The noise they made was ridiculous. I've never heard anything like it. There was one fish in particular that was constantly hurling itself out in the same spot, about 15 feet off the left side of the island and I couldn't ignore this, so in the end, I reeled in the left rod and tied the beetle to a longer hook length of about six feet. I was unsure of the depth but I did know it was weedy in the area where the fish was showing, so I just hoped that if I did land in the weed then my hook bait would still be sitting above it all.

I made a cast into the darkness and felt the lead touch down, not with a hard landing, but as if it had just landed in a bit of chod on the bottom. That was great because I knew my hook bait would be sitting pretty. I got back in the bag and tried to get some sleep. I had hardly slept, what with the circus act in the pond that night.

It was a stunning morning. The lake was covered in mist, the sun was creeping up on the horizon and as parts of the haze lifted from the surface, the lake looked like a silver mirror covered in thousands of bubbles caused by the carps' aerobic class during the night. Church is extremely photographable, and I spent a little while trying to improve my camera skills. It had all gone quiet now, though, and I thought the carp were probably knackered, as I was. It was 7am as I put the kettle on and I wondered what the day would bring.

A little while after I'd made my morning coffee, I heard a voice and looked to the end of the lake past the lodge bank. I saw Kev and Alan Blair who were on their way round to see how Gary and I had got on during the night. I was just firing up the cooker again, as I knew Kevin would want a cuppa, when totally out of the blue, the recast rod scared the life out of me when it burst into a one-toner. It was absolutely flying.

I picked up the rod and instantly had to pay out line or this fish would have just snapped my hook length. Alan was soon by my side, he loves his fishing and he's always so keen. "Jerreee!" he said, as he always does every time I see him. He was as excited as I was. Then I heard Kev's voice from behind me.
"How's it feel, mate?"
They had both heard the take and saw the way it had shot off. I knew this was something big and powerful, and I had to play it very carefully. It had found a weed bed now and wasn't moving, but I felt that if it decided to, it had the power to smash me up, no problem, so a bit of a stalemate was in order for the moment. I was keeping a steady pressure on the rod but not so much to cause me to lose it. There was a big kick of its tail and once again, I had to let it go, the fish taking line at will, and then it buried itself in a thick weed bed.

Alan started getting the boat and life jackets ready, and after a while, Kev said, "Best to get out on the boat. You'll have more of a chance if you're above the fish."
The use of the boat is always a last resort, but it must save a lot of fish from getting damaged. I kneeled at the front, with the net by my side, and Alan manned the oars. As he rowed toward where my line entered the water, I wondered just what might be on the end. Gary had joined Kevin on the bank, as well as Reedy and Tom from the office, and all were waiting to see if I'd land my fish.

Alan helped me to get the fish onto the bank safely.

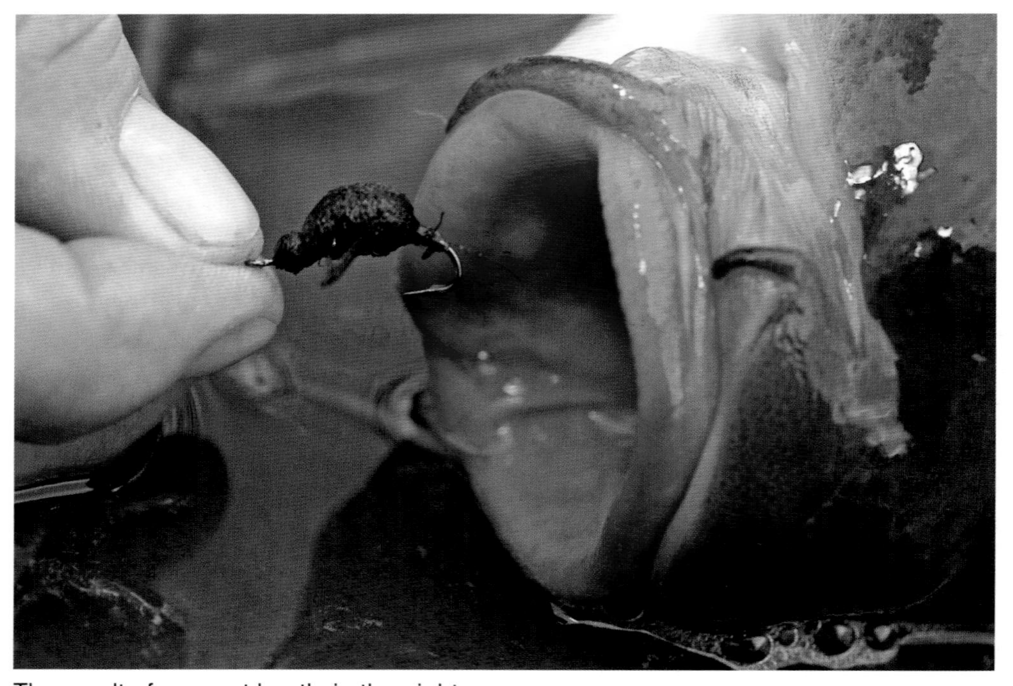

The result of a recast beetle in the night.

Gently, the boat glided along and, as I was winding down, I felt a hard kick. Before we'd even got over the fish it came up out of the weed bed and we saw this huge common, and it wasn't hanging about. In the clear water, I saw it steam off and hung on for dear life as Alan turned the boat and paddled it expertly in the direction of where the fish had taken off.
"Which common do you think that is, mate?" I asked him.
"That's the big 'un, Jerry," he said. "She hasn't been out for over a year and she's done 50lbs before."

Now I was crapping myself, and my 10lb hook link and that tiny hook were all I could think about, and then we were over where she had dived. From the boat, she was just visible, lying on top of the weed about four feet down with the whole of her back expossed and just her head buried. Now directly above her, I took up a bit more pressure and tried to lift her gently off the weed. Surprisingly, she just came up and this great beast of a fish was there for us both to see. I just kept repeating to myself, 'please don't come off'.

Alan got the net but she wasn't quite ready. She was on the surface thrashing about and did make a couple of vertical dives, but we were just pulled around in the boat. She tried one more dive and I thought 'this time when I get her up she's going in the net', otherwise I was sure she would just come off. Up she came and as soon as I had her on the top, I lifted the rod as high as I could while Alan reached out with the net. If she was going to come off, it would be now! It seemed to take forever to get her in, but in she went and we both gave a big cheer.

Halfway back, Alan shouted to the lads on the bank, "It's the big common!" I looked at her in the net as we paddled back and she was a huge carp, a fish of a lifetime. At the bank, one of the lads jumped on the boat to keep hold of the fish, and Kev was already congratulating me on my new PB. We got all the necessary bits of 'on the bank care' and weighing equipment ready, and I hooked the scales on one of the big weighing tripods. Now to get her in.

I had already bitten off my line. I checked that her pecs were tucked away and rolled up the net, then one of the other lads came on the boat to help, because it's not easy when you're leaning over the side. I lifted her high enough for Reedy to grab the other end of the landing net arms and we carried her to the mat. As I uncovered her, she looked even bigger, and there in the corner of her mouth was the bug. I unhooked it and the thin-gauge hook was bent out. I guessed that one more good lunge from her and she would have been off.

Never in my wildest dreams, could I have imagined this.

My super-bugged UK PB, at 51lbs.

The sling was zeroed, two of us carefully hooked the sling to the scales and I slowly let them take the weight. They span round, flying past 40lbs, settled at 51lbs, and sure enough, Kevin was right - a new PB! All the cameras were in position and I held out my prize, a 51lb common carp. What a touch! I then got into the lake with her on the mat for a couple of quick returners and as I let her go, she powered off to one of the weed beds and out of sight.

The capture of this incredible fish was fantastic, but what really made it was having all the lads there to help, and without Alan on the boat it would have been game over. Thanks lads. Eventually, everyone drifted off and I was left to have a brew and let the whole thing sink in. I checked my bag and I only had one beetle left. I needed to get a lot more made up, and with stronger hooks.

I tidied up the swim, cast out my last beetle, and then started to make the texts and phone calls. This is the great bit about a special capture. Neil and Charlie were due over in a few hours so I called Neil and told him. His reply was, "Jammy bastard" – as usual. I just chilled out for the rest of the day. The weather was pleasant and as far as I was concerned, I'd caught my fish, but I wanted to see Neil and Charlie get a nice one.

During the day, the lake was quiet with hardly any fish activity at all. Neil and Charlie turned up at around 3pm and came round to congratulate me on my huge common before going for a walk round. They reached the opposite end and I could see them just coming round the corner of the lake when my rod in the channel was off. I grabbed it and gave side strain as this fish was trying to get around the side of the island. I held on, giving no line and luckily, it turned away and came back into the channel. By this time, Neil and Charlie were back by my side. "Jammy bastard," Neil said as he grabbed the net.

The fish stayed in the channel throughout the fight and although it was weedy, I didn't have any trouble, so Neil scooped up a nice mirror. I already had all the bits ready from my earlier capture, so we lifted the fish out and on to the mat. What a stunning carp! This was a real beauty with large apple-slice scales; it was one of the nicest carp I've seen. This cracking mirror weighed 31lbs 10oz and we got some very good shots. I slipped her back and Neil and Charlie rushed off to get set up.

Neil set up outside the lodge and Charlie went on the opposite bank, so that we were all spread out. If they hadn't just arrived on the lake, I could easily have thanked Church Pool for my luck and left for home a very happy man.

Simply stunning!

Neil got off the mark with a 25lb mirror.

Over the next 48 hours, it went very quiet and I was even fishing a third rod, going right toward the shallows on a snowman rig, but all to no avail. It seemed that the lake had just switched off, which was a shame for the lads. I had to go on the Thursday but Neil and Charlie were to stay another night. The sun had been out each day and thankfully, Neil banked a nice 25lb mirror on a zig with black foam, so at least he was off the mark, and I hoped this was a break in the lull of activity.

I had nearly all my gear packed away with just the rods to bring in, when the rod in the same spot where I'd had the take from the big common was away. Talk about the lake being kind to me! Another bugged fish had made the mistake. Neil and Charlie came round to help out, Neil called me a jammy bastard again and another delicate tussle followed, including the usual circumstances whereby the fish weeded me up. I thought we may have to get out in the boat again but luckily, this fish didn't stay still and that was its downfall. Each time it twisted and turned in the weed, by using a steady pressure, I was able to get it moving and I soon had it close by. Neil waded out a short way with the net and as the fish rolled, the sun reflected off the golden scales of a linear mirror. I walked back with the fish now on the top, and Neil scooped her up.

Last cast beetle success!

What a way to end an amazing session.

What a way to finish what was already a mega trip! Sometimes when your luck's in, it's in. The last fish, the 31lbs10oz, was a cracker and then this one turned up. It really was a stunner. They don't come much better, and my leaving prize was a beautifully-scaled mirror of 35lbs 8oz. Happy days! After that fish, I stood and looked at the lake and wondered just what else lives in this remarkable water. That last fish, as far as I'm aware, had hardly been caught, and the lake is full of mysteries.

I felt as though I should have finished this chapter straight after the capture of the magnificent common, as the highlight was to have caught a 51-pounder but I just had to include the other two to finish the story properly. I have so much confidence in my bugs now that I'm sure I can catch on them, on any lake. I've always been a basic angler and tend not to get caught up in all the rig malarkey. I've been using the same rigs, or a variation, for years, and most of the time the right method is just staring us in the face. I seem to have to work hard for my fish, and you know the old saying, 'Work Hard, Play Hard'.

Throughout the book I've not delved too much into the tactical approach to my fishing, and it's something that I would like to do, perhaps by devoting a book to it. We'll see.

My daughter is about to have a baby and that outranks everything, so my fishing plans are definitely on hold. At some stage today, I'll become a grandad – and yes, I know I don't look old enough. If my grandson shows the slightest sign of taking a similar path in life as I have, then there's a little rod just waiting for him. For now, though, and for as long as I'm able, I'll carry on fishing for new memories and doing what I've loved to do all my life. Thanks for sharing my precious memories, and the very best of luck with catching your own.

Jerry

Stop press: With minutes to go before the deadline, I got this photo. Harley, who at 8lbs 9oz is the finest PB a grandad could wish for!

If Harley takes the same path as me in life, I have a rod already waiting for him with his name on it.